# PEER TALK in the

# Classroom
## Learning from Research

Jeanne R. Paratore
Boston University
Boston, Massachusetts, USA

Rachel L. McCormack
Plymouth, Massachusetts, Public Schools
Plymouth, Massachusetts, USA

Editors

International Reading Association
800 Barksdale Road, PO Box 8139
Newark, Delaware 19714-8139, USA

**Director of Publications**   Joan M. Irwin
**Assistant Director of Publications**   Wendy Lapham Russ
**Managing Editor, Books and Electronic Publications**   Christian A. Kempers
**Associate Editor**   Matthew W. Baker
**Assistant Editor**   Janet S. Parrack
**Assistant Editor**   Mara P. Gorman
**Publications Coordinator**   Beth Doughty
**Association Editor**   David K. Roberts
**Production Department Manager**   Iona Sauscermen
**Graphic Design Coordinator**   Boni Nash
**Electronic Publishing Supervisor**   Wendy A. Mazur
**Electronic Publishing Specialist**   Anette Schütz-Ruff
**Electronic Publishing Specialist**   Cheryl J. Strum
**Electronic Publishing Assistant**   Peggy Mason

**Photo Credits**   PhotoDisc, cover, p. i; Robert Finken, pp. 5, 25, 129; Image Productions, by Jeffrey High, p. 175

**Library of Congress Cataloging in Publication Data**
   Peer talk in the classroom: Learning from research/Jeanne R. Paratore, Rachel L. McCormack, Editors.
      p.   cm.
   Includes bibliographical references and indexes.
   1. Language arts (Elementary).   2. Reading (Elementary).   3. Peer-group tutoring of students.   4. Group reading.   I. Paratore, Jeanne R.   II. McCormack, Rachel L.
LB1576.P358     1997                                                          97-27908
372.6—dc21
ISBN 0-87207-181-2

# Contents

## Part Three: Examining Conflicts and Complexities in Peer Talk

## Part Four: Focusing on Ourselves

# Foreword

The title of this book is *Peer Talk in the Classroom: Learning from Research*. But, implicitly throughout the book and explicitly in many chapters, it is about teacher talk as well, and the all-important relation between the two.

Everything we read these days about classroom discourse tells us that students' talking is getting more attention from teachers and researchers, and that teachers are trying both to talk less and to talk in different ways. The danger in this period of exciting change—and I think it is a very real danger—is that we will slide too easily into yet another pendulum swing, and replace a "teacher-centered classroom" that we have inherited with a "child-centered classroom" that is advocated more out of opposition to the past than out of careful analysis of the needs of the present.

John Dewey issued a general warning about an earlier occurrence of this same pendulum swing in one of his last writings, *Experience and Education*. But figuring out positively what the changing role of the new teacher should be requires careful analysis of each curriculum subject and the kind of knowledge and skills that each entails.

More specifically than its title suggests, *Peer Talk in the Classroom: Learning from Research* is about elementary school children's understandings of and response to literature, often in classroom versions of "book clubs." The chapter authors give many examples of actual talk—among children by themselves and with their teacher, in small groups and large groups, in single lessons and over extended periods of time. The book should be a powerful resource for avoiding the pendulum swing by helping us understand how teachers must support students in *their* new role as active constructors of their own learning.

*Courtney B. Cazden*
*Harvard University*
*Cambridge, Massachusetts, USA*

# Contributors

JANICE F. ALMASI
Assistant Professor
State University of New York
    at Buffalo
Buffalo, New York, USA

FENICE B. BOYD
Assistant Professor
The University of Georgia
Athens, Georgia, USA

CYNTHIA H. BROCK
Assistant Professor
Texas Woman's University
Denton, Texas, USA

KAREN S. EVANS
Assistant Professor
National-Louis University
Brookfield, Wisconsin, USA

JAMES FLOOD
Professor
San Diego State University
San Diego, California, USA

LEE GALDA
Professor, Language Education
The University of Georgia
Athens, Georgia, USA

LINDA B. GAMBRELL
Professor and Associate Dean,
    College of Education
University of Maryland
College Park, Maryland, USA

SHEILA GARNICK
Title I Project Director
Boston University/
    Chelsea Partnership
Chelsea, Massachusetts, USA

SANDY KASER
Intermediate Multiage Teacher
Robins Elementary School,
    Tucson Unified School District
Tucson, Arizona, USA

WENDY C. KASTEN
Associate Professor, Curriculum
    and Instruction–Literacy
Kent State University
Kent, Ohio, USA

DIANE LAPP
Professor of Reading and
    Language Education
San Diego State University
San Diego, California, USA

TRINIDAD LEWIS
Doctoral Student
Boston University
Boston, Massachusetts, USA

RACHEL L. MCCORMACK
Consulting Teacher of Reading and
    Classroom Teacher
Plymouth, Massachusetts, Public
    Schools
Plymouth, Massachusetts, USA

JEANNE R. PARATORE
Associate Professor of Education
Boston University
Boston, Massachusetts, USA

WENDY RANCK-BUHR
Reading Specialist
San Diego City Schools
San Diego, California, USA

TAFFY E. RAPHAEL
Professor, Department of Reading
and Language Arts
Oakland University
Rochester, Michigan, USA

KATHY G. SHORT
Associate Professor
University of Arizona
Tucson, Arizona, USA

SARA SPACEK
Teacher, Middle School
Ida Price Middle School
San Jose, California, USA

JANICE VAN DYKE
Instructor, School of Teacher
Education
San Diego State University
San Diego, California, USA

SUSAN M. WALLACE
Research Assistant
Michigan State University
East Lansing, Michigan, USA

KATHRYN F. WHITMORE
Assistant Professor
The University of Iowa
Iowa City, Iowa, USA

# Introduction

∞

JEANNE R. PARATORE AND RACHEL L. McCORMACK

At the turn of the 20th century, Dewey (1900) commented on the social organization of schools. In comparing schools with society, he observed that schools did little to help students prepare to enter a society that, he believed, held people together through a common spirit and common aims. He believed that as a result of a lack of socialization, schools were not equipped to satisfy the impulses and instincts of students and failed to capitalize on their natural instincts. He described these natural instincts as *social instincts*, as shown in conversation and communication; *constructive instincts*, through making things and watching things happen; *investigative instincts*, through inquiry or finding out things; and *expressive instincts*, through art and artistic expression. Further, Dewey remarked on the effect of the lack of social organization of schools on the development of children's language. He called school language "recitation," where students repeated information learned from textbooks, and he called classrooms places where natural motives for language were seldom offered and natural purposes for speaking were taken away.

Based on his observations, Dewey stated that schools needed to reorganize to prepare students for society by bringing children into contact with more adults and other children "in order for there to be the finest and richest social life" (p. 59); focusing on schooling as a drawing out rather than a pouring in, to give direction to children's already intense activity; and teaching reading, writing, and oral language in a related way, as an outgrowth of a child's social desire and experiences.

Today, educators still are struggling with Dewey's ideas. Although schools may provide the social environments advocated by Dewey, research on the language and structure of classroom lessons suggests that teacher-controlled lessons continue to dominate the structure of classroom interactions (Cazden, 1988). Recitation-type lessons, following a pervasive, recurrent pattern of initiation act–reply act–evaluation act, with the initiation and evaluation acts practiced almost exclusively by the teacher, still prevail in many classrooms. And, although research suggests that teachers indicate a desire to change the social structure of classroom lessons by relinquishing some of the control, there is evidence that successfully accomplishing such change is difficult (Cazden, 1988; McCarthey, 1990).

The purpose of this book is to present classrooms where teachers have taken on the challenge to achieve a better balance in the talk structure of literacy lessons and have done so with notable success. Part One and Chapter 1 present the work of Lapp, Flood, Ranck-Buhr, Van Dyke, and Spacek, who create the context for looking at classrooms by joining literacy and language learning theory with practical ideas for getting started. This chapter uncovers the sometimes hidden connections between what we know about language and literacy acquisition and how we create conditions for learning in our classroom.

In Part Two, we focus directly on the students in classrooms where peer-led discourse contributes to children's opportunities to learn. Inviting us to listen in on the talk of her second graders in Chapter 2, McCormack argues that not only can these young children construct meaning by collaborating with one another, but they can also, in her words, "do much more." Indeed, the words of Tami, Jake, Allen, and other children convince us that she is right.

In Chapter 3, Kaser and Short challenge us to consider how to "respect and build on difference within an institution that is grounded in hierarchy and sameness." Sharing Kaser's experiences in her fifth-grade classroom, the authors explore the ways that she used peer talk to highlight diversity and children's own cultures in authentic ways.

In Chapter 4, Boyd and Galda cite compelling statistics about the rate of failure of students in U.S. high schools. They reason that, for many of these students, the path toward academic failure likely began with failure to learn to read and write. The authors remind us that children who struggle and who subsequently lack motivation to read and write are particularly poorly served by the traditional recitation model. With Boyd serving as the teacher researcher, the authors examine an alternative learning context in which high school students who find reading difficult engage in a cross-aged literacy project, and use oral and written language to construct meaning with fourth and fifth graders.

In the next two chapters, the authors explore and compare the power of peer talk in settings with both children and adults. In Chapter 5, Kasten examines three different contexts in which peer talk framed learning opportunities. She concludes that opportunities to think and speak collaboratively deepen critical thinking and extend learning.

Whitmore takes us into Mrs. Crowell's third-grade bilingual classroom and her own graduate seminar in Chapter 6. She relies on rich and varied transcripts from each of these settings to help us learn about and more fully understand the importance of providing students of all ages with opportunities to think about and articulate the ways their own experiences converge with the texts they are reading.

In Part Three, the authors continue to focus on students, but attempt to broaden the focus by exploring the conflicts and complexities that students confront as they engage in peer-led discussions. In Chapter 7, Almasi and Gambrell present data from several fourth-grade classrooms about the effects of peer-led and teacher-led discourse on students' ability to recognize and resolve sociocognitive conflict. Although it is these data that strengthen the authors' conclusions, perhaps it is the case study of young Derek that may cause us to rethink our literacy instructional strategies.

In Chapter 8, Evans takes us into two fifth-grade classrooms where, as a teacher researcher, she explored the ways gender influenced the type of talk and the participation patterns within the literature discussion groups. Evans's careful and thoughtful analyses remind us of the *diverse factors* that influence how children respond to texts and to one another.

In Part Four, we conclude our examination of peer talk in the classroom by shifting the focus from the student to the teacher. Raphael, Brock, and Wallace continue their investigation of "Book Club," the instructional program that Raphael and her colleagues began several years ago. In this chapter, they focus particularly on students with special learning needs who would have traditionally received instruction outside the regular classroom. In addition to looking at the nature of these learners' participation in Book Club and the influence of their experiences on their literacy learning, the authors also examine the roles teachers played in supporting these diverse students' opportunities to learn. Their extensive use of classroom transcripts helps us understand both teachers' and students' actions.

Finally, Paratore, Garnick, and Lewis shift the focus completely in Chapter 10 by examining what teachers observe as they watch children during peer-led discussions, and further, how the information they collect influences subsequent instructional actions. Children's transcripts and teachers' notes and interview comments provide persuasive evidence that the acts of watching and listening to our students is a critical step in learning to watch and listen to ourselves.

As we prepared this text and read and reread each chapter, we were struck by the many different ways in which peer-led discourse became a part of each teacher's instructional repertoire and by the variety of ways each of our colleagues chose to examine and think about peer talk in the classroom. We hope that by bringing these classroom contexts together in a single text we have extended an opportunity for you, too, to examine and think about peer talk in new ways.

## References

Cazden, C.B. (1988). *Classroom discourse: The language of teaching and learning.* Portsmouth, NH: Heinemann.

Dewey, J. (1900). *The school and society and the child and the curriculum.* Chicago, IL: University of Chicago Press.

McCarthey, S.J. (1990). *Talk about text: Changes in content and authority structures in peer response groups* (Research Report No. 90–5). East Lansing, MI: Michigan State University, National Center for Research on Teacher Education.

# PART ONE

## A Context for Peer Talk

# CHAPTER 1

# "Do You Really Just Want Us to Talk About This Book?": A Closer Look at Book Clubs as an Instructional Tool

∞

DIANE LAPP, JAMES FLOOD, WENDY RANCK-BUHR, JANICE VAN DYKE, AND SARA SPACEK

"Do you really just want us to talk about this book?" was one of the first questions a seventh-grade student asked during the initial introduction to book clubs. The students were convinced that there was some trick to the task of simply being asked to read a book. They were certain that a surprise quiz was going to be a part of the assignment. Much to their surprise, they found that by discussing their readings with others they enjoyed the book more and understood the reading much better than if they had been asked only to respond to specific questions about the story.

The role of "talking about books" in classrooms is the focus of much attention and research. Almasi (1996) states, "Students who talk about what they read are more likely to engage in reading" (p. 20). Statements such as this have caused classroom teachers to plan discussion time into their literacy program. However, implementing discussions into the regular instructional program entails more than just giving students time to talk about what they read. As Gambrell (1996) explains, "There is no one method or approach for implementing the ideal discussion; instead, research suggests that teachers who wish to implement book clubs have important choices to make" (p. 35). Some of these choices include deciding whether to use book clubs, determining how students can gain from book clubs, selecting materials that will be used for discussions, and determining how to manage and assess classroom book clubs. This chapter offers reasons to use book clubs as an instructional tool in the literacy classroom and outlines some of the issues surrounding the various aspects of book clubs.

# Why Book Clubs?

Readers construct meaning as they read. In doing so, Rosenblatt (1991) explains, "Each reader draws on a personal reservoir of linguistic and life experiences. The new meaning, the literary work, whether poetic or nonpoetic, is constituted during this actual transaction between reader and text" (p. 60). The reading experience is, therefore, a dynamic and ever-changing process.

Literature is a genre that is rich with opportunities for such personal interactions and provides readers with an important way to learn about their world and themselves. Literature both educates and entertains; it stretches the imagination, allowing readers the opportunity to see their world and other worlds in many different ways. Because literature has this power, Huck (1990) states, "We must do more than just teach our students to read. We must help them become readers who are completely absorbed in their books and look forward to a lifetime of pleasure in reading good books" (p. 12).

"Readers deepen and extend their interpretations of literature when they respond to that literature in a variety of ways" (Harste, Short, & Burke, 1988). Classroom book clubs that emphasize the discussion of literature are one means of response. Book clubs provide a powerful venue for student conversation because they are made up of small, heterogeneous groups of students. This arrangement provides the opportunity for every member of the group to speak and to be heard. Portions of the discussion can be student directed and other portions can be teacher guided. The discussions can focus on a book or piece of literature that is being read by all book club members. The major focus is on the reader and his or her personal responses to the text, and it is through these shared insights that each participant's world view is enhanced.

## Book Clubs Enhance Students' Growth and Understanding About Text and Self

Literature studies provide students with an opportunity to read about, discuss, and gain a better understanding of key issues that affect us all (Lapp, Flood, Kibildis, Jones, & Moore, 1995). In a study on students' perspectives of literature study circles (or discussion groups), Samway et al. (1991) found that literature studies influenced students' perceptions of their personal thoughts as well as others. Students in literature discussion groups viewed themselves as readers. The open-ended questions that helped focus the discussion groups allowed students to share their feelings and experiences as they related to the stories they read. They made connections with the literature and their own life. Also, when students were given an opportunity to reflect on the literature study groups, they commented on the importance of reading complete books, talking about books, being given some choice over which books they read, and having plenty of time to read.

In this same study, students spoke about disagreements with one another in their literature study group. However, even though they disagreed periodically, they realized that through discussion they gained new insights about what they read and had greater respect for the opinions of others. They emphasized how having opportunities to talk about books was a key element in helping them become knowledgeable readers and developing a better understanding of themselves.

## Book Clubs Enhance Oral Language Development

The best language lessons are good books and interesting discussions in which children are absorbed in the meaning of what is said to them or what is read. Quality literature cultivates language, provides language models, and facilitates language acquisition (Krashen & Biber, 1988). The use of quality literature within the structure of book clubs provides students with many opportunities for using language because book clubs are structured in a way that encourages rich conversations about literature among individuals and supports the learning of everyone in the group. Short (1990) describes book clubs as communities where there are opportunities for knowing one another; valuing what each group member has to offer; problem solving and inquiry; sharing responsibility and control; learning through action, reflection, and demonstration; and establishing a learning atmosphere that is predictable, yet full of real choices.

Book clubs enhance oral language opportunities for both first- and second-language English students; however, this nonthreatening environment is particularly beneficial for second-language English students (see Chapter 6 for further discussion on the benefits of conversation in second-language classrooms, and see Chapter 9 for further discussion of diverse students in book clubs). When working with students who are acquiring English, it is important to encourage their participation and to provide a stress-free, trusting environment for learning. Reducing anxiety is critical. Low anxiety is conducive to second-language acquisition, whether measured as personal or classroom anxiety. Krashen (1982, 1986) talks about reducing anxiety in terms of emotional engagement or keeping the affective filter low so that students will experience success in second-language acquisition. It is through these book club conversations that students get to orally try their ideas in a nonthreatening setting.

## Book Clubs Support Social Learning Theory

Current views and methods of reading instruction are based on social constructivist theory, which emphasizes learning as a social process. Based on this theory, children's reading and writing processes develop through interactions with adults and peers. Educators know that social interactions make up a child's school and home life. Vygotsky (1978) has shown that the kinds of social situations in which learners are involved have a major impact on their learning. He argued that the way we talk and interact with others becomes internalized and helps shape the way we think and learn:

> Each function in the child's cultural development appears twice: first, on the social level, and later, on the individual level; first, between people (interpsychological), and then inside the child (intrapsychological). (p. 57)

For example, during initial instruction, the teacher models, explains, clarifies, and supplies information. This instruction is controlled mainly by the teacher's interaction with the students. Once students understand the concept or skill, with some teacher prompting they can become responsible for applying the skill or concept to various learning contexts.

Through interactions with others, the student can demonstrate understanding of the concept:

> Real concepts are impossible without words, and thinking in concepts does not exist beyond verbal thinking. That is why the central moment in concept formation, and its generative cause, is a specific use of words as functional tools. (Vygotsky, 1986, p. 107)

As we begin to recognize the importance of social interactions and conversations in our classrooms, we begin to change our view of the classroom. We begin to explore this idea of a community of learners who interact with one another daily. "When opportunities to discuss the text are provided, the student gains the advantage of hearing other viewpoints and raising questions about interpretation" (Goatley & Raphael, 1992, p. 2).

Harste, Short, and Burke (1988) write that "talking about a piece of literature with others gives readers time to explore half-formed ideas, to expand their understandings of literature through hearing other's interpretations, and to become readers who think critically and deeply about what they read" (p. 293). It is important that readers understand that different interpretations of literature exist. In their discussions with their peers, students can explore their interpretations with one another to reach new understandings. "Book clubs help readers become literate" (Harste, Short, & Burke, 1988, p. 293).

Research conducted by Eeds and Peterson (1994) revealed two interesting pieces of information regarding the talk that takes place during book clubs. First, important topics in a story are discussed, and second, it is not necessary for a group leader to be present for the participants to discuss important topics. Both of these findings are important to consider as you begin to plan book clubs in your classroom; they support the notion that, given the opportunity to discuss books, students will have meaningful discussions on their own.

## Developing, Implementing, and Assessing Book Clubs

Developing book clubs in your classroom is a three-phase process that involves selection, implementation, and assessment.

1. *Selection*—This phase of the process encompasses all the tasks that must be completed before introducing the book club approach to students. Specific components of this phase include selection of books, seating arrangements, grouping, and management.

2. *Implementation*—This phase includes the specific sequence of instruction.

3. *Assessment*—This phase is ongoing throughout the book club discussions and includes teacher, peer, and self-assessments.

## Selection

Selecting books for use in book clubs is no different than selecting books for any other reading activity. Although your objective may be to develop comprehension strategies and oral fluency, you will need to begin by selecting books that have wide appeal and topics that will be of high interest to students. First, decide the type of materials you plan to read. Text length is an important consideration for successful book clubs. When you start your book club, it is best to start with short books or stories that can be finished in brief periods of time. Once the book club is operating, encourage members to attempt longer pieces of text and to suggest new titles.

We have found that collections of short stories and picture books work well for several reasons: they provide reading material for several discussions; they are short enough to be read in one sitting; and they cover a wide variety of topics. In addition, mysteries work well because they provide many opportunities for discussion as readers attempt to solve the mystery. The list of books in Figure 1 contains texts that we have used in our book clubs.

## Implementation

**Management and seating arrangements.** Seating arrangements are an important component of book clubs. In a large classroom where several discussion groups meet at the same time, it is best if the tables or desks in the classroom are arranged to accommodate small groups of students seated close together within their group and as far as possible from other groups. This type of arrangement not only reduces the noise level

# Figure 1 Book Club Selections

| Picture books | Short stories and short story collections | Novels |
|---|---|---|
| *The Eleventh Hour: A Curious Mystery* by Graeme Base | *The Tell Tale Heart* by Edgar Allan Poe (video available) | *The Man Who Was Poe* by Avi |
| *Finding the Green Stone* by Alice Walker | *Baseball in April & Other Stories* by Gary Soto (collection) | *The Giver* by Lois Lowry |
| *Chato's Kitchen* by Gary Soto | *Local News* by Gary Soto (collection) | *Nothing but the Truth* by Avi |
| *The Sign of the Seahorse* by Graeme Base | *Sadako and the Thousand Paper Cranes* by Eleanor Coates (video and play format available) | *I Am the Cheese* by Robert Cormier |
| *The Stranger* by Chris Van Allsburg | *Woman Hollering Creek & Other Stories* by Sandra Cisneros (collection) | *The Other Side of Dark* by Joan Lowery Nixon |
| *The Mysteries of Harris Burdick* by Chris Van Allsburg | *The Friendship* and *The Gold Cadillac* by Mildred Taylor | *Number the Stars* by Lois Lowry |
| *Two Bad Ants* by Chris Van Allsburg | *Song of the Trees* by Mildred Taylor | *Bless Me, Ultima* by Rudolfo Anaya |

of the discussions, but it also encourages students to keep their discussions within the confines of their own group until it is time to share ideas as an entire class.

In situations when you want to read a text with the entire class, be sure that students are seated so that they can see one another as well as they can see you. This arrangement is important because it demonstrates that students' comments are as important as the teacher's comments in a book club discussion.

**Grouping.** Students' personalities and reading fluency should to be taken into account when creating groups for book club discussions. It is important to balance reading fluency within each group so that the more fluent readers can provide support for the less fluent readers. Additionally, students' willingness to talk in a small-group setting needs to be considered. Be certain to distribute the most talkative and the quietest students among the groups that you create. If you have students who are acquiring English as a second language in your class, be sure to provide group support by having more than one ESL student per group and by seating them beside very fluent English speakers. You also may wish to include partner discussions before group discussions since this ensures participation from everyone and it provides a safe setting for reluctant speakers.

**Procedures.** Conducting a book club discussion requires some structure to ensure the book club is a student-centered experience that permits members of the group to have opportunities to share and reflect on the reading. Our research on book club discussions with teachers and preservice teachers (Flood et al., 1995; Flood, Lapp, & Ranck-Buhr, 1993; Flood, Lapp, Ranck-Buhr, & Moore, 1995; Van Dyke, 1997) has led to the development of a series of procedures for conducting book talk discussions. Using these procedures, coupled with the 10 research-based practices described in the next section of this chapter, we found that students' discussions moved beyond the traditional summarizing of text and toward more personal responses to text. The procedures for book clubs that we have used successfully are outlined in Figure 2.

**Ten Research-Based Practices.** Through our research with book clubs, we have found that the following 10 practices are beneficial for enhancing the quality and quantity of students' discussions.

> 1. Begin with picture books and videos. This allows students' discussions to be based on something that is concrete. Students often are more comfortable participating in a discussion about something that is concrete as opposed to a text that requires, at least

## Figure 2  Procedures for Book Clubs

| Procedure | Time | Grouping format | Size of group |
|---|---|---|---|
| *Prior to the book club sessions:* | | | |
| Participants read the selection and write a response in their journal to the text being read. | 20–30 min. | individual | 1 |
| *During the book club sessions:* | | | |
| 1. Participants review their journal entries and revisit the text by scanning; | 1–2 min. | individual | 1 |
| 2. Participants read what they wrote and do one of the following: underline or highlight words or phrases that they want to share with their partner; write a brief new entry that is a reflection about their written response; or write a new thought or question based on their review of the text. | 3–4 min. | individual | 1 |
| 3. Participants share responses with a partner. | 2–4 min. | pairs | 2 |
| 4. Moderator leads a discussion with the group. Moderator begins the discussion by asking participants to share their thoughts based on their reading or writing and discussion of text with their partners. Content-specific questions should be prepared by the moderator in advance to focus the discussion if it strays or becomes too bogged down on a point that seems to be unresolvable. | 10–15 min. | group | 7–8 |

*(continued)*

## Figure 2 Procedures for Book Clubs (continued)

| Procedure | Time | Grouping format | Size of group |
|---|---|---|---|
| 5. Journal writing—When the discussion seems to have run its course, ask participants to write a response to a pointed question. For example, what surprised you most about the discussion of the text? (i.e., what caused you to say "wow!"?); or what questions do you have about the text or discussion at this point? (i.e., what's still puzzling you?); or what word or phrase caught your attention enough for you to have savored it? (i.e., why do you think it was so memorable?). | 4 min. | individual | 1 |
| 6. Participants share responses with a partner. | 10 min. | pairs | 2 |
| 7. Participants return to a large-group discussion. Responses based on the previous writing can be invited. | 2–4 min. | group | 7–8 |
| 8. Participants can be asked to write a journal entry based on the following: Write about your own growth in interpreting this text. Be sure to think based on your journal writing and the discussions. You also are invited to compare how you see the text at this point. | 2–4 min. | individual | 1 |

in the student's mind, that he or she understand and interpret the reading selection prior to the discussion.

2. Keep the procedures simple. This allows students to become comfortable with the process of book club discussions and to focus on the talk that takes place rather than the assignment that needs to be completed.

3. Model discussions for students. Raphael, Goatley, McMahon, & Woodman (1994) reported that students need to learn how to participate in book clubs. Modeling book club discussions allows students to see and hear what a book club discussion should sound like prior to being asked to practice the technique on their own.

4. Use a phase-in, phase-out model. Use a model of instruction that slowly relinquishes control of the book club process to students. With proper support, given at appropriate times throughout the teaching cycle, students eventually will be able to carry out the discussions on their own.

5. Reward students for talking about text. Students need to learn what is expected of them during the discussion process. This can be taught to them by providing them with simple and immediate feedback while they are participating in book club discussions. One method for doing this requires the teacher to circulate among the discussion groups and monitor the conversations. If students are on task and discussing the text, the teacher places a marker, such as a dry pinto bean or plastic chip, on the table. The marker indicates that students are on task and allows them to monitor their own discussions without interference. At the end of the book club session for that day, students can trade their markers for an incentive such as extra credit or a new pencil. Some teachers may elect to use the markers to monitor progress over time. For example, some book clubs may earn only three markers on the first book club session but by the sixth book club discussion the same group may earn ten markers or more.

6. Select literature carefully. Literature selection is a key element in motivating students. As mentioned earlier, select a wide range of literature to which students can relate in some way (topic, culture, interest, or author). It also is helpful to select authors who have

written various types of literature, such as picture books, short stories, and novels. This allows students to have the familiarity of an author's style as they expand their reading to more difficult selections.

7. Be patient, be observant, and change as needed. Implementing book clubs into a classroom is relatively easy, but it does not always work as planned. Watch students carefully. Listen to what they are saying during their discussions and modify your instruction based on your observations.

8. Pair and group students strategically. When you first implement book clubs in your classroom, plan how the students will be paired and grouped. Put students together by matching their strengths and weaknesses, as mentioned earlier. Try different arrangements and observe changes in students' discussions.

9. Arrange your classroom in a way that encourages discussions. Arrange the tables and chairs in your classroom to allow student groups to be as far from one another as possible. This arrangement will prevent students from interrupting others during the discussion period.

10. Develop rules of operation prior to discussions. Students will be more active participants and will follow the procedures more readily if they have some input regarding the development of the book club rules of operation. Encourage students to keep the rules to a minimum so that everyone can follow them. Also encourage students to help one another accept and follow the rules.

## Assessment

Assessment of students' learning via a book club discussion is sometimes difficult to monitor. Observations and anecdotal records are helpful, but these methods of assessment do not provide students with opportunities to reflect on their own learning experiences.

Reflection and metacognitive thinking involve both thinking about one's own thinking and learning and relating ideas to previous experiences. Reflection and metacognition involve critical and creative thinking. A person who thinks reflectively is able to "link ideas to previous and current and predicted experiences, question and self-question, and assess self and the situation" (Wilson & Jan, 1993, p.113). Self- and group assessment requires that students examine their own behavior and work and the behavior and work of their peers. When students assess their behaviors in learning, they can learn to establish goals to improve their individual learning (Wilson & Jan, 1993).

Reflection takes many forms. When readers make predictions about the content of the book, question what will happen next in a story, think about the author's message, and examine literacy devices, they demonstrate a form of reflective evaluation. "Reflective evaluation is demonstrated by many people in the classroom—by teachers as they think out loud about their own reading and writing experiences, and by other students as they share their self-evaluations" (Ames & Gahagan, 1994, p. 57). The following examples represent some of the methods that teachers can use to encourage students to participate in self-reflections about book club discussions.

The work sample presented in Figure 3 is an example of a reading-response journal that students complete on their own while they are reading and after the discussion. The teacher or another observer can write comments as shown in the completed example. This also can become a dialogue journal between teacher and student because the teacher comments can be shared with the student. Although this example has been designed as a result of reading *The Giver*, it can be used to respond to any selection.

Following each book club's discussion, students can be asked to respond to a series of open-ended questions, as shown in Figure 4. These questions provide students with the opportunity to reflect on their own group process, monitor their own behavior, and take responsibility for their own learning. Students should be asked to review their responses to these questions prior to beginning the next book club session. This procedure encourages students to set goals within their group and to work toward improving their discussions.

The Self- and Group Evaluation, shown in Figure 5 on page 21, was designed to be used after students complete the book club sessions for a complete novel. This evaluation gives students the opportunity to share what they feel is important to the operation of their group discussions and also allows them to reflect on their own learning as a result of their participation in the book club. Through this evaluation process, the stu-

# Figure 3 Sample of Student Reading-Response Journal

Name: Cesar Martinez

Novel title: _The Giver_          Author: Lois Lowry

Chapter #/Title: _____5_____

### Student Reflection

| Reflections while reading | Reflections on group discussion and process | Reflection on next session |
|---|---|---|
| I felt that the way everyone was assigned a life wasn't good because you lived how someone told you. I think Jonas is not going to get an assignment that he would like. I also wonder why they didn't tell more about housing. | I thought it was perfect. I felt I participated well, but one person didn't participate that well. I don't know why. | I hope it goes as well. |

**Teacher's comments about discussion**

Terrific! You recalled details from the novel easily and often helped your fellow readers when their details were not accurate. You also stated that the novel was difficult to understand in the first few chapters. You had more questions about the strangeness of the community. You stated that, "No action…I don't like it. It's a dead book. It's hard for me to get into this book." You're doing very well at reflecting on your thoughts during reading and discussion. Thanks for sharing.

**Teachers' comments about behavior**

You also referred to certain pages and chapters from the novel as you recalled certain issues Andrew had questions with. You also seem to look to him for the lead on the discussion. You can be a leader as you demonstrated when you took on the role of leader when Andrew seemed to lose the topic of discussion. You were well prepared for the discussion. You also mentioned the chapter you were reading and asked the rest of the group where they were in their reading. You confirmed that the discussion was finished.

## Figure 4　Reflection Prompts for Group Discussion and Process

Name: _____

Book title: _____

Date: _____

1. What did I do well today (and/or improve) during group discussion?

2. What do I still need to improve during group discussion?

3. How did the group function today in the discussion?

4. What could the group do to improve the discussion?

5. How could I be an even better group member?

6. How am I perceived by the other group members?

dents are able to monitor their group's performance, and they also are able to assume responsibility for their own learning.

Prior to selecting the assessment tools you are going to use for your book club, you should ask yourself two questions. First, what outcomes do you want your students to achieve as a result of their participation in book clubs? Second, what are the best methods for measuring those outcomes? With these two questions to guide you, select methods of assessment that match your school's expectations and your own teaching style. For example, if you use portfolio assessment in your classroom, you will want to consider a form of assessment for your students that could be included in their portfolios such as an audiotape or videotape of a book club discussion with an accompanying teacher and student reflection.

# A Final Note

Book clubs hold promise as an instructional tool that enables students to enhance their understandings of text. Through book clubs, students are able to construct meaning from text that is consistent with current theories of reading. Teachers who use book clubs in their classroom will be able to provide learning experiences that develop students' skills in all areas of the language arts and provide a solid foundation for their future as lifelong readers.

# Figure 5  Self- and Group Evaluation

Name: _____ Date: _____

## Evaluate Yourself and Your Group

Give each member of your group a grade for his or her participation in the discussion. Think about the quality of their comments, ability to bring up new topics for discussion, listening, skills, staying on topic, and overall knowledge of the literature. Use the rubric below.

+ = excellent
√ = average
- = very little contribution

Name: _____Score: _____

1.

2.

3.

4.

5.

6.

## Write your responses to the following questions:

1. What have you learned from book club discussions?

2. How have you changed the way you read and the way you respond to literature?
   Compare your journal responses from the beginning of book club to the end of book club. Are there any developments in your thinking about literature? What are some of the differences? Has your comprehension of the literature changed?

3. Review your reflections. What developments do you see throughout your reflections with the different groups you worked with? Discuss.

4. Reflect on the last several weeks. What is your overall evaluation of book clubs and your participation? What are the values of doing book clubs versus whole-class reading and discussions?

5. Comments and recommendations:

_____

_____

_____

_____

# Questions for Reflection

1. Think about the students in your classroom or students who are at the grade level you hope to teach. What are their interests, cultural composition, and range of reading fluency? Based on your answer, expand the list of book club selections in Figure 1 on page 12 to accommodate your students.

2. Continuous assessment is a major factor in planning effective instruction. Please reread the section of this chapter that introduces a variety of assessment measures. Now, think about the goals of the book club you are planning or already have implemented in your classroom. Which of these assessment measures seem appropriate? Why? You may want to design some additional measures that will provide you with the insights you need to inform your classroom book club instruction.

# References

Almasi, J.F. (1996). A new view of discussion. In L.B. Gambrell & J.F. Almasi (Eds.), *Lively discussions! Fostering engaged reading* (pp. 2–24). Newark, DE: International Reading Association.

Ames, C.K., & Gahagan, H.S. (1994). Self-reflection: Supporting students in taking ownership of evaluation. In R. Routman (Ed.), *Invitations: Changing as teachers and learners K–12* (pp. 52–66). Portsmouth, NH: Heinemann.

Eeds, M., & Peterson, R.L. (1994). What teachers need to know about the literary craft. In N.L. Roser & M.G. Martinez (Eds.), *Book talk and beyond: Children and teachers respond to literature* (pp. 10–23). Newark, DE: International Reading Association.

Flood, J., Lapp, D., Alvarez, D., Romero, A., Ranck-Buhr, W., Moore, J., Kibildis, C., & Lungren, L. (1995). *Teacher book clubs: A study of teachers' and student teachers' participation in contemporary multicultural fiction literature discussion group* (Reading Research Report No. 22). Athens, GA: National Reading Research Center.

Flood, J., Lapp, D., & Ranck-Buhr, W. (1993, March). *A study of teachers' participation in contemporary multicultural fiction reading discussion groups.* Paper presented at the Annual Meeting of the American Educational Research Association, Atlanta, GA.

Flood, J., Lapp, D., Ranck-Buhr, W., & Moore, J. (1995). What happens when teachers get together to talk about books: Gaining a multicultural perspective from literature. *The Reading Teacher, 48*(8), 720–723.

Gambrell, L.B. (1996). A new view of discussion. In L.B. Gambrell & J.F. Almasi (Eds.), *Lively discussions! Fostering engaged reading* (pp. 25–39). Newark, DE: International Reading Association.

Goatley, V., & Raphael, T.E. (1992). *Moving literature-based instruction into the special education setting: A book club with nontraditional learners* (Report No. CS 301 824). East Lansing, MI: Center for Learning and Teaching of Elementary Subjects.

Harste, C.J., Short, K.G., & Burke, C. (1988). *Creating classrooms for authors*. Portsmouth, NH: Heinemann.

Huck, C.S. (1990). The power of children's literature in the classroom. In K.G. Short & K.M. Pierce (Eds.), *Talking about books: Creating literate communities* (pp. 3–15). Portsmouth, NH: Heinemann.

Krashen, S.D. (1982). *Principles and practice in second language acquisition*. Oxford: Pergamon.

Krashen, S.D. (1986). Bilingual education and second language acquisition theory. In *Schooling and language minority students: A thematic framework* (pp. 3–49). Los Angeles, CA: California State University; Evaluation, Dissemination and Assessment Center.

Krashen, S., & Biber, D. (1988). *On course: Bilingual education's success in California*. Sacramento, CA: California Association for Bilingual Education.

Lapp, D., Flood, J., Kibildis, C., Jones, M.A., & Moore, J. (1995) Teacher book clubs: Making multicultural connections. In N.L. Roser & M.G. Martinez (Eds.), *Book talk and beyond: Children and teachers respond to literature* (pp. 42–49). Newark, DE: International Reading Association.

Raphael, T.E., Goatley, V.J., McMahon, S.I., & Woodman, D.A. (1994). Promoting meaningful conversations in student book clubs. In N.L. Roser & M.G. Martinez (Eds.), *Book talk and beyond: Children and teachers respond to literature* (pp. 66–79). Newark, DE: International Reading Association.

Rosenblatt, L.M. (1991). Literary theory. In J. Flood, J. Jensen, D. Lapp, & J.R. Squire (Eds.), *Handbook of research on teaching the English language arts* (pp. 57–62). New York: Macmillan.

Samway, K.D., Whang, G., Cade, C., Gamil, M., Lubandina, M., & Phommachanh, K. (1991). Reading the skeleton, the heart, and the brain of a book: Students' perspectives on literature study circles. *The Reading Teacher, 45*(3), 196–205.

Short, K.G. (1990). Creating a community of learners. In K.G. Short & K.M. Pierce (Eds.), *Talking about books: Creating literate communities* (pp. 33–52). Portsmouth, NH: Heinemann.

Van Dyke, J. (1997). *A group case study of student teachers' reactions to multicultural discussion group reading*. Unpublished doctoral dissertation, San Diego State University, Claremont Graduate School, San Diego, California, USA.

Vygotsky, L.S. (1978). *Mind in society: The development of higher psychological processes* (M. Cole, V. John-Steiner, S. Scribner, & E. Souberman, Eds. and Trans.). Cambridge, MA: Harvard University Press. (Original work published 1934)

Vygotsky, L.S. (1986). *Thought and language* (A. Kozalin, Trans.). Cambridge, MA: MIT Press. (Original work published 1934)

Wilson, J., & Jan, L.W. (1993). *Thinking for themselves*. Portsmouth, NH: Heinemann.

# PART TWO

❧

## Focusing on Students

# CHAPTER 2

# Eavesdropping on Second Graders' Peer Talk About African Trickster Tales

∞

## RACHEL L. McCORMACK

Four second-grade children, two boys and two girls, are sitting close together on the floor of a classroom that is filled with activities and chatter. They surround a small tape recorder that records their talk as they reconstruct the events in the African folk tale *A Story A Story* (Haley, 1970). The story tells of the origin of African tales, which is a result of a series of tricks that a frail character named Ananse, the Spider Man, plays on the Sky God, keeper of all the stories.

The students are in awe of Ananse, the Spider Man. They are animated in their interpretations of his actions, but they have many questions. How does he think of all those tricks? How does he make a spider web? Does it come out of his mouth? Why would the leopard want to eat him? After all, Ananse looks like he's a thousand years old. He wouldn't even taste good! After much give and take, the children come to an agreement and provide a reasonable explanation for their questions. If Ananse is indeed a thousand years old, then he must be wise. "When you're that old, you can do anything," said one student.

The students in this peer-led literature discussion group had been working together for three weeks. They talked about the things they liked in the stories they read, they pointed out things they did not understand, and they challenged one another's ideas. In the absence of an adult to lead the discussions, the children chose their own topics to develop and they negotiated their own turns. They even provided their own explanations for things, feeling satisfied with the interpretations they made. Everyone talked and everyone listened. They constructed meaning together first by bringing their own interpretations to the group, then by revising them with the help of their peers. Each voice was heard, but many voices became one.

In this classroom, the construction of meaning was a dynamic process of associations and transactions. Rosenblatt (1978) defined a transaction as an "ongoing process in which the elements or factors are aspects of a total situation, each conditioned by and conditioning the other" (p. 17), and she related this definition to a number of situations. For example, in speech, transactions occur among speakers who share similar rules for communication and a common knowledge of language; this results in changing an utterance, a string of words, into a speech act. Similarly, when readers interact with text, the experience is not a solitary one. Readers connect what they know with what the author has written. Further, when readers interact with one another to respond to text, a new transaction occurs as the readers' constructed meanings merge.

The social constructivist perspective places such learning in the context of a learner's interaction with the environment and community (Gavelek, 1986; Mead, 1934; Vygotsky, 1978; Wertsch, 1985). Social constructivism views social acts as critical to the creation of communication and language, and fundamental to the construction of meaning. Key tenets of this perspective studied by Vygotsky (1978) as mentioned in Chapter 1, and outlined by McCarthey (1994, p. 201) are as follows:

- Knowledge and knowing have their origins in social interaction;

- Learning proceeds from the interpsychological plane (between individuals) to the intrapsychological plane (within an individual) with the assistance of knowledgeable members of the culture; and

- Language mediates experience, transforming mental functions.

The idea of mediated experience is the basis for Vygotsky's theory of the Zone of Proximal Development (1986), which posits that all learning has a previous history embedded in the child's development and experiences, and that some mental functions, not yet fully matured, can be helped along with interaction with more capable peers or under the guidance of an adult.

Guided practice through scaffolded instruction makes it possible for students to engage in authentic experiences with a movement toward independent practice. In literacy learning, these independent experiences are enhanced by contexts in which socialization is a key element. If learning is socially constructed, it stands to reason that the optimal condition for literacy learning is a context in which instruction not only is aimed at the highest level of performance, but also is a situation in which students are given ample time to engage in guided practice and are given opportunities to practice independently or with their peers. This gradual release of responsibility results in a dynamic, interactive process in which transactions take place.

Where do these transactions take place? In typical classrooms, students are given little time to socially construct meaning. As mentioned in the Introduction to this book, most lessons are offered as recitations, with participation structures resembling the predominantly used teacher initiation–student response–teacher evaluation (IRE) format for instruction (Mehan, 1979). These teacher-dominated lessons prevail despite evidence that in order for children to become competent language users, they need opportunities to engage in talk in the classroom (Cazden, 1988; Cullinan, 1993; Short, 1992). Encouraging student talk helps children clarify their thoughts, assists them in understanding what they have read, and helps them develop confidence as language users (Cullinan, 1993). Without opportunities for practice, students are unable to engage in the language functions in the classroom: the language of curriculum, the language of control, and the language of personal identity (Cazden, 1988). Further, there is evidence that because students are given fewer opportunities to talk in school than at home, they initiate fewer conversations, ask fewer questions, make utterances that are syntactically less complex, and draw on a narrower range of meaning in the classroom than they do at home (Wells, 1986).

The lack of opportunities given to children to engage in classroom discourse and to practice the functions of language has implications when investigating how students, especially younger ones, perform when responding to literature. Holland, Hungerford, and Ernst (1993) reported that younger children had not been the subjects of research studies on literature response until 1978 because it was thought that children did not have the experience or capabilities to respond adequately to literature. When studies were conducted with younger children, the results of their performance often were correlated with age and developmental stage, suggesting that younger students are limited in their ability to respond to text analytically (Applebee, 1978).

Results of more recent studies offer evidence that supports Vygotsky's theory and supersedes developmental studies by suggesting that the ability of students to respond to text is affected by the type of instruction and environment in which students participate when responding to literature (Dysthe, 1993; McCarthey, 1990; Villaume, Worden, Williams, Hopkins, & Rosenblatt, 1994). Results from these studies suggest that students benefit from explicit modeling and guided practice in talking about books that improve their performance over time. In addition, frequent opportunities for peer interaction in small, peer-led or teacher-facilitated groups aid students' ability to construct shared meaning, resulting in more intertextual connection—responses drawn from personal experiences and related texts (Eeds & Wells, 1989; McMahon, 1992; Tierney & Rogers, 1989).

Although research supports the value of peer interaction in story discussions, the evidence on younger students' participation has been scarce. The following study supports the view that younger students not only can accomplish what their older peers can do, but they also can often do more when certain instructional conditions are in place.

# Teacher as Researcher

## Promoting Peer Talk

In this study, I explored the influence of the social structure of the classroom on young students' response to literature. In addition to investigating the role of the teacher in guiding students' learning, I examined the influence of peers on language learning, self-expression, coconstructing meaning, and language use. As I observed the children and their language, I asked the following questions: What are the characteristics of group interaction that support students in the process of responding to literature? and How do second-grade students use intertextuality to construct shared meaning in peer-led literature discussion groups? To address these questions, I observed my 27 second-grade students as they participated in 9 peer-led discussions over a 5-week period at the end of a school year. The classroom for my work was in a middle-income community of predominantly Caucasian students.

I used a flexible grouping model to organize the students for reading instruction (Paratore, 1991). The grouping model used a number of configurations beginning with whole-class instruction and moving to smaller, needs-based groups, peer dyads, and interest groups. The students followed a similar daily procedure as they moved through these groups and were expected to do five things as they read each day. The procedure was named "Take Five" by the students because of its five components: (1) Get Ready, (2) Read, (3) Reread, (4) Respond, and (5) React.

Every aspect of the lesson framework promoted peer talk. For example, the first component, "Get Ready," typically consisted of helping students devise a cognitive map of the subject introduced in the reading selection. This activity frequently caused the students to challenge one another about what they should include on the map. Just as I often deviated from the norm in the typical IRE participation structure when I led the prereading discussions, so, too, did the students when they were offering their suggestions for additions to the map. These dialogues often led to informal chatter among the students about predictions for the next story, questions to think about, and personal experiences that were related to what they were about to read.

Peer discourse also was an integral part of the children's first encounter with the story, causing it to be interactive and somewhat noisy. I usually read the story aloud first while I modeled and encouraged thinking aloud (Brown & Lytle, 1988), a comprehension strategy in which readers verbalize their thinking. Consequently, the students knew that it was acceptable for them to think aloud spontaneously while I read. In fact, I often elaborated on their think-alouds and invited others to do the same. The students occasionally extended their think-alouds by offering more predictions and adjusting them throughout the story by saying, "I know what will happen now."

Student talk was most evident in the discussions that followed the reading of the stories. Their participation in story discussions had been scaffolded during the months preceding the study. At first, all story discussions were teacher led, providing models and examples for students to use when they ultimately would lead their own discussions. Teacher-facilitated discussions gave the students guided practice in negotiating turntaking and other functions of talk, including initiating topics, seeking clarification, and elaborating. When they moved their discussions to small, peer-led groups, the students were given a prompt to talk about the stories and were given more opportunities to practice the functions of language. In these instances, I circulated from group to group to offer assistance, facilitate the discussions that needed help, and give new prompts. The students again used an informal style to discuss the books, relying on my assistance if they needed help in sustaining the discussions. I was guided by the work of Galda, Cullinan, and Strickland (1993) as I demonstrated the kinds of questions I might like my students to discuss in the groups, discussed and demonstrated the group processes that I wanted them to encourage, clearly demonstrated my expectations, discussed and demonstrated the group dynamics I wanted to promote, and asked the students to assess their group's progress.

After 8 weeks of assisting the children in peer groups, I helped the students form peer-led discussion groups. I explained to the children that they would be spending the next 5 weeks in these groups talking about books. The groups of 4 to 5 students were heterogeneous in regard to gender, reading ability, and verbal performance. However, I made certain that each group had evidence of a leader who could help keep the discussions going. Last, I checked the dynamics of the groups to help ensure that personalities would be compatible.

## Collecting Evidence

Although the African tales chosen for this work were retold by different authors, all had the same features and themes. Consistent with their reputation as "trickster tales," the stories involved characters outwitting one another. In most cases, the smaller or weaker characters managed, through a series of well-planned events, to trick the larger or stronger characters. I hoped that the similarities between the stories would make it easy for the students to make intertextual connections when talking about the stories in their peer groups. Other than the obvious similarities among the stories, they also were chosen for their appropriate reading levels of beginning to end of second grade, the quality of the retold versions, and the quality of the illustrations.

The children followed the same five steps each day as they read a new African tale, practicing the Take Five plan. To get ready, all the students gathered at the easel with a copy of the book to be read that day. The lesson typically began with prereading activities. For example, the title and author were discussed, and the students made predictions after skimming through the text and looking at the illustrations. Vocabulary was introduced and developed. Then, the children added their ideas to a cognitive map they had been devising since the onset of the unit. They began by offering information about what they already knew about folk tales. Each day, they were invited to add to the map as they became more familiar with the unique features of the African tales. While they did so, they asked many questions: Were the illustrations unique? What about the language—the repetition of onomatopoeic words so prevalent in the folk tales? What were the characters' motivations for tricking one another?

After getting ready to read, I read the African tale aloud in its entirety while the children followed along in their own copies. The students next were asked to reread the story silently at their seats or form peer dyads to reread the selection, while I assisted the less able readers with the rereading of the story. The children then wrote responses in response journals. When it came time for them to discuss the tale, the children arranged themselves into their newly formed peer discussion groups. Each group was given a tape recorder to record the discussion. They were given no prompts when asked to discuss the story, but they were required to bring their copy of the story to the group with them. The students knew that I was not available to facilitate the discussions in any way. My purpose was to see how they interacted independently, without prompts. The students had 10 minutes to discuss the story and were instructed to turn off the tape recorders after 10 minutes.

## Examining the Evidence

The second graders had participated in 9 peer-led discussions of the African tales over a period of 5 weeks. Although I listened to each tape, only the third, sixth, and ninth discussion of each peer group were transcribed. While reading the transcripts, I paid close attention to two aspects of the discussions. First, I was interested to know how the children used their turns when talking about the stories. I hoped that determining their purposes for talking, then examining those purposes to see how they connected to one another, would inform me of the ways they constructed meaning together. For this aspect of the discussion, I used categories suggested by Roberts and Langer (1991) to formally code the data. Next, I was interested to know exactly what the children said. Once again, I looked for connections. I hoped that by investigating the content of the discussions, then looking to see if what they said connected to what others said, I could discover the ways the children linked texts to construct meaning. For this part of the discussions, I used categories of intertextuality offered by Bloome and Egan-Robertson (1993). These classifications included types of texts, such as literary genre and personal experience, and imitation, such as referencing through words, phrasing, and text structure. A complete list of coding categories is included in the Figure below.

## Coding Categories

| *Speaker's Purpose** | *Intertextuality*** |
|---|---|
| Agree | Text-Based |
| Challenge | Genre |
| Check | Language |
| Clarify | Illustrations |
| Confirm | Instruction |
| Disagree | Semantic Features |
| Expand | Text Structure |
| Help (Focus, Hint, Modify, Shape, | Reader-Based |
|    Summarize, Tell) | Experience |
| Invite | Prior Knowledge |
| Orchestrate | |
| Present | |
| Recycle | |
| Restate | |
| Upping the Ante | |

* Adapted from Roberts and Langer, 1991
** Adapted from Bloome and Egan-Robertson, 1993

# Rendering the Evidence

**Connecting voices.** The young students debuted as timid investigators of the stories they read when they first met in their newly formed peer discussion groups. They began their discussions with trepidation, producing unsophisticated utterances indicative of what Applebee (1978) described as typical responses for 7- and 8-year-olds. In most instances, the students used their turns to offer retellings that were often mimicked or extended by the next students who spoke. At other times, the students used their turns to introduce a new topic, yet each new discussion topic was rarely ever sustained by the other students or revisited by the student who introduced the topic. Once the students had a chance to speak, they did not know what to say, except to give detailed summaries of the story. In many instances, it appeared that the challenge for the students was to somehow maintain control or, better yet, to seize it from another speaker. As a result, the discussions often took a turn for the worse, as impatient groupmates engaged in antics and "metatalk," talk about talk (O'Flahavan, Wiencek, & Marks, 1993), sabotaging any attempts the speaker might have for developing a topic.

In the following interaction, two students illustrated this type of unproductive interaction. The first speaker, Tami, took control of the discussion and used her turn to begin a lengthy retelling of the story *Why Mosquitoes Buzz in People's Ears* (Aardema, 1975). Another student, Kris, possibly annoyed at listening to another retelling of a story, began making sound effects similar to the ones in the book to accompany Tami's narrative.

Tami:    We read a book. It was called *Why Mosquitoes Buzz in People's Ears.*

Jake:    Tami, you're blocking your voice with the book. It's going over the microphone…

Tami:    …and it's about snakes and all these animals and it has all these dark pages. It's about a monkey who killed an owlet and the monkey killed the owlet because the branch fell because the hawk…

Allen:   …the crow…

Tami:    …the crow was crowing…

Kris:    CAWWW—CAWWW…AWWW—AWWWW

| Tami: | It wasn't the monkey's fault. It was the mosquito's because at first it started telling about… |
|---|---|
| Kris: | ZZZZZ—ZZZZZZZ—ZZZZZZZZZZZZ |
| Tami: | He was talking about how someone digged up the kind of potato and he blocked his ears with sticks and then at the end they killed the mosquito. |
| Kris: | WHAPPO! |
| Allen: | Come on, Kris! |
| Cathy: | You're messing up our group! |

By the sixth and ninth discussions, the discussions had evolved into more conversational-style discourse. The children's purposes for speaking represented a wide range of objectives, and all the groups increased their ability to sustain a topic or theme. Each group had moved from an individualistic structure, as evident in the first transcribed discussions, to a more cooperative structure. In addition, with each successive discussion, the contents of the discourse improved. Utterances became speech acts, with the students connecting and building on the ideas of others. The students abandoned summaries and retellings and replaced them with related comments, providing explanations for the events that occurred in the stories.

The following sequence, which involved all the students in one group, illustrates the overall improvement in the cooperative structure of the discussions. The children had moved from merely presenting an idea and abandoning it, to speaking for a number of different purposes.

| Allen: | I have a question. I wonder why Manara was so mean to Nyasha. |
|---|---|
| Jeff: | Because she didn't like her. |
| Tami: | She got treated the best. |
| Cathy: | I don't know if everyone agrees but the mean sister, Manara, I think she was greedy and mean. |
| Jeff: | Wicked mean! |
| Cathy: | I know! She kept saying mean things like, "Someday I'll be the queen and you'll be my servant in my household." |
| Jeff: | But they turned around at the end. |
| Cathy: | I know. At the end, the king picked Nyasha as the queen. And I don't know if Manara knew she was the queen. |

The second graders, through practice, became responsible for the content and direction of their interactions and were flexible in their use of strategies to construct group meaning.

**Connecting discourse.** As the second-grade students improved the cooperative structure of the literature discussions, they also refined and amended their use of language. Their use of intertextual connections, personal experiences, and numerous other influences affected the type of discourse they used while they participated in the groups. They developed a unique speech register, a particular way of talking, when speaking to me or another adult, unlike the ways they spoke to their friends on the playground.

Much like adults do when participating in academic situations, these young learners left their informal language behind. They adopted a sophisticated discourse style for the discussions, and they avoided slang. The second graders freely practiced the academic discourse, or "teacher talk," that had been modeled in the classroom.

Bakhtin (1986) explained the assimilation of discourse in two ways. The first explanation for assimilation he called "reciting by heart" or authoritative discourse. Authoritative discourse originates from instructions, rules, directions, and models. The students demonstrated authoritative discourse in many ways. One way was through their references to the universal features of the African folk tales. Throughout the transcripts, there was evidence that the children aligned what they had learned about the particular characteristics of folk tales, which they had graphically depicted on the cognitive map, with reasonable explanations for why certain things occurred. For example, when one child asked another how she knew that one character would outsmart the other, she responded by saying, "This is an African tale. The weak character always outwits the stronger one." Identification of other features of the tales were similarly woven into their conversations. The students made references to the repetition of sounds and words found frequently in the stories, things happening in threes, episodes involving trickery, the characters learning a lesson, and the events often coming full circle.

Another example of authoritative discourse was manifested through the children's use of language referencing, both from the instructional talk and from the texts read. I often could hear my voice echoed in the conversations the students had about the stories. Just as I often challenged students' remarks by saying, "Why do you say that? Can you give me a reason?" so, too, did students use this tactic to get their peers to elaborate. Another example was the types of questions and comments the students made that mirrored those that I typically made in the whole-class discussions. The children knew when we met as a large group that most of my questions were reader based. Consequently, in the peer groups, they made introductory statements that marked their questions as reader based. They introduced new topics by saying, "This story reminded me of…," "I don't understand why…," "One thing I think is…," and "I like the way they…."

The language of the text also greatly influenced the students' language use in the discussions. While making intertextual connections to describe events from story to story, they used the precise language from the texts to embellish the discussions. For example, when discussing the story *Why Mosquitoes Buzz in People's Ears*, the students referred to the broken branch as a "dead limb," talked about the rabbit "running for its life," and recounted the actions of the monkey who was "toppling through the treetops." They rationalized the actions of the iguana, explaining that "he would rather be deaf than listen to such nonsense." They endorsed the mosquito's demise by saying that when he was slapped on the man's ear he was "getting an honest answer." Specific words from one tale were used to describe events, characters, and actions in others. Characters were described as "greedy" and "clever." The children remarked about characters "outwitting" each other, and they experimented with unusual words like "calabash" or colorful language like "the stinging bees" that they encountered in the texts. They left their informal "kid talk" behind and were more likely to use carefully constructed school language, peppered with the language of the texts, when discussing the tales with their peers.

Bakhtin's second explanation for the assimilation of discourse is referred to as "telling in one's own words" or internally persuasive discourse. The students used the words of their peers to inform, reword, and rework their own ideas, making the discourse "half theirs, half someone else's." They made zealous attempts to coconstruct meaning for events and actions that they found confusing or unexplainable. They continually reflected on their own lives to provide help to those who were perplexed during the discussions, and, like adults, they persisted until they were sure everyone understood.

For example, when reading *Mufaro's Beautiful Daughters* (Steptoe, 1987), all the groups at one point during the discussion of the story expressed their dismay about the unfair treatment of the two sisters. In the following excerpt, two students tried to make sense of the situation, possibly drawing from their own experiences to provide an explanation.

Hillary: If the daughters loved each other, then why would one person make fun of the other? I didn't understand why Manara made fun of Nyasha.

Erin: Probably because the older sister is Manara. She probably grew up before her and she probably didn't want to have another sister or probably didn't want to share anything. She was fine by herself and probably just a little sister came along.

Hillary: It's not fair that Manara got to do everything. Manara got to get everything but Nyasha was really the nicest one. So it wasn't fair that Manara was making fun of Nyasha, but Nyasha was the one who was being nice.

Another time the children used internally persuasive discourse to provide explanations for events in the stories was when they tried to rationalize the actions of the animals in the stories. African folk tales almost always use animals for characters. This caused problems for these young learners who, knowing that animals do not have human characteristics, were willing to anthropomorphize them for the purposes of the stories. However, if the animals were going to act like people, then why did they do such foolish things? For example, why didn't Iguana know that putting sticks in his ears would make him deaf? Wouldn't Mosquito know that biting a person hurts? Why didn't Osebo, the leopard-of-the-terrible-teeth, know that he was being tricked? In the following excerpt, the students painstakingly tried to convince one another that the events in the story had some logical explanation.

Todd: That was a stupid thing for the iguana to put sticks in his ears—so dumb.

Melinda: He just didn't want to listen to all that nonsense that mosquito was telling him.

Todd: Yeah.

Brett: He coulda gone deaf, anyway.

| Sean: | If somebody told me a lot of nonsense, I wouldn't want to listen to it. But, I just wouldn't want to put sticks in my ears. |
|---|---|
| Melinda: | Well sticks would be too big for our earlobes. |
| Amanda: | Yeah. |
| Kim: | Yeah, but the iguana's earlobes might be bigger and the sticks— |
| Melinda: | You would have to put cotton balls in our ears. |

Although they initially appeared to have an understanding of the limitations of animals as human characters, the young students did not successfully articulate their grasp of the concept. They continued to confuse fantasy and reality as the discussion progressed. They could not understand, for example, why mosquitoes were not accountable for their actions, as shown in the following dialogue.

| Sean: | I know mosquitoes have no brains—not much brains. But I don't know why they just buzz in people's ears. |
|---|---|
| Melinda: | They just want attention. |
| Kim: | Yeah, that's what the story says and I agree with Melinda. |
| Todd: | Me, too! They have fruit for brains. |
| Melinda: | They just like to bite us—like we like to chew gum. |
| Brett: | Mosquitoes don't have eyes. |
| Kim: | Mosquitoes should know that every time they bite a person it hurts the person. |
| Melinda: | It itches! |
| Brett: | They put poison in there. |

The students made use of their personal experiences and understandings about events that occurred in the stories first to construct individual meaning, then to contribute to the group construction of meaning. The discourse became a melding of ideas from peers, their own personal experiences, and the language of text and instruction. Their limited understanding and knowledge about the motivation for the characters' actions served as a catalyst for the group discussions. Multiple influences played into the children's interpretations of the events in the stories.

# Lessons Learned from Classroom Research

In what ways did these young learners improve my understanding of how students construct meaning? An important lesson I learned was that the students had the ability to choose their own topics and themes when talking about literature. Although it had been common practice to allow them to develop their own topics under my careful supervision, I never really understood the consequences until I read and analyzed the transcripts of their discussions. The students' choice of topics had a profound effect on my own perceptions of children's understanding of stories. The second graders raised many questions and introduced themes that I would not have considered had I been leading the discussions. For example, I found their unyielding attention to rules and fairness—a characteristic of 7- and 8-year-olds—enlightening, and I was delighted when they developed those themes in their discussions. Consequently, when talking about the characters in *Mufaro's Beautiful Daughters*, the students had a supportive community in which to parallel the motivations of the characters to specific circumstances in their own lives. I was pleased to hear them support the "underdog" and at times take an opposing point of view.

The context in which the students were allowed to discuss the stories, without intervention or interruption from an adult, gave them an opportunity to adopt a different demeanor. As teachers, we often direct students to perceive things from another perspective. Yet, when we do, we provide the focus and circumstances. Within these confines, we might not have confidence in second graders' ability to independently adopt a different stance. However, these young learners repeatedly took over the role as teacher and demanded from their peers a closer look from another point of view.

As I would have suspected, the small, peer-led groups gave more students the opportunity to contribute their ideas to the group discussions. In every discussion, all members of the group contributed, at least in part, to the group construction of meaning. Still, there were some surprises. I was amazed to hear the strong voices and opinions of some of the students, including those who rarely spoke in whole-class discussions. I found that once they took the risk and were not scrutinized by their peers, they were less reluctant to contribute and their convictions became loud and clear. I learned critical lessons about what was important to these students. I found myself asking how we, as educators, are to know what is important to students unless we purposefully ask them or provide them with a context in which to investigate, examine, and probe their own questions.

Perhaps the greatest lesson I learned from observing my own second graders participating in peer-led discussion was the fragile balance of roles that a teacher researcher must assume. As a researcher, I was somewhat surprised at the unsophisticated ways in which the children initially interacted when talking about the African tales with their peers. I was aware of the kinds of instruction that preceded the formation of the peer groups. I knew ample time had been given for the students to observe and practice conversation-like discussions about stories. I knew the kinds of questions and discourse the students had come to know as "talking about books." What I could not understand was why, given this systematic instruction, the students were behaving in a less than desirable way.

However, looking at the situation as a teacher, I understood why. Despite my best efforts, the children, without my help, were not quite ready to assume all the responsibility. They needed more time and practice, settling into their new circumstances, before they could feel confident about employing the strategies they had learned to the new context in which they were expected to perform. They needed to revert to the old behaviors that felt comfortable to them and that gave them the most security. They needed to try the functions of talk one at a time before combining them into a repertoire of connected behaviors. Consequently, as teacher, I was not surprised at the outcome. The children had repeatedly shown me that, with sufficient instruction and frequent opportunity for guided and independent practice, their performance in demonstrating understanding of a new skill would indeed improve over time.

## Conclusion

The peer-led groups gave the students a context in which to explore their own topics and place them in their own worlds—real and imagined. Drawing on their own experiences as children and taking into account their limited knowledge and understanding of the world, they attempted to explain characters and events that were not consistent with what they believed to be true. They confronted their fears and addressed their confusions without intimidation or evaluation by an adult, and they developed those topics according to their own frame of reference. Without an adult leading the discussions, the students neither adopted an adult stance nor dismissed their peers' choice of topics as trivial or irrelevant. Using their scholarly language and sophisticated demeanor, they were still allowed to react to the literature like second graders.

Because young children thrive in an imagined world, their perceptions of fantasy versus reality are not always developed. Somehow, the African folk tales contributed to the second graders' acceptance of make-believe. The challenge for these children was to put the stories into the perspective of their own young lives.

# Unanswered Questions

As I reflected on this work, I was left with many questions. Primary among them were questions about the amount of instruction needed to prepare students for independent practice in literature discussion groups.

This study was based on an assumption that second graders needed a great deal of assisted instruction. What would happen if second graders participated in peer discussions without such preparation? How would the discourse change? What about third-, fourth-, and fifth-grade students? Is there a point at which students acquire skills and strategies beneficial to response without demonstration and modeling by the teacher? Should teachers immerse children in response groups and expect that they will get better with practice? Were these second graders successful because of the foundation laid prior to the start of peer-led response groups? Although existing studies support the first point of view, there are, yet, few studies from which to form firm conclusions.

## Questions for Reflection

1. The students in this class focused on themes of rules and fairness. What themes would you want your students to develop? How would you help them develop those themes?

2. In what ways can we help students develop turntaking skills? How can we use literature discussion groups to help our students become more competent language users?

# References

Applebee, A.N. (1978). *The child's concept of story: Ages two to seventeen*. Chicago, IL: University of Chicago Press.

Bakhtin, M.M. (1986). *Speech genres and other late essays* (V.W. McGee, Trans.). Austin, TX: University of Texas Press.

Bloome, D., & Egan-Robertson, A. (1993). The social construction of intertextuality in classroom reading and writing lessons. *Reading Research Quarterly, 28*(4), 305–334.

Brown, C.S., & Lytle, S.L. (1988). Merging assessment and instruction: Protocols in the classroom. In S.M. Glazer, L.W. Searfoss, & L.M. Gentile (Eds.), *Reexamining reading diagnosis: New trends and procedures* (pp. 94–102). Newark, DE: International Reading Association.

Cazden, C.B. (1988). *Classroom discourse: The language of teaching and learning*. Portsmouth, NH: Heinemann.

Cullinan, B.E. (Ed.). (1993). *Children's voices: Talk in the classroom*. Newark, DE: International Reading Association.

Dysthe, O. (1993, April). *The heteroglossic classroom: Interactions of writing and classroom discourse in American history*. Paper presented at the Annual Meeting of the American Educational Research Association, Atlanta, GA.

Eeds, M., & Wells, D. (1989). Grand conversations: An exploration of meaning construction in literacy study groups. *Research in the Teaching of English, 23*(3), 4–29.

Galda, L., Cullinan, B.E., & Strickland, D.S. (1993). *Language, literacy and the child*. Fort Worth, TX: Harcourt Brace.

Gavelek, J. (1986). The social context of literacy and schooling: A developmental perspective. In T.E. Raphael (Ed.), *The contexts of school-based literacy* (pp. 3–26). New York: Random House.

Holland, K.A., Hungerford, R.A., & Ernst, S.B. (1993). *Journeying: Children responding to literature*. Portsmouth, NH: Heinemann.

McCarthey, S. (1990). *Talk about text: Changes in content and authority structures in peer response groups* (Research Report No. 90–5). East Lansing, MI: Michigan State University, National Center for Research on Teacher Education.

McCarthey, S. (1994). Authors, text, and talk: The internalization of dialogue from social interaction during writing. *Reading Research Quarterly, 29*(3), 200–231.

McMahon, S. (1992). *Book club: A case study of a group of fifth graders as they participate in a literature-based reading program*. Unpublished doctoral dissertation, Michigan State University, East Lansing.

Mead, G.H. (1934). *Mind, self, and society from a standpoint of a social behavioralist*. Chicago, IL: University of Chicago Press.

Mehan, H. (1979). *Learning lessons*. Cambridge, MA: Harvard University Press.

O'Flahavan, J.F., Wiencek, B.J., & Marks, T. (1993, December). *Social interpretive development in third grade teacher-assisted and peer discussions about literature*. Paper presented at the Annual Meeting of the National Reading Conference, Charleston, SC.

Paratore, J.R. (1991). *Flexible grouping: Why and how*. Needham Heights, MA: Siver Burdett Ginn.

Roberts, D.R., & Langer, J.A. (1991). *Supporting the process of literary understanding: Analysis of a classroom discussion* (Report Series 2.15). Albany, NY: Center for the Learning and Teaching of Literature.

Rosenblatt, L. (1978). *The reader, the text, the poem.* Carbondale, IL: Southern Illinois University Press.

Short, K. (1992). Intertextuality: Searching for patterns that connect. In C.K. Kinzer & D.J. Leu (Eds.), *Literacy research, theory, and practice: Views from many perspectives* (Forty-first Yearbook of the National Reading Conference, pp. 187–198). Chicago, IL: National Reading Conference.

Tierney, R.J., & Rogers, R. (1989). Exploring the cognitive consequences of variations in the social fabric of classroom literacy events. In D. Bloome (Ed.), *Classrooms and literacy* (pp. 250–263). Norwood, NJ: Ablex.

Villaume, S.K., Worden, T., Williams, S., Hopkins, L., & Rosenblatt, C. (1994). Five teachers in search of a discussion. *The Reading Teacher, 47*(6), 480–489.

Vygotsky, L.S. (1978). *Mind in society: The development of higher level psychological processes* (M. Cole, V. John-Steiner, S. Scribner, & E. Souberman, Eds. and Trans.). Cambridge, MA: Harvard University Press. (Original work published 1934)

Vygotsky, L.S. (1986). *Thought and language* (A. Kozalin, Trans.). Cambridge, MA: MIT Press. (Original work published 1934)

Wells, G. (1986). *The meaning makers.* Portsmouth, NH: Heinemann.

Wertsch, J.V. (Ed.). (1985). *Vygotsky and the social formation of mind.* Cambridge, MA: Harvard University Press.

## Children's Literature References and Other Suggested African Folk Tales

Aardema, V. (1969). *Who's in rabbit's house?* New York: Dial.

Aardema, V. (1975). *Why do mosquitoes buzz in people's ears?* New York: Dial.

Aardema, V. (1985). *Bimwili and the zimwi.* New York: Dial.

Aardema, V. (1989). *Rabbit makes a monkey out of lion.* New York: Dial.

Haley, G.E. (1970). *A story, a story.* New York: Macmillan.

McDermott, G. (1992). *Zomo the rabbit.* New York: Harcourt Brace Jovanovich.

McKissack, P. (1988). *Monkey-monkey's trick.* Boston, MA: Houghton-Mifflin.

Steptoe, J. (1987). *Mufaro's beautiful daughters.* New York: Scholastic.

Wolstein, D. (1981). *The banza.* New York: Dial.

# CHAPTER 3

# Exploring Cultural Diversity
# Through Peer Talk

∞

## SANDY KASER AND KATHY G. SHORT

When both of us entered the classroom as young children, we were expected to be ready for school—either we adjusted to school or we were left behind. Along with our classmates, we marched through the same set of materials and everyone arrived at the same end point (or dropped out of school). Upon graduation, we were considered educated to become citizens who could contribute to society. Unfortunately, many people viewed a "citizen" as monocultural with one set of acceptable characteristics.

When we entered the classroom as teachers, schools had begun to change, most notably in recognizing the different experiences that children bring to school. Our initial experiences with multicultural education were characterized by a superficial focus on ethnicity in which each ethnic group was studied in isolation as a theme study, an activity in a learning center, a set of books, or a special monthly focus. We soon grew dissatisfied with this approach because it set people apart with the assumption that more information would lead to more understanding which, in turn, would bring about the valuing of cultural diversity and a change in behaviors (Banks, 1994). The approach defined culture narrowly and eliminated important characteristics that shape each of us as people. It also implied that ethnicity was static and uniform rather than a dynamic feature of children in classrooms.

Our dissatisfaction led us to explore other approaches to multicultural education. We took time to investigate our students' home experiences, building on research that shows that all children have literacy experiences (Taylor & Dorsey-Gaines, 1988) and that all households have funds of knowledge (Moll, 1992). We changed our definition of readiness to ask how we could create classrooms that are ready for specific children, instead of believing that children must be ready for school.

Through reading and talking with others, we became convinced that recognizing the diversity in students' home experiences was not enough; we also needed to understand how students go about learning in more diverse ways. We created flexible class structures so that students could make decisions about how they would accomplish the work of school. *What* they learned often was still not negotiable, but *when* and *how* they learned that content was more flexible and open. One example of this flexibility was encouraging children to make and share meaning through a variety of sign systems, such as art, music, mathematics, movement, and language (Leland & Harste, 1994). We also highlighted dialogue and created opportunities for children to talk openly and critically with peers about many issues.

However, our thinking about diversity was restricted because our schools continued to define outcomes narrowly. Diversity builds on strengths and we could not always predict the exact outcomes of learning, which made administrators and parents nervous. The message we received was that schools value diversity, but *only if* students can still speak standard English, write a persuasive essay, pass the standardized tests, and meet society's standards for excellence. Our students were led to believe that schools value who they are, but then we were expected to lead them toward becoming monocultural citizens in order to be judged successful (Short & Burke, 1994).

We believe that although schools have begun to recognize and accept diversity, difference is still not respected or addressed. Schools continue to focus on the same educational outcomes for all students despite the fact that it is difference, not sameness, that makes a democracy strong and creates powerful learning environments (Edelsky, 1994). Through building on the different ways of living that students and teachers bring to the classroom, new possibilities are created in everyone's life. We wanted to explore classroom settings that valued everyone's strengths.

Of course, the difficult issue is how to respect and build on difference within an institution that is grounded in hierarchy and sameness. This perplexing question is one that we have explored through reading and talking with other educators as well as through working with students. In this chapter, we want to share experiences that reflect Sandy Kaser's attempts as a teacher to highlight diversity and children's own cultures in more authentic ways. To highlight Sandy's voice and her role as a teacher researcher, the "I" voice throughout the article is hers and the "we" voice reflects both authors.

The chapter is divided into two major sections: The first section examines an expanded view of children's connections to culture, and the second section explores issues of "kid culture." The experiences we share particularly highlight the role of talk about literature as a way for children to consider diverse perspectives (see Chapter 9 for further discussion on peer talk with diverse students). Ultimately our goal is social change in how children view their world and one another. We believe that dialogue about literature is one means of supporting this change.

## Exploring Children's Connections to Culture in the Classroom

I began to explore alternatives to the multicultural unit in my fifth-grade classroom because I wanted to encourage my students to bring their lives into school. I teach in a Tucson, Arizona, USA school that serves a diverse multiethnic working-class community. Although my students reflect a wide range of ethnic backgrounds including African American, American Indian, European American, and Mexican American, I could not recall any of them ever making a personal response to multicultural lessons or units. There never had been occasions of powerful classroom sharing about their cultural connections from these activities.

I searched for a vehicle that would connect home and school—a way to signal to children that how they came to be who they are is of value in school. After reading research and talking with Kathy Short, I devised a cross-curricular, literature-based Family Studies Inquiry to encourage students to explore their own experiences and family background in an effort to better understand themselves (Kaser, 1995). Kathy and I hoped that this curriculum would support children and allow them to value their diversity in experiences, ways of learning, and outcomes as essential to our classroom community and their own learning. The students and their lives became the central focus of the curriculum, with the study of family as a framework and literature discussion as a vehicle for response. Although I developed an initial curriculum framework, the flowchart presented in Figure 1 shows how the curriculum developed with students over the year.

I saw one of my responsibilities as providing students with access to books that might contextualize diverse perspectives in very personal and concrete terms. Books were chosen to encourage students to explore their own cultures and those of others inside and outside the classroom. Although I collected the books, students always were given choice in selecting books to examine more closely. They also had the freedom to explore issues within those books that were of greatest importance to them at that moment. In their literature circles, I hoped that students would share issues relating to the literature in an authentic way through personal response, collaboration, reflection, and dialogue, with questions such as "How does my family compare to the family in the story?" "How do my traditions compare to your traditions?" and "What would I like to know more about?"

The literature circles consisted of small groups of four to five students who engaged in conversation and dialogue about a book (Short & Pierce, 1990) (see Chapters 5, 6, and 10 for further discussion of peer talk in literature circles). Sometimes students used discussion strategies, such as webbing, Sketch to Stretch, and Save the Last Word for Me (Short & Harste, 1996) to facilitate their thinking. Throughout these activities, I collected student artifacts, took field notes, kept a teaching journal, and tape recorded literature circles. To make sense of the data, I constructed profiles of three students to document individual responses across the year. I also examined several whole-group discussions of literature at different points in the year.

Throughout this process, Kathy and I talked frequently about a wide range of curricular and research issues—how to select books, organize the data collection and analysis, and formulate research questions. Kathy's role was both to support and to provide another perspective for me as a teacher researcher. She provided articles about issues of culture and suggested other ways to view children's responses as we examined

## Figure 1    Curriculum Flowchart of Family Studies Inquiry

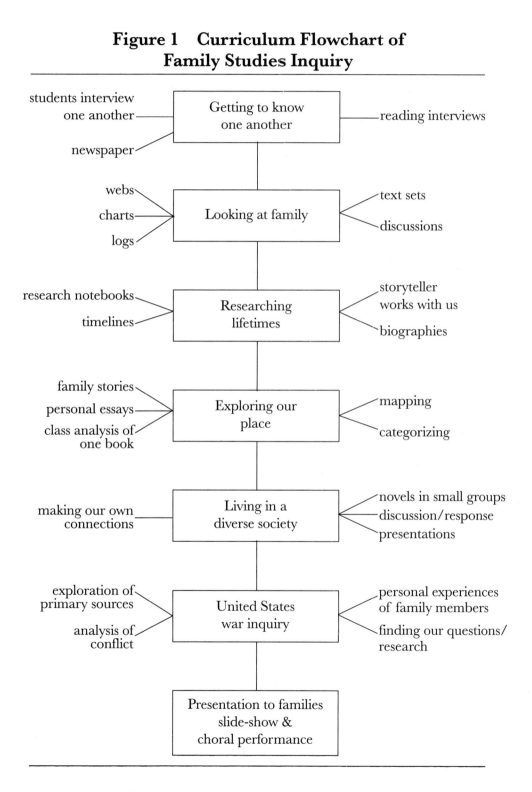

student artifacts and transcripts of children's talk. Although issues of culture pervaded the entire curriculum, we decided to focus solely on literature discussions to examine children's talk and thinking about culture. From previous experiences, we knew that these discussions were particularly generative for this type of talk. Examining literature circles allowed me to focus my data collection, but because I was the classroom teacher I also was aware of the broader context of the classroom.

As students shared issues that were significant to them, I realized that I was still operating under a restricted view of culture. I had assumed that because the students came from such diverse ethnic backgrounds, issues of ethnicity would be the most important aspect of culture that they would want to explore. I spent hours searching for children's books and making sure that they reflected many different ethnic perspectives. What the students taught us was that culture never can be defined that narrowly for *any* person. Although ethnicity mattered to them, other aspects of their own cultures such as gender, religion, family, community, and social class sometimes were of greater importance or were interwoven with issues of ethnicity and race.

## Examining Children's Connections to Culture

In order to understand the aspects of culture that were most significant to children, I examined three students closely to see what issues occurred repeatedly in their conversations and writing across the year (Kaser, 1994). By looking closely at Rosanna, Brad, and Joe, I hoped to better understand how children thought about these connections to culture.

**Rosanna's connections to family.** Rosanna connected with the Family Studies Inquiry immediately. Learning about her family history and traditions and sharing them with the class gave Rosanna a reason for dialogue with family members throughout the year. As she shared her heritage and her stories, the whole class gained a rich sense of her values as a Mexican American. The children saw her stories as authentic knowledge based on the experiences of a member of the classroom community rather than a unit of study mandated by me or the school district.

Yet, from the beginning, Rosanna was most interested in issues of family structure. Although Rosanna's focus on family obviously was intertwined with her ethnic heritage, family structures as culture became her most significant area of inquiry that year. While exploring conceptually related sets of picture books on families, Rosanna chose the set of books on family issues. Her group made a list of what they considered to be the most important family issues: the possibility of Dad being laid off, kids with two families, favorite belongings of families, expectations for boys and girls, families of different races, and foster families.

Foster families became Rosanna's focus immediately and remained so throughout the year. She expressed this interest in an early literature log entry:

> I like the books on foster families because I want to learn about how to help people. I think it is really sad that kids have to be put into foster care.... I want to do a report on foster families for our newsletter.

Rosanna pursued a number of inquiries and selected more literature on foster children. It was Rosanna's self-directed research and discussion of family structures that moved the class a step further in considering situations different from their own—an essential move if they were to fully understand and respect difference. Students began to see their family structures as part of their personal heritage rather than valuing one kind of family over another.

**Brad's connections to family and religion.** Brad began the year with a strong focus on family and generational cultures as he pursued books and conversations about grandparents. The first text set Brad chose to explore dealt with grandfathers. After a literature discussion relating to these books, he wrote the following excerpt:

> Today I made a connection with the books. My grandpa used to take us fishing in Pinetop. We did a lot of stuff like that with him. He died and we don't do that, well, sometimes we do things like that and fish, but I miss him.

When Brad shared this entry with others in the group, it led to the following discussion:

Joe:     I just wish I could have done things with my grandfather. I wish I knew stories that my grandfather would have told me.

| Dan: | Me, too. Brad, you were lucky. I will have to wait and see if my grandfather will tell me stories in heaven. But it is still sad for you. |
|---|---|

Brad later chose the novel *Racing the Sun* (Pitts, 1988) to read in a literature circle. This novel deals with a grandfather and grandson relationship. He continued to work through the death of his grandfather in the first few sessions of the group and made a web in his log about his connections (see Figure 2).

The Family Studies focus gave Brad the opportunity to revisit the death of his grandfather through literature, talk, and writing. Within his discussion group, he found a friend in Joe who shared stories of his own grandfather. Discussions of grandparents led naturally to discussions of heritage, and although Brad had a strong Mexican American and European American heritage, religion was the cultural aspect that seemed to be of greatest importance to him throughout the year.

Midway through *Racing the Sun*, Brad began to look at religion and view it as a significant piece of his culture. He made this log entry:

> I connect with the book in a religious way. People say that the point of time we're in now is the new age. My family and I have to keep our Christian ways as does the grandfather in *Racing the Sun* who has to keep his Indian ways. Next time we may want to talk a little about people in our families who do and don't keep up with the family's background.

Brad did a considerable amount of writing on religion, and he later took leadership in a whole-class discussion comparing his view of God to his perceptions of American-Indian views of God. His interest in these views grew out of his friendship with Joe, a Pima Indian. Here is an excerpt from the whole-class discussion:

| Miguel: | I think that corn dancers are like our folklorico dancing. |
|---|---|
| Joe: | No, they are not the same. When an Indian dances, it is a kind of prayer. We pray by dancing. |
| Brad: | Right, that is what Indians do. But why do you still do that? You pray to the sun and stuff, and you are supposed to pray to God. I am Christian and I pray to God. |
| Murmurs: | We are Catholic and we pray to God. |
| Joe: | I am Catholic and I am Indian also. We pray to one God, but we believe his spirit is in all of nature. There is like a spirit God for each thing in nature. Indians dance all their |

## Figure 2    Brad's Connections to *Racing the Sun*

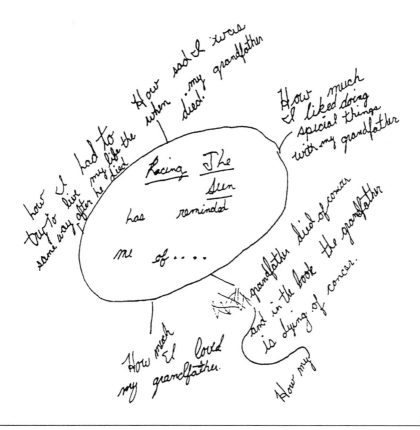

lives, like from age 3. The whole tribe goes to dances. It's not like you can choose.

The Family Studies Inquiry allowed Brad to explore his family's religious belief system and what it might mean in the future. He spoke thoughtfully about religious traditions within the larger class community. Brad contributed in an authentic way to the class's understandings of cultural diversity and encouraged others to share and ask questions. In the past, he always had taken a leadership role in group situations and often ignored others' perspectives. Perhaps because of the personal nature of his inquiry into religion and his grandfather's death, he became more respectful of others' viewpoints and contributed to the group instead of feeling he had to be the group leader.

**Joe's connections to ethnicity.** Throughout all of the class discussions, Joe was a significant contributor to the dialogue. Joe became eagerly involved in the Family Studies Inquiry as soon as books were placed in his hands. He quickly chose the "grandfathers" text set to discuss. Joe enjoyed the format of literature circles and wrote in his log after the first session, "It went really well. Everybody just jumped right in."

Joe "jumped in" during this first session by talking about his favorite book in the set, *Knots on a Counting Rope* (Martin, 1987). He explained that his grandfather had been an eagle dancer and stated that the grandfather in the book was telling a story. He talked about attending Indian gatherings with his family where the old people tell stories. He referred to the illustrations to help his classmates imagine what his grandfather looked like as he danced.

The second book Joe read was *Racing the Sun*. Although Brad chose this book because it was about grandparents, Joe was drawn to the fact that the main characters were Navajo. He made the following observations in the group discussion:

| | |
|---|---|
| Kaser: | I wonder why he [the grandfather] wanted to go back. |
| Joe: | Earlier in the book he says he misses the smell of the sagebrush. |
| Brad: | He didn't feel comfortable in the city. |
| Marcus: | It said he was feeling sick but he felt better at home. |
| Brad: | He wanted to die in his hometown. |
| Joe: | His reservation. |
| Brad: | Maybe it's a custom of the Navajos. On page 116, it says he looks better because he was happy. |
| Joe: | In the city, he was home alone with the family working. He wanted to go to people who were more into their culture, like he was. |
| Brad: | "The father did not want to go," it says on page 117. For the same reasons—each one wanted to stay in his own culture. |
| Joe: | The father said he didn't want the grandfather to be in a car. |
| Brad: | But that was just an excuse. |

Joe:        Brandon [the grandson] wanted to go because he was getting interested in his culture. He was getting closer to the grandfather. The grandfather shared stories, chants and jogging, and growing plants. And besides the father did go back.

After the group spent a few minutes discussing the family's trip to the reservation, Joe brought up an issue that was important to him:

Brad:       Well, anyway, I think the book is about how to take on the new ways without having to give up the old.

Joe:        You shouldn't give up on your heritage.

Brad:       Yeah, but, sometimes people aren't proud of heritage because traditions seem silly.

Randy:     It doesn't seem up-to-date. He even calls it "the old ways."

Brad:       I think the father was just trying to get away from the stereotyping of Indians—riding horses, shooting arrows.

Joe:        Yeah, well, I still think people should stay in their heritage, but no one in my family is into it. Like that guy in the story, they want to go on with life and pretend they are not Indian. I feel more like Brandon. I'm interested.

Marcus:   I'm like Brandon, too. I want to remember.

In this discussion, Joe took on the stance of an authority as the only American Indian in the group and drew upon his connections to his own ethnicity. It was apparent throughout the year that Joe was thinking through what being an Indian meant to him. He developed an awareness of how people around him view their own ethnic heritage and how they, in turn, are viewed by the broader society. Joe clearly saw the Family Studies Inquiry as a place where he could articulate his concerns and understandings. He felt a sense of identity with the Indian characters in the books he read, and he was more participatory in group discussions that centered on these books. He expressed disappointment that his family seemed to place more importance on becoming part of mainstream society than on developing their own ethnic uniqueness. I introduced Joe to a resource teacher who supported him in finding people and materials to further his personal inquiry. He felt a sense of status in the classroom as the "resident expert." His focus on ethnicity contributed to and was interwoven throughout class discussions of culture. As a result, the Family Studies focus helped draw him into rather than set him apart from his community of peers.

Because Kathy and I did not decide ahead of time what issues students needed to study or how they should respond to what they read, students were able to create meaning for themselves. Although teachers need an instructional framework through which to offer support, learning takes place when students are able to make connections to their knowledge and personal experiences, searching for new information based on their interests and needs.

The use of quality children's literature that was enjoyable and representative of cultural diversity was crucial to the Family Studies Inquiry. The literature selections enabled a range of issues relating to culture to surface, and students knew they could do their own thinking and enter into dialogue with others to make sense of the literature and their own life.

## Expanding the Definition of Culture

As we examined children's talk and how they chose the aspects of culture that were most significant to them at a given moment, we realized the importance of defining culture as all the ways in which people live and think in the world. "Culture can be understood as the shared patterns that set the tone, character and quality of people's lives" (Geertz, 1973, p. 216). These ways of living and thinking include language, religion, gender, social relationships, socioeconomic status, ethnicity, race, family structures, region, and rural, suburban, and urban communities.

Fleck's (1935) discussion of thought collectives helped us think about culture more broadly. He defined thought collectives as groups of people who learn to think in similar ways because they share a common interest, exchange ideas, maintain interaction over time, and create a history that affects how they think and live. Because most individuals think and act within several thought collectives at a time, this view captures the dynamic, evolving nature of culture as each person interacts with, and is changed through, transactions with other cultures.

These understandings about culture were important to us for several reasons. One reason was that they allowed us to see the diversity of children's own interconnected talk and issues of culture. Another reason was that they removed the "other" within the classroom. When culture within multicultural education is defined only as ethnicity and race, then many people view culture as a characteristic of particular groups and as outside the experience of everyone else; multicultural curriculum remains a separate unit or book, not a characteristic of the classroom learning environment. What we found was that when students and teachers recognize the cultures that influence their own life and thinking, they become more aware of how and why culture is important to everyone else. These understandings do not devalue culture or promote cultural sameness but highlight differences across cultures as important and valued in creating community and providing multiple perspectives that enhance everyone's learning.

In examining children's talk, we also noted that it was important that children chose the aspects of culture they did and did not want to discuss. Sometimes students did not talk about the issues of their cultural identity that seemed to be most significant to them. We respected their right not to discuss these issues. Other times, we noticed that students were able to voice their concerns by talking about a character from a book rather than about themselves.

## Understanding the Role of "Kid Culture"

As we examined the transcripts, Kathy and I noticed that there was one aspect of culture that we had overlooked consistently. Students often discussed how a topic or book related to the culture they shared with members of their age group. These issues went beyond differences in their personal histories and cultural identities to a set of shared "kid" values.

### Talking About Issues of Kid Culture

One day I read aloud *Angel Child, Dragon Child* (Surat, 1983), the story of a Vietnamese girl who is laughed at in school because of her ethnic dress. I hoped the book would spark a discussion about accepting differences; instead, the class was incensed that someone had not told the girl how children dress in school. It was clear that the students judged their peers by the way they dressed and that they knew how to dress in order to send a desired message to others. The class discussion about the book and this issue follows on the next page.

Rosanna: It was sad in the book when they teased her because she was different. They said she wore pajamas.

Manny: Yeah, that was pretty dumb. Somebody should have told her to dress like all the other kids. She has to fit in more. How you dress in school is important.

Rosanna: It's important because people look at you and judge you by what you are wearing on the outside.

Sophia: Your hair is also part of how you are dressed. Hairstyles are *really* important.

Rosanna: Mexican girls wear their hair different than other kids. It's usually bushier and more teased.

Joe: Most people dress according to their personality. Like some people are all laid back and some come to school like fashion plates.

Manny: Nerds dress different—like pocket protectors or bow ties—just to say, "I'm part of the nerd group."

Brad: And you can tell gang members by how they dress. And the gang wanna-be's dress like gang members and act all cool, but everyone knows they are not in the gangs.

Rosanna: Like if you are a nature person who goes hiking and stuff, you wear khaki clothes and hiking boots even if you are not hiking that day.

Manny: And she just walked in and communicated, "Hey, look at me. I'm different." She was different enough.

Brad: If it was us in Vietnam, then *we* would be the different ones.

The next day Dan brought up the book again. He said he felt sorry for the girl because "when you go to a new school you don't always know the rules." From his comments, it was clear that he meant the implied rules known only by students, not the school rules. He shared his own experiences moving to a new school, and many of the students told stories about moving. They agreed that going to a different school was one of the most difficult things a child has to do and was not understood by adults. "They just walk in the door and tell you, boom, 'you have go live with your Dad,' and boom, your whole life is different," said Dan. The discussion then dealt with the lack of power children feel around adults.

The class felt that children made up rules for one another because it gave them power.

In later literature discussions students talked about other issues such as the importance of parents considering how names will affect children and how certain names can become embarrassing. They talked about the difficulty of making decisions because of divided loyalties among family, peers, and their desires as a child. They especially felt strongly about situations in which parents disagree and the child's decision can be seen as siding with one parent over the other.

## Recognizing the Importance of Kid Culture

Kathy and I realized that students were connecting cultural diversity with the expectations and culture of their own age group. Although today's students are bombarded with issues of ethnicity, the story of growing up that each student creates also is an important focus in their life. The struggle to determine who they are as individuals is a struggle all children share, irrespective of differences in their cultural characteristics. This behavior is consistent with Bullivant's (1989) definition of culture as "a social group's design for surviving in and adapting to its environment" (p. 27).

Even as early as elementary school, children define and view one another through their shared definitions of "kid culture." Essentially kid culture is the underground peer culture of how children of a certain age think about themselves. Lurie (1990) points out, "Anyone who has spent time around children and observed them carefully, or really remembers what it was like to be a child, knows that childhood is also a separate culture, with its own rituals, beliefs, games, and customs, and its own, largely oral, literature" (p. 194).

Children often use peer talk to judge and control the behaviors of classmates. These kid culture issues of acceptance and rejection touch all aspects of the lives of young people—music, talk, appearance, behavior, values, and priorities, as well as ways to maintain and achieve status. This culture is revealed only in classrooms where space is provided for conversation on significant issues.

Newkirk (1992) discusses the culture of children through examining first and second graders' talk about literature. Children brought a discourse into discussion groups that he initially found annoying and believed was off-task talk. However, in reexamining this talk, he became convinced that it was a valid form of discourse from children's own culture. Children came to groups "not as total novices but as members of a rich oral culture that has its own repertoire of responses" (p. 9).

As adults, we teachers are excluded from this kid culture, and we found that we had to work hard to understand and value the ways in which this culture entered into children's talk about literature. Although we wanted to encourage children to accept and understand differences, significant changes in their attitudes often could not occur because they had another more powerful agenda that we were not taking into account. Kid culture has a tremendous influence on children and frequently involves values that conflict with other aspects of their cultures and with the teacher's values. Yet this culture is left out of curriculum designed to explore cultural diversity. Either we teachers are unaware of it, or we assume that children will grow out of this developmental stage. Other times we find kid culture in conflict with the values of cultural diversity that we are trying to promote, so we ignore or judge it. Children respond by taking their culture underground so that it becomes a secret code known only to one another, rather than examining it critically as they talk freely about issues in school. We also knew that as adults we could not force children to discuss kid culture issues. We could, however, create an environment in which they felt free to discuss this aspect of their identities among themselves.

The students' talk about literature allowed us to identify what was missing in other aspects of the curriculum. One day a substance abuse officer talked with students about drugs and saying "no" to those who offer drugs. The students had family members who used drugs and belonged to gangs, and they knew that life on the streets among their peers just was not that simple. The role playing they were asked to do involved adult language that would be viewed negatively or ignored within their kid culture. They needed language and strategies to avoid drugs that fit their own culture of peers and the street. Because the officer's comments did not connect to their world, they simply rejected the comments as irrelevant and repeated what he wanted them to say without engaging with the issues.

Our experiences convinced us that children feel that the discourse common in their kid culture has no place in the classroom. When they do not talk in adult discourse, they are judged by teachers, not as different, but as deficient. Nodelman (1992) asserts that adults attempt to speak for children, even through children's literature, because adults believe children are incapable of speaking for themselves; they see children as different from, and presumably inferior to, adults as thinkers and speakers. Nodelman suggests that some adults view children as innocent rather than lacking in intelligence, but this assumption still allows adults to have power over children.

## Acknowledging Kid Culture in the Classroom

We found that instead of urging children to get back on task when they engaged in talk from kid culture, we needed to provide structures to support them in exploring this talk openly and critically with one another. When presented with an alternative perspective, students need to find where it might fit with what they already know, understand, or have experienced. If social change is implied, then social context is significantly relevant to our curriculum. As teachers, we wanted to provide a place for talk about kid culture to intermingle with other concerns of cultural heritage and with acceptance and understandings across cultures. Time and opportunity for this talk is essential for children if we really believe that they need to bring their lives into the classroom.

Nodelman (1992) points out that, as adults, we never will completely escape the "imperialist" tendencies that are at the heart of our discourse with children. We also never can completely understand kid culture because the culture changes with each generation and, by its definition, excludes adults. However, we can become aware of the ways in which we oppress and deny kid culture and move beyond thinking children are like us or seeing them as different from us. Because kid culture is generational and separate from the cultural identities children share with adults, we must respect their need to keep some of this discussion private. We believe that students need to talk about kid culture in order to understand and critique its role in their lives.

During the Family Studies Inquiry, a strategy that worked well was to listen to children's comments and ask questions when I did not understand or value what they were saying. In the past, I would have rejected or ignored their discussions of topics such as the importance of children dressing in particular ways in favor of what I saw as more direct connections to the book being read. Instead of judging students, I tried to reply to their comments out of a sincere desire to understand what they were saying (Barnes, 1976). As they expanded on their comments, the students could explore those aspects of kid culture together and discuss social attitudes within their own contexts. However, if my comments or questions were interpreted as being judgmental, the students immediately stopped sharing any connections to or reflection on their kid culture.

Kathy and I also found that children needed to talk in small groups where teachers were not present. No matter how carefully I tried to listen empathetically, I was viewed as an outsider and there were certain aspects of kid culture that were not discussed when I was present. Their humor, for example, was rarely shared with me because they presumed I would not understand or like it; however, the talk surfaced when students met in small groups without me.

"If the only talk that matters is that which is patterned off adult conversation, students can conclude that what matters most to them, their culture, has little place in the classroom" (Newkirk, 1992, p. 10). Educators have known for years that when children of diverse ethnicities feel their culture has no place in the classroom, they often reject the curriculum and resist the learning experiences of that classroom. We believe that these same findings apply to children who feel that adults deny or devalue their kid culture. They have learned to be silent about their culture around adults, and, in so doing, the culture becomes even more powerful in their lives. In these situations there is no opportunity for students to explore or critique kid culture or to make connections across all aspects of their cultures. One of our goals is that students can bring together the cultures of home, school, and peers and explore the connections and the disjunctions across those cultures. In order for this to occur, children need space to share issues of kid culture through peer talk.

# Implications for Schools and Classrooms

In thinking about children's responses to the Family Studies Inquiry, we identified what seemed to be key characteristics of the curriculum that provided room for valuing differences in experiences, ways of learning, and outcomes in the classroom. One characteristic is the importance of setting up engagements that allow teachers to really listen to students. We found that ways of listening needed to be planned into the day or the busyness of teaching would cause teachers to miss hearing what children said. Teachers need a sense of students' thinking in order to support them in making connections and building from their own experiences to new ideas. In addition, both dialogue and storying are essential for children to make connections and consider new ideas. Children need to be constantly encouraged to share oral, written, and visual stories from their lives so that they can explore their own personal connections and thoughts. Through this sharing of stories, they develop a sense of community that allows them to enter into dialogue with one another. Dialogue involves thinking with others so that their ideas and connections are considered thoughtfully and critically. Dialogue focuses on inquiry and critique and takes learners beyond their own ideas to consider new perspectives and ways of viewing the world (Peterson, 1992). Dialogue about literature in literature circles provides children with multiple perspectives as they enter the world of the story and share their interpretations with one another. They make connections to their personal lives and cultural identities, but they also examine other possible worlds through the characters in books and the talk of their peers.

In encouraging dialogue, we are aware that for some students, disclosure of themselves through dialogue or writing is not culturally appropriate. Our belief in the importance of literature and dialogue is the result of our own cultural values. Although we remain committed to their role in children's learning, we also believe that we have no right to force children to make personal disclosures. Should students choose not to discuss personal issues, they still can benefit from hearing others' perspectives and can become better able to make thoughtful decisions about what they read.

Another essential characteristic is that the classroom curriculum should be focused on inquiry, on children searching for the questions that are significant to them, instead of on covering a particular topic through sets of activities. Even when the topic is mandated by the school, children still can find their own questions within that topic. American history was part of the mandated school curriculum for fifth grade, but I waited to see where it would fit with children's questions. Their interest in timelines and family histories led the students to the realization that their own family members had participated in significant events in American and Mexican history. When the class began this study, I did not decide on the topics of study or have children sign up for groups based on my topics. Instead, students spent time reading and talking so they could develop questions; then they formed groups based on those questions.

Research that involved children's own families and communities was integral to all their inquiries. Children collected oral family stories, researched their family timelines, and interviewed family members. Their experiences in school led them to ask questions and gather data from their families. Sharing this data with one another led them to new questions and research in books and other sources and then back to their families.

# Conclusion

These characteristics of curriculum are based on our belief that cultural diversity is a strength for building strong learning contexts, not a problem to be solved. Difference, not sameness, makes a classroom and society strong. Along with Sleeter and Grant (1987), we believe that our goal is not multicultural education as an additive to the curriculum, but an education that *is* multicultural.

The goal of schools in our modern global society is to create productive citizens who have marketable skills. The goal of education in traditional oral societies is for children to learn how to become human beings—to figure out who they are and where they fit in the broader scheme of things (Oleska, 1995). We believe that both goals are essential in schools today. To become a citizen, but lose your personal identity, is not acceptable within school contexts. If schools truly respect and build on difference, diversity can become a strength for creating powerful classroom learning environments and a stronger democratic society.

## Questions for Reflection

1.  What are the cultural identities that are significant in your life that shape your thinking and learning?

2.  How might a consideration of children's multiple cultural identities, including their "kid culture," influence curriculum in your classroom context?

# References

Banks, J. (1994). *Multiethnic education: Theory and practice*. Needham Heights, MA: Allyn & Bacon.

Barnes, D. (1976). *From communication to curriculum*. Portsmouth, NH: Heinemann.

Bullivant, B.M. (1989). Culture: Its nature and meaning for educators. In J. Banks & C. Banks (Eds.), *Multicultural education: Issues and perspectives* (pp. 27–48). Needham Heights, MA: Allyn & Bacon.

Edelsky, C. (1994). Education for democracy. *Language Arts, 71*, 252–257.

Fleck, L. (1935). *The genesis and development of a scientific fact*. Chicago, IL: University of Chicago Press.

Geertz, C. (1973). *The interpretation of cultures*. New York: Basic Books.

Kaser, S. (1994). *Exploring cultural identity*. Unpublished educational specialist thesis, University of Arizona, Tucson.

Kaser, S. (1995). Creating a learning environment that invites connections. In S. Steffey & W. Hood (Eds.), *If this is social studies, why isn't it boring?* York, ME: Stenhouse.

Leland, C., & Harste, J. (1994). Multiple ways of knowing: Curriculum in a new key. *Language Arts, 71*, 337–345.

Lurie, A. (1990). *Don't tell the grown-ups: Subversive children's literature*. Boston, MA: Little, Brown.

Moll, L. (1992). Bilingual classroom studies and community analysis: Some recent trends. *Educational Researcher, 21*(2), 21–24.

Newkirk, T. (1992). *Listening in*. Portsmouth, NH: Heinemann.

Nodelman, P. (1992). The other: Orientalism, colonialism, and children's literature. *Children's Literature Association Quarterly, 17*(1), 29–35.

Oleska, M. (1995). *Communicating across cultures* (videotape series). Juneau, AK: University of Southeastern Alaska.

Peterson, R. (1992). *Life in a crowded place*. Portsmouth, NH: Heinemann.

Short, K., & Burke, C. (1994, July). *Curriculum as Inquiry*. Presentation at the Annual Whole Language Umbrella Conference, San Diego, CA.

Short, K., & Harste, J. (1996). *Creating classrooms for authors and inquirers*. Portsmouth, NH: Heinemann.

Short, K., & Pierce, K.M. (Eds.). (1990). *Talking about books*. Portsmouth, NH: Heinemann.

Sleeter, C., & Grant, C. (1987). An analysis of multicultural education in the United States. *Harvard Education Review, 57*, 421–444.

Taylor, D., & Dorsey-Gaines, C. (1988). *Growing up literate: Learning from inner-city families*. Portsmouth, NH: Heinemann.

## Children's Literature References

Martin, B. (1987). *Knots on a counting rope*. New York: Holt.

Pitts, P. (1988). *Racing the sun*. New York: Avon.

Surat, M. (1983). *Angel child, dragon child*. New York: Scholastic.

# CHAPTER 4

# Lessons Taught and Lessons Learned: How Cross-Aged Talk About Books Helped Struggling Adolescents Develop Their Own Literacy

∞

## FENICE B. BOYD AND LEE GALDA

The need to explore alternative literacy-learning contexts for adolescents who struggle with reading, writing, and schooling has never been greater. Approximately 48% of students in the United States dropped out of grade 12 in 1992, and many adolescents as young as 15 decide to discontinue their schooling before grade 12, 31.3% dropping out in grade 11, and 20.9% dropping out in grade 10 (National Center for Education Statistics, 1992). These alarming statistics suggest that U.S. high schools are failing to help many students continue their education successfully. Individuals who drop out of school will not have adequate literacy skills to sustain themselves in an ever-changing advanced technological society. Likewise, society will inherit many consequences due to dropouts because the nation will not benefit from the potential and talent of many adolescents. This chapter explores an alternative program for literacy learning based on dialogue and discussion that enlists students who struggle with literacy as teachers of younger students. The data reported here are part of a larger study by Boyd (1996); the chapter is written in her voice.

# Lessons Already Learned:
# Effective Literacy Instruction

Students drop out of school for countless reasons, and failure in literacy acquisition and development certainly is an underlying cause for many (Allington & McGill-Franzen, 1993). Researchers have documented several indicators of long-term difficulty with literacy learning:

- More than 90% of the children placed in the lowest reading group in first grade are still poor readers in the upper grades (Juel, 1988).

- Children labeled as poor readers and writers during primary grades are among those children most likely to be retained (Shepherd & Smith, 1989).

- Children who are retained are those who are most likely to be classified as handicapped or learning disabled (Ysseldyke, Thurlow, Mecklenburg, & Graden, 1984).

- Low academic achievement, retention, and special-education placement all are associated with dropping out of school, teen parenthood, and unemployment or limited earning power in adulthood (Edelmann, 1988).

Often, the type of instructional approaches provided to poor readers and writers contributes to why these students do not achieve academically. Instruction for students who do not read and write well typically has been based on behavioral theories. This perspective limits definitions of success to the products of literacy activities, such as oral fluency or the ability to answer literal comprehension questions, rather than the processes of reading and writing. Many of these theories have ignored the social nature of literacy learning. Both behavioral and cognitive theories pervade instructional programs that emphasize decontextualized skills-based instruction. This is especially true for students who read and write poorly.

This type of literacy instruction has been criticized because of its reliance on practicing skills in isolation (Allington & McGill-Franzen, 1989), tracking students into low-level literacy experiences (Applebee, 1991) and not providing opportunities for working with a variety of literary genres (Walmsley & Walp, 1990). Scholars have noted the limited success of skills-based instructional programs (Carter, 1984; Glass, 1986), suggesting that there are consequences for the students' development of higher cognitive processes. The very nature of traditional literacy instruction is narrowly focused because it does not encompass strategies that might enable students to develop critical thinking skills. Because many adolescents remain trapped in traditional skills-based programs (such as remedial reading) throughout their high school years, we need to change our thinking about approaches to literacy instruction for students who do not read and write well and who, all too often, drop out of school.

Other scholars (see, for example, Au & Mason, 1981; Cazden, 1988b; Michaels, 1981) document the differential treatment of diverse and minority learners in school contexts and argue that such differential treatment negatively affects students' achievement in literacy learning. Others note the overrepresentation of students from diverse cultural and ethnic backgrounds in traditional skills-based literacy programs (Kennedy, Jung, & Orland, 1986).

There is a lack of opportunity for low-tracked students to initiate interactions with their teachers or peers. Interactions that do occur follow the pattern of teacher-controlled initiation, response, and evaluation (IRE) (Cazden, 1988a), mentioned in earlier chapters in this volume. Although such procedures appear to work well among high achievers and students who are well motivated, they do not appear to benefit low achievers (Applebee, 1989). With such prescribed literacy activities from the teacher, low-achieving students have little voice about what they read or write about in their literacy programs and have few opportunities for discussion. Their development in literacy learning is contingent upon working on decontextualized basic skills in order to reach a specific level of reading ability; it involves little or no opportunity to develop the control or the motivation they will need for their long-term literacy education.

Because traditional skills-based approaches to literacy instruction have not been sufficient for ongoing literacy development of many poor readers and writers, it is imperative that we identify reasonable options to assist our students in developing their own literacy education. This endeavor requires that we think about what we know about current conceptions of language, literacy, and learning, and about the population of students about whom we are concerned.

# Establishing a Context for Literacy Instruction

Many scholars suggest that, because human development and learning are intrinsically social and interactive (Wells & Chang-Wells, 1992), literacy learning is enhanced when students have opportunities to engage in natural, meaningful context-embedded interactions. Becoming literate involves social interactions with other readers and writers, as well as individual cognitive achievement. Collaborative modes of social interaction and learning acknowledge the central role of language (Bakhtin, 1986; Vygotsky, 1978; Wells, Chang, & Maher, 1990) as reading, writing, speaking, and listening. These literacy activities are means to communicate intentions and meanings between the reader and text, and among people involved in the reading act. Background knowledge, experiences, and multiple voices play a significant role in how all readers construct meaning from what they read. Much of this research has been conducted with young children. This chapter considers what benefit meaningful and purposeful interactions have for the literacy learning of low-achieving adolescents who are at risk of school failure. Emphasizing the cognitive *and* social aspects of literacy has direct implications for work with adolescents who struggle with reading, writing, and schooling.

# Theory and Rationale for a Cross-Aged Literacy Program

The purpose of the larger study, a portion of which is reported here, was to investigate the experiences of adolescents who struggle with reading, writing, and schooling as they participated in alternative literacy-learning contexts constructed around fundamental principles of social constructivism. As mentioned in earlier chapters, social constructivism stresses the importance of language and social interaction in learning (Vygotsky, 1978). Three principles undergird social constructivist theories in learning: (1) Higher psychological functions such as reading and writing are both social and cultural in nature; (2) Knowledge is constructed through the interactions among individuals within the social context; and (3) Learning is fostered through the assistance of more knowledgeable members of the community and culture.

Whether students are gifted or low achieving or attend elementary or high school, the principles of social constructivism acknowledge the role of oral and written language. Oral and written language are significant to consider when emphasizing the cognitive and social nature of learning for students who struggle in their literacy development.

For this study, literacy-learning experiences for low-achieving high school students occurred within multiple contexts of the Cross-Aged Literacy Program. The adolescents were provided opportunities to use oral and written language for learning and meaning construction with fourth and fifth graders in goal-embedded, task-oriented settings. All students engaged in literary discussions and responded and reacted to their peers' ideas. Participants in this cross-aged literacy program came from different academic, cultural, ethnic, and social backgrounds. The discussion groups created rich contexts in which older and younger students could interrelate, generate meanings, and transform and negotiate their own values.

# Lessons Taught: Description of the Cross-Aged Literacy Project

The Cross-Aged Literacy Program developed by Boyd (1996) extends and modifies concepts articulated by McMahon, Raphael, Goatley, and Pardo (1997) in the Book Club Program and by Topping (1988) in his discussions of peer tutoring. Basic components of the program were preparation seminars, which included debriefing sessions and cross-aged literary discussion groups. The preparation seminar supported the cross-aged activities of the high school and elementary school students by preparing the high school students to work with the younger children. It also allowed the high school students to consider their experiences in previous cross-aged discussion groups and to think about themselves as both teachers and literacy practitioners. The cross-aged discussion groups consisted of a high school student who led, facilitated, and actively participated in a conversation about a piece of literature with four to six children.

## The Preparation Seminar

The first component of the program was the preparation seminar. The purposes of this component were threefold: (1) to facilitate literacy-learning activities and tasks with the high school participants one to two times per week in a small group, (2) to plan the literacy activities and tasks that the high school students would do with younger children, and (3) to conduct debriefing sessions with the high school participants after each session they conducted with the younger students. Debriefings enabled the high school students to assess the strengths and weaknesses of previous cross-aged sessions. The intent underlying the preparation seminar was to prepare the high school students to engage in literacy-learning activities before meeting with younger children, and to provide a context for them to monitor and assess the nature of the social interactions and their overall experience as participants in an alternative literacy program.

The preparation seminar was part instructional and part collaborative learning between the high school students and me. Instructionally, my overarching goal was to help them develop much-needed skills and strategies relating to fluency and expression in oral reading, comprehension, and response. Learning centered around these literacy areas as students collaborated to prepare for their upcoming work with the fourth and fifth graders, work that would parallel our activities in the preparation seminar.

The instructional activities spanned from selecting the literature to creating contexts for the high school students to read, respond to, and discuss the selected texts. There were five instructional foci:

1. select and read children's literature together orally,
2. write personal responses in reading logs,
3. share and discuss written responses among members of the group,
4. plan and prepare the agenda before meeting with the elementary students, and
5. conduct debriefing sessions to reflect and analyze the group dynamics after meeting with the elementary students.

The following sections explain these instructional activities and decisions, then describes the collaborative activities in which the students engaged to prepare for the cross-aged literacy events.

**Selecting and reading literature.** Scholars suggest several determining factors (such as, emotion, story understanding and liking, and empathy with a certain character) that influence how students engage in a piece of literature (Black & Seifert, 1985; Golden & Guthrie, 1986; Hansen, 1986; Jose & Brewer, 1984). These ideas influenced me as I selected the literature for the cross-aged literacy program. For this project, we read two picture books: *Tuesday* (Wiesner, 1991) and *June 29, 1999* (Wiesner, 1992). In addition, we read two novels: *Song of the Trees* (Taylor, 1975) and *Journey to Jo'Burg* (Naidoo, 1986). I selected the picture books because they are virtually wordless. The wordless picture books provided the students with an experience in which they were not able to rely on learned patterns of response such as IRE, and instead took risks in their oral and written responses. The novels were selected because they center on themes and issues that address conflict and multicultural understandings. I believed that these novels would encourage rich discussions between the adolescents and me, and between the high school students and the younger students. In addition, since the high school participants for this program were minority students, I selected literature that might raise some issues of personal relevance and interest to them (Purves & Beach, 1972).

In our preparation seminar, the high school students read orally on a voluntary basis. If students did not wish to read aloud, I did not push them. If they chose not to read, I read orally to them, using the occasion as an opportunity to model fluency, intonation, and expression. Sloan (1991) suggests that when adults read orally to young children, this assigns a special role to reading, signaling to the child that adults find reading worthwhile and enjoyable. This notion also applies to high school students who are less motivated to read. As our project and relationships progressed, the high school students eventually began to take risks and read orally. In fact, they reached a point where they were willing to volunteer to read orally in the preparation seminar as well as in the cross-aged sessions. The students would proceed by turntaking, using a pause or end of a section or chapter to change readers. An exciting time of the study occurred when students showed initiative to read. It appeared that they had gained enough confidence in themselves to read orally in public.

**Writing.** I wanted to provide a context that would give students an opportunity to express themselves personally by writing responses to literature. This entailed providing a means to respond that was more than fill-in-the blank answers to questions. To do this, students wrote entries in their reading logs in response to questions that either I or their peers raised, a key issue or event in the story that they wanted to discuss, or an idea selected from the Reading Log Ideas response sheet developed by members of the Book Club research project (Raphael, Pardo, Highfield, & McMahon, 1997). The response sheet enabled them to write their reactions from a broad range of options, giving them opportunities to choose and make decisions about what ideas to share and how to share them (Goatley & Raphael, 1992). I modified the response sheet to include ideas that high school students and elementary students might find interesting to write about. Options that students might choose from included drawing pictures, developing a character map, and writing about a character's point of view.

The reading logs we used were based on the ideas proposed by researchers who suggest that journals are a significant tool for students to reflect about their reading, to encourage close reading, and to prepare for later sharing of their ideas (Atwell, 1987; Blatt & Rosen, 1982; Fulwiler, 1982). Students wrote a response to a particular piece of the text they wanted to share in the preparation seminar as a way to prepare for our discussion once or twice per week.

**Discussion.** The discussion component of the preparation seminar promoted two goals: (1) focusing on key issues or events in the literature, and (2) preparing students to engage in a literary discussion with younger children. For example, when reading the picture books *Tuesday* and *June 29, 1999,* I decided to focus on helping students learn more about using picture books to create meaning (Galda, 1988). Because *Tuesday* is wordless, I asked students to concentrate on creating their own story using the illustrations in the book as a frame. The detailed illustrations provided an opportunity to examine the reading experience closely, focusing on what students observed in the illustrations and how they interpreted them. My role during the discussion component was that of facilitator; I provided the students with an opportunity to respond personally to the text and experience open-ended discussions with their peers and me before going to the elementary school. As we participated in our discussion together, I modeled with them what their role and interactions might look like with the fourth and fifth graders as they discussed their novels.

After the students had an opportunity to read, write, and personally respond to the literature, we reflected on the activities, brainstormed, and planned literacy activities they might do with the fourth and fifth graders.

This resulted in another phase of discussion designed to plan literacy activities and tasks for the younger children.

**Planning the lessons.** The high school students were expected to conduct discussions with the children in their small groups in ways similar to the discussions in the preparation seminar, so we planned lessons and procedures to guide them in facilitating a literary discussion with the fourth and fifth graders. We began the planning component of the preparation seminar by talking about the reading, writing, and discussion activities in which we engaged (for example, who read, what was read, what key issues were raised, and what they might talk about with younger children) as a model to help us develop lesson plans. Therefore, planning for the cross-aged literary discussions centered around who would read orally at Angelou Elementary, what chapter(s) or section(s) would be read, and what key questions, issues, and events would be raised. A variety of ideas emerged relating specifically to what key issues and events students might talk about in their small groups. After debating what would be discussed and developing questions, we made final decisions. I typed the lesson plans for the high school students to use as a guide when they worked with the younger children in their individual groups.

**Debriefing of previous discussions.** A final focus of the preparation seminar, the debriefing, centered on analysis and reflection to assess the nature of the cross-aged interactions during previous discussions. I planned the debriefing phase of the preparation seminar to talk with the high school students about their roles and responsibilities in their small groups, the strengths and weaknesses of the cross-aged sessions, and what they learned about themselves as facilitators of cross-aged discussion groups with fourth and fifth graders.

To generate discussion of roles and responsibilities as participants in the study, I gave students a list of guidelines that briefly outlined what good tutors do when they work with young children (see Figure on page 75). Together, the high school students and I read and discussed the guidelines. I explained to them that they were role models for the children at Angelou Elementary, and that the guidelines should be used as a reference for appropriate behavior that role models should display. Over the course of the study, discussions about students' roles and responsibilities emerged based on the experiences that they encountered in their

# 15 Things a Good Tutor Does

1. Smiles often and is friendly at all times.
2. Asks friendly questions before each session.
3. Is on time.
4. Is prepared for the tutoring session.
5. Uses time efficiently.
6. Gives clear instructions.
7. Keeps correct, up-to-date records.
8. Remembers to praise partner(s), never criticizes.
9. Says things like "Very good," "Right," "You are doing very well," and "Nice job."
10. Thinks of other ways to praise so he or she does not always say the same thing.
11. Never says "That's wrong" or "No."
12. Never does or says anything to make the partner(s) feel bad.
13. Helps partner(s) feel he or she is doing well so he or she will enjoy being tutored.
14. Gets the job done.
15. Has a good time.

small groups. For example, if a high school student had one child who dominated discussion time during the cross-aged session, we brainstormed for ideas as a group to help that student handle the situation in an appropriate manner. Students stored the guidelines for good tutors in their folders and used them as a reference during the course of the study.

Roles and responsibilities were related to academic encounters as well as social interactions and role modeling. In order to study and learn about themselves as facilitators and coparticipants in cross-aged literary discussions, students viewed videotape to observe themselves as they worked with their group. To assess what we thought was happening in the videotape, either a student or I would pause the tape whenever we saw an event that we wanted to discuss. The student or I would describe the event to the group, focusing on whatever we wanted to talk about from the videotape. After rendering a description, we talked about the events, highlighting the strengths and weaknesses. We discussed strengths to reinforce the positive things that both older and younger students did and how they worked together to have a productive discussion. We discussed weaknesses to brainstorm for ideas about what might be done differently when the students met for another cross-aged session. For example, if a student encountered a dilemma within his or her group, we discussed the problems, what was believed to be the source of the problems, and how things might be done differently. Occasionally, the high school students thought a literature discussion was not done very well. We used debriefing sessions to discuss ways to help them engage the younger children in a discussion about text the next time they met.

Finally, students discussed how the younger children's various oral and written responses to the literature engaged them and extended or shortened discussions. For instance, the high school students observed occasions when children responded to a question, and they saw how that response sometimes influenced how and what another group member said. Debriefings relating to this aspect of the cross-aged discussions enabled the high school students to learn strategies and skills they might use to help the children and themselves have productive literary discussions. Further, the debriefings enabled the high school students to consider some ideas made by the younger children about which they had not thought. A reflection and analysis of others' ideas helped students consider what the activities, tasks, and discussions meant for their own literacy learning and social and cognitive development.

**Summary of preparation seminar.** The instructional and debriefing focus of the preparation seminar gave the high school students an opportunity to develop their oral communication skills by discussing the literacy activities, tasks, lesson plans, and debriefings. The debriefings gave them a chance to reflect and critique themselves as learners and as teachers and to receive feedback from one another and from me. Debriefing sessions also allowed the high school students to rethink and reformulate their literacy activities before their next visit with the elementary children. Overall, the preparation seminar component offered opportunities for low-achieving adolescents to engage in literacy-learning tasks and activities for meaningful purposes, and to develop their planning, organizational, and decision-making skills within a social setting.

## Cross-Aged Literary Discussion Groups

Twice per week, the high school students went to Angelou Elementary School to conduct literacy-learning activities with pupils in a fourth-

and fifth-grade combination classroom. The small groups consisted of one high school student facilitating and coparticipating in literacy activities with four to six elementary students. The cross-aged literary discussion sessions were composed of three interrelated literacy activities: (1) oral reading, (2) writing, and (3) discussion. The high school students conducted the cross-aged sessions, modeling the interactions we experienced in the preparation seminar.

**Oral reading.** Oral reading was shared among the older and younger students. They took turns, changing at a pause or at the end of a chapter or section of the text. On occasion, I read to all the students (older and younger) at Angelou Elementary to continue working with them on fluency, intonation, and expression.

**Writing.** After reading orally, a high school student wrote questions from his or her lesson plan guide on the chalkboard so that all students could read them. After reading the questions on the board, the high school student asked the younger children to write their responses to the questions in their reading logs. Students were given the option of responding to two to four questions. The high school students wrote responses in their reading logs as well, continuing to model the process and further considering their own ideas about the literature. During some sessions of the cross-aged discussions, students were given an opportunity to write a response using the Reading Log Ideas response sheet instead of the questions. The high school students and younger children kept records of their personal responses and reactions to the literature in their reading logs. Written responses occurred in a range of ways: a response to specific question(s), a response or reflection to a comprehension strategy, a response to a specific literary element such as a critique of the book, or a personal response about something that the book reminded students about.

**Discussion.** When all students completed their personal responses, they assembled in their small groups. In the groups, the high school student began the session by reading a question and asking one child to share his or her response with the group. If students had selected an idea to write about from the Reading Log Ideas response sheet instead of responding to a question, they read their personal response. Likewise, the group facilitator read his or her response, contributing ideas to the group as well. Each high school student facilitated the discussion in his or her small group by

- asking the children if they had questions or comments to make about a group member's response;

- asking questions to clarify ideas;

- making comments about shared ideas;

- initiating new topics;

- offering alternative views; and

- taking critical positions.

In turn, the elementary children assisted in facilitating the discussion by responding and commenting to one another as they talked about the literature.

**Summary of cross-aged literary discussion groups.** The cross-aged literary discussion group sessions provided several features that are significant for the literacy education of the high school students. First, this component of the project placed the students in a literacy-learning context in which they had to make informed and spontaneous decisions during interactions with the children. Second, the social context of the project was designed so that high school students could enhance their leadership strategies and skills. Finally, the cross-aged setting provided the high school students with a second opportunity to deepen their social and cognitive literacy education in a context designed to read, write about, and discuss the same literature that was used in the preparation seminar.

# Lessons Learned: Adolescent Reflections

During this study the adolescent participants talked about what they were doing in their cross-aged discussion groups. From the transcripts of their talk, it is apparent that they learned many lessons. They developed knowledge about the procedures of reading, writing about, and discussing a book, and about literacy as a process. They also learned lessons about the potential of social interaction around books.

# Procedural Lessons

Debriefing sessions offered the adolescent participants an opportunity to define what they felt was a good discussion and offered guidance on how to manage these discussions. The students relied on the procedures practiced in the preparation seminars to manage their cross-aged discussion groups, which increased their repertoire of strategies that they could use in their own meaning making.

After the first few visits to Angelou Elementary School, three of the participants, Michael, Teresa, and Mark, met with me to discuss their experiences. They began to talk about what constituted a good book discussion and how to promote good book discussions. Mark talked explicitly about his observations of the elementary students in his cross-aged group. He noticed that most of the students contributed to the discussion by pointing out different but specific details in the illustrations of *Tuesday*, and they used their imaginations to construct meanings of those illustrations. Similarly, Michael commented on how the students in his group incorporated current television comedy into their observations. Michael and Mark modeled their discussion techniques on the practices they learned in the preparation seminars.

After a debriefing session in which the participants identified and solved the problems they had encountered in the cross-aged discussions, Michael used what he learned and subsequently modified his procedures. He employed the read-write-talk procedure that he experienced in the preparation seminar to assist his group in discussing the literature.

Fenice:    Think about the different reading, writing activities, the discussions that you've had with the fourth and fifth graders in your small group at Angelou Elementary. Explain to me what kinds of things you do that are important to you and why they're important.

Michael:    It's important for me, um, for when we have our discussions, to discuss with them because when I discuss with them, I feel like I'm, you know, that they can talk. The more I talk to them, the more they feel that they can talk to me. Like 'cause when I first started, they really, you know, didn't talk much because I felt that they, I guess, they felt they didn't know me. But the more we, you know, had our discussions, the more I talked to them, the more they talked back and that made, so that made like the next time we read a book or their discussion, when the discussion part came around, that made our discussions more, you know, interesting, because they weren't really scared of me. They were able to talk to me.

Not only did the seminars and discussions help adolescent participants improve their skills as discussion leaders, they also began to change the students' attitudes about reading and started to influence their ability to profit from discussion about books. Michael summarizes these ideas during a debriefing session in the following excerpt:

[Discussion] helps me to know what to write, and for me to be able to understand where my group is coming from when they talk about different things. I want to read more. The reading is helping me a lot. I used to think that reading is boring. I really just started. It relaxes me and helps me to take my mind off of different things. I know why I'm there and I just do it.

These comments suggest that the adolescent participants for this study learned a variety of procedural lessons about how they might facilitate a discussion. Included in their observations and comments was awareness of how the younger children interacted with the text, such as using their imaginations to construct meaning. These comments also suggest that the high school students were engaged through scrutiny of group dynamics, talk about text, and how one might construct meaning from text and peers. Their comments show that they were thinking about a piece of text beyond the literal level of comprehension. In addition, it is significant to note that Michael, Teresa, and Mark discussed the procedural lessons they learned within a social context with knowledgeable others. They were provided with multiple contexts and opportunities to develop their understanding about their own literacy learning.

## Literacy Lessons

Talking with the fourth- and fifth-grade students about *Tuesday* resulted in at least two important literacy lessons for the adolescent participants. Mark, Teresa, and Michael talked during a debriefing session about how the students acted as resources for their own meaning making.

Mark: But I mean, yeah, that's another thing. When he [Michael] said the older kids thought it [*Tuesday*] was so stupid, we thought it was stupid. But when we got around them [fourth and fifth graders], they brought out, they helped us bring out what they really thought about the book. It helped us see that the book could be what we want it to be because they thought it was fun. They found the fun parts in it that … which we didn't see. And that's the good thing about it.

Teresa: Like the cat. I didn't see the cat.

Michael: Yeah, I never saw the cat neither…[laughter] and I never saw the swan…the frog swinging on the thing….

Mark: That's the only thing I seen, was the cat.

Their experience with the basic text of *Tuesday* helped them realize the effect of other peoples' ideas on their own reading and understanding. They changed their opinions and enlarged their views about the text and about reading and responding. They began to develop an understanding of the importance of social interaction around books.

Teresa: We don't have picture books in high school or anything. It was something different.

Michael: Yep, we can't use our imaginations.

Mark: You can't use your imagination.

Michael: Sometimes it's good to use your imagination.

Mark: But when we read the book without the words, we imagined, we seen the, we seen the pictures but still we imagined, we imagined words and we imagined everything that was goin' on. We didn't imagine, we didn't imagine just the words. Or how do I say….

Fenice: What with *Tuesday* you imagined everything that was going on?

Mark: Was goin' on. Like, we seen the pictures, but we still got to imagine like what the people would really say, or what we think they would really say. Even what the people in the picture were thinkin'. That's the, that's another thing we got to do.

Teresa had been labeled as learning disabled and a dyslexic reader during elementary school and was reluctant to read orally; she felt at a great disadvantage when reading in front of her peers. The wordless nature of *Tuesday* allowed her what may have been her first unencumbered encounter with a piece of literature.

> Teresa: You feel under pressure when you read it, like Michael said. But um when you're doing a picture book, you can think of what you want. You don't feel any pressure. It's your imagination. I mean, nothin's wrong. You can't get nothin' wrong. You can't just say a word or anything.
>
> Fenice: You say you don't feel the pressure?
>
> Teresa: 'Cause when you're reading you're like, everybody's gonna see...see if you messed up so they can laugh or somethin'. When doing a picture book, it's not like that. You can see you own words. You won't mess up on the words.

Reading *Tuesday* and discussing it with younger students offered Teresa the opportunity to act like a reader; she created her own meaning as she "read," and then discussed it with others. Neither difficult text nor peer competition interfered with her reading experience.

The experience with *Tuesday* also helped Teresa, Michael, and Mark realize that books are full of multiple possibilities that can be understood from a variety of perspectives. Because they had to think and talk about books as the leaders of their cross-aged groups, they were forced to listen to what others had to say and others listened closely to them. There had been few opportunities for this kind of reciprocal, respectful interaction in their previous school experience.

## Social Lessons

The procedural and literacy lessons the adolescent participants learned were interconnected and embedded in the social roles they assumed as group leaders and participants in the project. Perhaps the procedural and literacy lessons were possible only because of the social nature of the cross-aged literacy program. Having to talk about what they were reading, how they were thinking, what they were doing, what the younger students did, and how they could do things differently was a new experience for these young adults. The social interactions that were necessary for the success of this program were the kind necessary for the success of these learners.

The adolescent participants also learned to accept and appreciate the responsibility they had as group leaders. During our preparation seminar, Devon, Michael, and Mark were present. I asked them to explain their perceptions of these sessions:

Devon: Oh, it's um, it makes the session [cross-aged discussion group] at Angelou like much easier because like if we didn't have these preparation seminars, I'd be all confused.

Michael: It does. I'm not even tryin' to say that to make you, to make you know…. But honest, sometimes when I first started comin, I think the first two sessions, I was lost.

Mark: It helps me not only, you know, just in my little groups. It helps me in school, too, because you know, um, most of the time I just have one idea or whatever. But you know, ever since I started comin' to the prep sem, you know…. They make me get more ideas like in my classes and stuff. Yesterday, I didn't have not one idea whatsoever and I was and I had to write my last reflection thing, in my reflection log, and I was thinkin' to myself, how can I get mentored. I was just thinkin' these kids always come up with these good ideas, and I was just thinkin' about the little kids' book, and I had to write a short story…and I was like, I could use a little kid's story…and it won't be so hard. Them kids helped me. Show me right!

By taking responsibility for the learning of others, the adolescent participants learned how to learn. They learned how to participate in and direct discussions. They learned that stories contain much more than one prescribed meaning and are full of multiple possibilities, and that talk with others can provide insight for alternative points of view. They learned that they, too, could be successful readers. And they learned to take responsibility for their own and others' learning.

# Lessons Learned: Cross-Aged Interactions and Literacy Learning

We, too, can learn from this study. Certainly the responses of the adolescent participants to their experience working with younger students exemplify the principles of social constructivist theory. Reading and writing were embedded within the social and cultural context of the cross-aged program. The participants constructed knowledge about themselves as readers and writers and about the process of reading and meaning making as they interacted with others in the program. They also discovered that they could learn from themselves and others, even when the others were younger than they were. All of this learning "floated on a sea of talk" (Britton, 1993).

This talk was meaningful because the participants were engaged in literacy activities that had real purposes: They cared about what they were doing because they were responsible for the success of the project. The participants were disconnected from their school experiences and they brought their resistance with them to this project. It was only after they began to work with the fourth- and fifth-grade students and they saw how much responsibility they really had, that this resistance changed into commitment. Although the processes and procedures were important, the social nature of the cross-aged literacy program was the key to its success. The adolescent participants wanted to learn and be successful because they had an enormous responsibility for the others.

If we want students who have been labeled as low achievers to excel in their literacy education and schooling career, we must make them responsible for their own learning. The cross-aged literacy program is one way of doing that.

## Questions for Reflection

1. How do the social interactions in an alternative literacy program help educators to rethink, reconstruct, and redefine literacy learning for adolescents who struggle with reading, writing, and schooling?

2. How might educators build upon the strengths of low-achievers to assist them in reaching their full potential for academic success?

# References

Allington, R.L., & McGill-Franzen, A. (1989). Different programs, indifferent instruction. In A. Gardner & D. Lipsky (Eds.), *Beyond separate education* (pp. 75–98). Baltimore, MD: Brookes.

Allington, R.L., & McGill-Franzen, A. (1993). Placing children at risk: Schools respond to reading problems. In. R. Donmoyer & R. Kos (Eds.), *At-risk students: Portraits, policies, programs, and practices* (pp. 197–217). Albany, NY: State University of New York Press.

Applebee, A.N. (1989). *The teaching of literature in programs with reputations for excellence in English* (Report No. 1.1). Albany, NY: State University of New York, Center for the Learning and Teaching of Literature.

Applebee, A.N. (1991). Environments for language teaching and learning: Contemporary issues and future directions. In J. Flood, J.M. Jensen, D. Lapp, & J.R. Squire (Eds.), *Handbook of research on teaching the English language arts* (pp. 549–556). New York: Macmillan.

Atwell, N. (1987). *In the middle: Writing, reading, and learning with adolescents.* Portsmouth, NH: Heinemann.

Au, K.H., & Mason, J.M. (1981). Social organizational factors in learning to read: The balance of rights hypothesis. *Reading Research Quarterly, 17*(1), 115–152.

Bakhtin, M.M. (1986). *Speech genres & other late essays.* Austin, TX: University of Texas Press.

Black, J., & Seifert, C. (1985). The psychological study of story understanding. In C. Cooper (Ed.), *Research response to literature and the teaching of literature* (pp. 190–211). Norwood, NJ: Ablex.

Blatt, G., & Rosen, L.M. (1982). *The writing response to literature.* Paper presented at the 30th Annual Meeting of the Michigan Council of Teachers of English, East Lansing, MI.

Boyd, F.B. (1996). *The cross-aged literacy program: Extending the boundaries for adolescents who struggle with reading, writing, and schooling.* Unpublished doctoral dissertation, Michigan State University, East Lansing.

Britton, J. (1993). *Language and learning.* Portsmouth, NH: Boynton/Cook.

Carter, L.F. (1984). The sustaining effects study of compensatory and elementary education. *Educational Researcher, 12,* 4–13.

Cazden, C.B. (1988a). *Interactions between Maori children and Pakeha teachers.* Aukland, NZ: Aukland Reading Association.

Cazden, C.B. (1988b). *Classroom discourse: The language of teaching and learning.* Portsmouth, NH: Heinemann.

Edelmann, M.W. (1988). Forward. In *Children's Defense Budget.* Washington, DC: Children's Defense Fund.

Fulwiler, T. (1982). *Language connections: Writing and reading across the curriculum.* Urbana, IL: National Council of Teachers of English.

Galda, L. (1988). Readers, texts and contexts: A response-based view of literature in the classroom. *The New Advocate, 1*(2), 92–102.

Glass, G.V. (1986). The effectiveness of special education. *Policy Studies Review, 2,* 65–78.

Goatley, V.J., & Raphael, T.E. (1992). Non-traditional learners' written and dialogic response to literature. In C.K. Kinzer & D.J. Leu (Eds.), *Literacy research, theory, and practice: Views from many perspectives* (Forty-first Yearbook of the National Reading Conference, pp. 313–323). Chicago, IL: National Reading Conference.

Golden, J.M., & Guthrie, J.T. (1986). Convergence and divergence in reader response to literature. *Reading Research Quarterly, 21*, 408–421.

Hansen, E. (1986). *Emotional processes engendered by poetry and prose reading.* Stockholm: Almquist & Wiksell.

Jose, P., & Brewer, S. (1984). Development of story liking: Character identification, suspense, and outcome resolution. *Developmental Psychology, 20*, 911–924.

Juel, C. (1988). Learning to read and write: A longitudinal study of 54 children from first through fourth grade. *Journal of Educational Psychology, 80*, 437–447.

Kennedy, M.M., Jung, R.K., & Orland, M.E. (1986). *Poverty, achievement, and the distribution of compensatory education services.* Washington, DC: U.S. Department of Education, Office of Educational Research and Improvement.

McMahon, S.I., Raphael, T.E., Goatley, V.J., & Pardo, L. (1997). *The book club connection: Literacy learning and classroom talk.* New York: Teachers College Press; Newark, DE: International Reading Association.

Michaels, S. (1981). "Sharing time": Children's narrative styles and differential access to literacy. *Language in Society, 10*, 423–442.

National Center for Education Statistics. (1992). *Dropout rates in the United States: 1992* (NCES 93-464). Washington, DC: U.S. Department of Education, Office of Educational Research and Improvement.

Purves, A.C., & Beach, R. (1972). *Literature and the reader: Research in response to literature, reading interests, and the teaching of literature.* Urbana, IL: National Council of Teachers of English.

Raphael, T.E., & McMahon, S.I. (1994). Book club: An alternative framework for reading instruction. *The Reading Teacher, 48*(2), 102–116.

Raphael, T.E., Pardo, L.S., Highfield, K., & McMahon, S.I. (1997). The Book Club: A literature-based curriculum. Littleton, MA: Small Planet Communications.

Shepherd, L.A., & Smith, M.L. (Eds.). (1989). *Flunking grades: Research and policies on retention.* Philadelphia, PA: Falmer.

Sloan, G.D. (1991). *The child as critic: Teaching literature in elementary and middle schools.* New York: Teachers College Press.

Topping, K. (1988). *The peer tutoring handbook: Promoting co-operative learning.* Cambridge, MA: Brookline Books.

Vygotsky, L.S. (1978). *Mind in society: The development of higher psychological processes.* (M. Cole, V. John-Steiner, S. Scribner, & E. Souberman, Eds. and Trans.). Cambridge, MA: Harvard University Press. (Original work published in 1934)

Walmsley, S.A., & Walp, T.P. (1990). Toward an integrated language arts curriculum in elementary school: Philosophy, practice and implications. *The Elementary School Journal, 90*, 257–294.

Wells, G., Chang, G.L., & Maher, A. (1990). Creating classroom communities of literate thinkers. In S. Sharan (Ed.), *Cooperative learning: Theory and research* (pp. 95–121). New York: Praeger.

Wells, G., & Chang-Wells, G.L. (1992). *Constructing knowledge together: Classrooms as centers of inquiry and literacy*. Portsmouth, NH: Heinemann.

Ysseldyke, J.E., Thurlow, M.L., Mecklenburg, C., & Graden, J. (1984). Opportunity to learn for regular and special education students during reading instruction. *Remedial and Special Education, 5*, 29–37.

## Children's Literature References

Naidoo, B. (1986). *Journey to Jo'burg: A South African story*. New York: Harper.

Taylor, M.D. (1975). *Song of the trees*. New York: Bantam.

Wiesner, D. (1991). *Tuesday*. New York: Clarion.

Wiesner, D. (1992). *June 29, 1999*. New York: Clarion.

# CHAPTER 5

# Learning Is Noisy: The Myth of Silence in the Reading-Writing Classroom

∞

## WENDY C. KASTEN

On an early September morning in 1973, a kindly gentleman walked me down the hallway of an old brick school building, our feet echoing from the freshly polished floors. This principal beamed with pride as he showed me his school during my first job interview for an elementary teaching position. He paused in front of the door where a substitute teacher tended the classroom that was lacking a permanent teacher on the first days of the new school year.

I peered in the door, which was standing ajar, to see children quietly sitting in rows of tan-colored desks, writing on a piece of paper on their desktop. The only sounds were those of pencils scraping and feet shuffling even though it was less than 30 minutes into the school morning. The principal sighed and said with heartfelt conviction, "That's a master teacher at work." He smiled and added, "It takes experience to be able to handle a class like this teacher does!" I smiled and nodded, being in need of a job, but also understanding that this man valued silence and I doubted I could be the kind of teacher he was looking for. Clearly pleased with the silent room and the silent halls of his building, he completed the tour and my interview concluded.

I was not offered a job there.

In my subsequent travels, I discovered that most principals I encountered in the 1970s, and even some I have met recently, believed to varying extents that a silent classroom was a productive one. To them, it meant the teacher was clearly in control and the students were busy. In the elementary school where I later taught sixth grade for several years, the principal of our school was mildly tolerant of my nonsilent room. However, I never stopped worrying about the noise and about what he would think of my teaching if my room were too noisy. I found echoing words of my first job interview a bit haunting. Did the fact that my room was noisy mean that I was a less effective teacher? My reflections spoke to my self-doubts, and I began to look more closely at the talk in my classroom. I wondered why people assumed, without listening to what students were talking about, that talking was not part of learning.

I began to watch my students more closely during various activities, although not in any systematic fashion, because at that time I did not understand that everything a teacher does to learn more in the context of her classroom is a form of teacher research. However, I listened to the talk, especially during writing and reading, because these were the two activities I had observed being conducted in silence in other classrooms.

What I heard seemed to me to be productive types of talk. I listened during writing and heard students talking about the activities and saw them complete stories in spite of the noise. I could not honestly say they were off-task, yet I still worried about what other teachers would say when they walked by the buzzing room. I listened during reading and again discovered that students were talking about their work, whether it was the story or the accompanying activities. They seemed to me to be very much engaged, and yet I still had lingering doubts about the noise.

Listening to children talk, an area of interest that had its origin in my own classroom teaching years, became a line of inquiry that I pursued in graduate school and in my own later research. In this chapter, I present a chronology of how I came to understand the role of peer talk in the reading-writing classroom. My purpose is twofold: to share what I learned through more than a decade of inquiry into peer talk in classrooms, and to give educators the impetus to listen to talk more carefully in their own classrooms. I hope that they might share what they discover with those around them who may not understand the importance of talk in the learning process.

In this chapter I also briefly summarize three areas of inquiry with which I have been involved that all relate to talk in the reading-writing classroom. The first two involve peer talk during writing, and the third involves talk during literature circle activities.

# The First Line of Inquiry:
# The Tohono O'Odham Study

As a graduate student, I had the privilege of working on a research study with Yetta Goodman and fellow graduate students at the University of Arizona. The two-year study took place on the Tohono O'Odham Indian Reservation southwest of Tucson. For two years (1981–1983), we made long weekly treks into the Sonoran desert to the Indian Oasis School District where we studied the writing process of elementary-age children while they were in third and fourth grade. This study has been written about extensively (Goodman & Wilde, 1992), but here I focus on what we learned about the role of talk in the process of writing (Kasten, 1984, 1990). Connecting to my own questions as an elementary teacher and the talk I had listened to and worried about in my classroom, my questions were as follows: Does the talk represent on-task or off-task behavior, how do I know, and how do I document it?

The subjects for this study were six students who we followed throughout their third- and fourth-grade years. We collected in-class writing samples, narratives that had been written while the children were observed by one of the members of the research team. We observed everything that accompanied writing, including talk.

The one-on-one observations were accomplished using a technique first proposed by Donald Graves at the University of New Hampshire and modified by Yetta Goodman for the purposes of this study. As they wrote, children were observed by a researcher seated close enough to them to be able to observe and hear all that was taking place. Using a detailed coding system (Goodman & Wilde, 1992), we recorded the students' writing and verbal and nonverbal behaviors that accompanied it. The incidents of student talk recorded during the observations became part of the focus of my dissertation. To look at the nature of the talk that had accompanied the writing, I selected a random sample (25) of all the writing that had been collected during the two-year study (more than 200 pieces).

Analysis of students' writing and talking was based on the process that I defined as having three parts: prewriting or consideration, the actual invention of text, and the reconsideration or revision of writing. I examined each piece of writing to see if the comments were related to prewriting, invention, or revision or if the comments were unrelated to writing.

Table 1 summarizes the outcome of the analysis of peer talk during writing. I discovered that nearly all talking (90%) was related to the act of writing, and the talk was purposeful. The young writers discussed topics, checked their spelling with others, clarified assignment expectations, solved problems with mechanics, sought opportunities to collaborate, sought an audience for their writing, and listened to the sound of their own writing, as they read aloud their work. I concluded that when children shared ownership in the writing process, engaging in talk as they wrote generally assisted them in the process of composing.

# The Second Line of Inquiry: The Sarasota Oral Language and Writing Study

In reflecting on the first study, I wondered if I would obtain similar results with other populations, especially in view of the fact that all subjects in the first study were members of the same ethnic group. A colleague and I decided to examine similar questions in a Florida community with a school population that was diverse both ethnically and economically. We spent a year using the same data collection methodology that had been

### Table 1    Classroom Talk During the Writing Process: First Study

| | |
|---|---|
| Consideration of language | 46% |
| Language during writing | 10% |
| Reconsideration | 18% |
| Other related comments | 16% |
| Language related to writing | 90% |
| Unrelated language | 10% |

From "Oral Language During the Writing Process of Native American Students," by Wendy Kasten, 1990, *English Quarterly, 22*, pp. 149–156. Reprinted by permission.

## Table 2    Classroom Talk During the Writing Process: Second Study

|  | Semester 1 (5th grade) | Semester 2 (5th grade) | Semester 2 (3rd grade) | Average |
|---|---|---|---|---|
| Consideration | 19.6% | 27.6% | 20.2% | 22.5% |
| Text invention | 37.0% | 17.0% | 15.0% | 23.0% |
| Reconsideration | 12.1% | 22.3% | 14.5% | 16.3% |
| Other related | 24.0% | 27.1% | 21.2% | 24.1% |
| Unrelated | 5.6% | 5.0% | 1.1% | 10.2% |
| Undetermined | 1.7% | 1.0% | 28.0% | 10.2% |
| Total on-task | 94.4% | 95.0% | 98.9% | 96.1% |
| Total off-task | 5.6% | 5.0% | 1.1% | 3.9% |

used in the Arizona study. This time we collected data from third graders during one semester and from fifth graders over the course of two semesters. More than 50 writing episodes were observed in all.

All writing artifacts first were analyzed in the same manner used in the Arizona study. The results presented in Table 2 are highly similar to those in the previous study. Nearly all talk was related to the writing process and judged to be on-task. As in Table 1, the parts of the writing process are listed on the left with the percentage of talk that related to that area on the right. Because of occasions when language was not intelligible to the researchers, one category, "undetermined," was added to Table 2. Such instances did not occur in the earlier study.

In addition, a second analysis was conducted, this time using Halliday's (1978) functions of language: interactional, informative, heuristic, imaginative, personal, instrumental, and regulatory. As can be seen in Table 3, where data are arranged in rank order from most frequent to least frequent, talk that was interactional, informative, and heuristic was the most common. These results signal that talk during writing was very purposeful, helped solve problems, and made use of the social nature of the classroom. These three functions far outweighed others that occurred during writing. Utterances that were personal, instrumental, regulatory, or imaginative were infrequent (Kasten & Clarke, 1987).

What I learned in this study was that my results from the Arizona study were more typical than I might have thought. Both analyses suggest

## Table 3　Halliday's (1978) Functions of Language During Writing

|  | INT | INF | HRS | PER | IST | REG | IMG | UND |
|---|---|---|---|---|---|---|---|---|
| All 5th grade | 29.0 | 23.0 | 16.0 | 7.4 | 2.8 | 0.8 | 2.0 | 29.0 |
| 5th grade Year 1 | 18.9 | 21.4 | 12.1 | 8.5 | 2.0 | 1.4 | 1.0 | 35.2 |
| 5th grade Year 2 | 19.7 | 24.1 | 19.7 | 6.2 | 3.8 | .03 | 3.4 | 23.1 |
| 3rd grade | 26.7 | 21.5 | 18.8 | 1.8 | 7.1 | 2.9 | 1.3 | 19.9 |

INT = interactional    PER = personal
INF = informative      IST = instrumental
HRS = heuristic        REG = regulatory
IMG = imaginative      UND = undetermined

that the process of writing is so engaging that there is little room for frivolous talk. Purposeful talk does, however, support the process of the individual writer and the community of writers as they assist each other. Based on these two studies, I concluded that the language that accompanied writing was highly related to the writing process and facilitated valuable learning opportunities; I further concluded that the talk during writing was mostly on task. Peer talk supported the process by providing opportunities for collaboration and by creating an audience for emerging works (Kasten, 1984, 1990; Kasten & Clarke, 1987).

# The Third Line of Inquiry: Peer Talk During Literature Discussions

In recent years, my exploration of peer talk has broadened to include its function in literature discussion groups, particularly in the context of literature circles. Intrigued by the rich and stimulating nature of literature discussions and response, especially in contrast to the quiet classrooms of the 1970s, I have observed both the oral discussion and the reflective responses from a variety of sources. These data have been less systematic and more informal than the studies I described earlier. They were part of my own process of refining the use of literature circles in elementary classrooms where I have spent time with teachers who are implementing them, and part of my own college teaching, where I have used literature circles in graduate and undergraduate teaching. In the following sections, I outline how I pursued my interests in literature circles, explain the model by which I use them, and share my insights to date about the talk within.

## Learning About Literature Circles

My visits to classrooms, my use of literature circles with adults, and my mining of elementary students' response logs for good examples to show my university students all have been concurrent and interrelated. Working with the younger learners enabled me to understand literature circles in more depth in order to teach this as a method of proceeding with literature-based reading instruction in teacher education. As I implemented literature circles with preservice and inservice teachers, I had several goals. First, I wanted to model a cutting-edge strategy for elementary reading that university students would experience sufficiently and later implement with confidence. Second, university students frequently are products of unexciting reading instruction. The richness and engagement I was beginning to observe and savor among children had not been the experience of today's adults when they were in school. Many university students privately admitted to disliking or even hating reading—a situation unacceptable in a new reading teacher. My goal of turning on the students to reading in the same way I saw children responding to this methodology became paramount.

With undergraduate students, I used young adult literature selections. The last 30 minutes of a weekly three-hour class were spent in literature circles, while I circulated around the room, participating in each group occasionally. With graduate students, we jointly selected current adult novels that class members had heard about and not yet had the time to read. In these cases, I assigned myself as a member of one of the groups. I felt that in doing this I could gain an insider's view of literature circles and I also could feel fairly confident that my presence would not cause the group dynamics to change as it might with preservice teachers.

During these class periods, I also was visiting a multiage primary classroom twice a week and modeling the use of literature circles with fluent readers for the teacher in that classroom. Since I had never worked with the circles with children prior to this, visiting this classroom gave me an opportunity to try the strategies I was teaching to college students. I kept photocopies of the journal entries from the multiage primary students and also collected and photocopied the journals from a fifth-grade class where literature circles were proceeding very well.

**How literature circles work.** Literature circles have been found to promote engaging conversations about literature and informational texts (Borders & Naylor, 1993; Kasten, 1995; Peterson & Eeds, 1994) and are now often implemented in various ways with students from kindergarten through adult (see Chapters 3, 6, and 10 for further discussion of literature circles). Unlike the days when "discussion" really meant the teacher asked questions and students gave answers, literature circles provide opportunities for genuine reflections and dialogue about books. Whether working with younger or older learners, the procedures are similar. Groups of students select quality trade books and meet in small groups to read those titles together. Each meeting consists of some oral sharing of the text without the presence of a teacher (only by choice, no one reads aloud who does not want to). Following a determined length of reading time (perhaps 10 to 30 minutes), group members immediately respond in a journal about what they are thinking and feeling. Sometimes, good, open-ended questions such as "What does it remind you of?" get students thinking about what to write (Borders & Naylor, 1993). These literature responses form the basis for discussion when group members choose to talk about or share their entries. Discussions take many directions as a result (Kasten, 1995).

Because classroom time is limited for elementary students and for college students, sometimes group members agree to read certain portions of the book between class meetings. They further agree not to read ahead of one another in order to experience new parts of the book together. This reading outside of class also facilitates the group's completion of the task by a deadline. Deadlines may be needed so selections are completed by the end of the course, or by a particular date when the task is completed.

At the end of a book, literature groups prepare a presentation that depicts to others what the story means to them. These presentations provide for active student involvement as the group must negotiate, plan, selectively reread, and rehearse their presentation. These presentations are extremely entertaining and exciting, and they can be used as part of assessment where needed. Groups might act out portions of a story, dress as story characters and interview one another, create murals or video presentations based on some part of the story, put words to music, or even dance their interpretation.

**Peer talk in literature circles.** In my work with literature circles at elementary and postsecondary levels, I have observed how similarly the process proceeds no matter the age or maturity of the learners. Both children and adults use discussion to sort out and clarify story events and characters and to arrive at a consensus about exactly what took place. This characteristic of discussion is especially common early in the experience when the opening chapters of a new book present more challenges to readers. For example, 8-year-olds reading *Sarah, Plain and Tall* (MacLachlan, 1985) determined which characters in the story lived in Maine where Sarah came from, and which resided in the prairie setting of Sarah's new life. Adult graduate students in a reading course also had to work at sorting out Pat Conroy's many various colorful characters in his story *The Water Is Wide* (1972) which is based on his early teaching experience in a poor, rural South Carolina island community.

For both younger and older learners, one function of the talk in literature discussion groups clearly supports basic comprehension, as readers sort out and confirm the nature of the role of different characters. Higher level comprehension is supported in other instances as students work together to make judgments about people, events, and authors. Elementary teachers who have implemented literature circles report that this type of talk occurs often.

Another common characteristic of the discussions and response surrounding literature circles involves valuing and judging. As readers join to discuss characters and events, they offer opinions and compare reactions. These critical and in-depth discussions are especially valuable as learners, young and old, respond and react to people and events based on their own schema. The result is multiple perspectives about the topic of discussion. Group members often comment with surprise at the differing reactions and perspectives and admit that those differences stretch their thinking.

In *Sarah, Plain and Tall*, some of the 8-year-old readers could relate to the different ways Anna and Caleb came to accept a new female adult replacing their deceased mother. Several classmates lived in blended families and had experienced similar feelings. Some judged Anna's cautious distance more harshly while others understood and legitimized Anna's reactions.

In the adult literature group of which I was a member, Pat Conroy's coteacher and principal often was the focus of discussion and debate. Unlike the advocacy and high expectations Conroy was trying to practice in his classroom in *The Water Is Wide,* his coteacher at times humiliated students and assumed her learners would never amount to anything. This character's behavior was viewed with shock by graduate students and teachers who were members of the group. These discussions easily led to personal accounts of negative schooling experiences and individuals associated with those memories.

Within my adult literature group, judgments also were made frequently about Conroy's writing. Some members of the group had a deep appreciation of his prose and chose to spontaneously read aloud favorite lines or paragraphs. Others perceived Conroy's vocabulary as "highbrow" and wondered if he wrote "seated next to a dictionary" in order to select larger words. On occasions when Conroy's vocabulary included a word that no one in the group could define, all were reminded that becoming more literate is indeed a lifelong process; this was a good lesson for teachers to experience themselves.

Children are no strangers to making judgments either. Four 11-year-olds girls reading *Lottery Rose* (Hunt, 1976) expressed anger with the author for letting a mentally challenged character in the story die. "How could Irene Hunt write such a sad story?" a little girl lamented in her journal and subsequently to her group. Another student in the same group realized Hunt's talents when she concluded, "I thought no book could bring more emotions from me than *Bridge to Terabithia,* but I guess I judged too soon." (Paterson, 1977).

As in the adult examples, some comments by younger learners also are highly critical. One 11-year-old boy who was part of a group reading *Dragonwings* (Yep, 1975) decided that Yep "must have written pages 95 to 112 in a hurry" because he "didn't put the same feeling into them as with the rest of the book." This young reader thought he detected a change in the author's style when he added that those pages "are more like a history lesson than part of a story."

**Delving into the heart of fiction.** Donald Graves (1989) reminds us all that the heart of fiction is characterization. In addition to supporting the process of literal comprehension and becoming critical of literature, the discussions surrounding literature circles enables readers to delve deeply into the characters of fiction. Although traditional comprehension activities have tended to have a greater focus on plot and events, it is the vivid characters we have visited in our favorite books that stay with us for years and make reading the most memorable.

Although characterization weaves its way into many literature response discussions and journals, it is most memorable in the class presentations after the stories are finished. I have dressed as a reluctant student portrayed in *The Water Is Wide* (1972), as an older illegal immigrant in *Journey of the Sparrows* (Buss, 1993), and as the heroine of medieval Europe in *On Fortune's Wheel* (Voigt, 1990), but my more relevant memories come from the words of students.

Preservice teachers, after being touched by *Across Five Aprils* (Hunt, 1964), dressed and talked as members of the family, each delivering a poignant monologue from the character's viewpoint. Similarly, after discussing *Tales of a Fourth Grade Nothing* (Blume, 1972), a self-contained class of 8- to 12-year-olds labeled "emotionally handicapped," formally appointed one class member to be a television talk-show host. Others in the group decided to become the characters of Peter Hatcher, his friend, and his mischievous little brother Fudge. Using video-camera filming to add authenticity, the talk-show host interviewed the story characters on his show. The normally shy student playing the show host prepared and delivered detailed, intricate questions for his guests that not only demonstrated his literal comprehension of the story, but also showed a thorough understanding of the characters. The students playing the guests made decisions about how to dress, how to talk, and how to behave to represent their characters; the actor playing Fudge even went to the extent of falling out of his chair several times during the show because he was certain Fudge would have done that in the same situation.

Although the examples mentioned are only samples of my experiences with oral language in literature circles, I hope they illustrate how student talk enables the exploration of characterization and other critical issues related to books and authors.

## Summary and Conclusions

A decade of research on peer talk in various contexts has led me to some important conclusions about the place of peer talk in reading-writing classrooms. First, I learned that writing is not always best accomplished quietly. Young writers, like professional writers, often talk to themselves and to others. Donald Murray speaks of his own writing process when he says that "I hear the words as I use them. Revising is an act of talking to myself" (in Graves & Murray, 1981, p. 17). When they talk to others, young writers assist one another in the writing process, learn more about parts of writing, and share and trade ideas. Language accompanies and nurtures the act of writing. In classrooms, students who are writing need opportunities to talk, to interact, and to try their words aloud.

Second, I have learned that although reading may be a wonderful process as a private act, interacting with others about what we read also is a compelling and rewarding process. After participating in a literature circle in my graduate class, one of my students reflected, "I have always been a very good reader. Literature circles really got me to thinking: If I'm a good reader, and I learned so much from doing this, then what would it be like for someone who is not as good a reader?" This student's reflections emphasize the power of discussion that results in hearing and understanding the viewpoints of others, stimulates and broadens one's own thinking, and results in personal growth. Peer talk in the process of reading aids and broadens comprehension. Talk contributes to meaningful and lasting engagements with books that not only enhance the act of reading and the experience of literature, but also are in themselves highly rewarding and satisfying.

Third, I have learned that collaboration and social interaction take place in reading, writing, and other areas of classroom life through peer talk. Teachers and principals of the past who worked hard to keep children quiet (myself included) did not know how critical social interaction and collaboration are in learning. Piaget (1928/1977) said that social life is a necessary condition for the development of logic. More recently, Wood (1988) noted that "I believe that adults, social interaction, and communication play a far more formative role in the development of children's thinking than his [Piaget's] theory allows" (pp. 15–16).

The work of Vygotsky (1978) reinforces the same ideas. He suggested that the act of collaboration in the Zone of Proximal Development enables learners to forge ahead more effectively than they can when problem solving lacks collaborative efforts. Others, such as Trudge and Rogoff (1989), explain that "higher moral processes, such as meaning of voluntary attention are created and sustained by social interaction" (p. 21). Hooper (1968) had similar sentiments: "Cognitive change is made possible by the active interaction of the child and his surrounding physical and social environment. Experiences in classrooms are no exception to this" (p. 429).

In other words, peer talk and the social interaction it mediates are not separate from other classroom learning and the goals of schooling. Social development affects academic development and academic development affects social development, both in positive and accumulative ways (Bornstein & Bruner, 1989; Doise & Mugny, 1984; Trudge & Rogoff, 1989; Webb, 1977; Wood, 1988). These are as interrelated as the reading-writing process. As teachers, we must recognize that talk is a vital part of the social development that affects academic development, and all of these are integral parts of teaching and learning.

If we consider that reading, writing, listening, and speaking are the four language arts, then peer talk is a critical aspect of speaking and listening. It is amusing that the teachers of another era spent so much time keeping their classes quiet and then wondered why so many students were terrified of occasional oral reports and even continued into adulthood to be uncomfortable speaking to a group. The evidence from my own work and that of others is persuasive. Children and adults benefit from opportunities to talk as they read and write. Silence as evidence of effectiveness in the reading-writing classroom is a myth. Learning is noisy.

## Questions for Reflection

1. When I observed peer talk during writing, I concluded that the talk facilitated learning opportunities. Observe your students as they read, write, and talk. In what ways are your observations similar to or different from those described in this chapter? What do you learn as you listen to your students talk during reading and writing?

2. What books would you choose to help your students "delve into the heart of fiction?" What books would you choose to share with colleagues for the same purpose?

### References

Borders, S., & Naylor, A.P. (1993). *Children talking about books*. Phoenix, AZ: Oryx.

Bornstein, M.H., & Bruner, J.S. (1989). *Interaction in human development*. Hillsdale, NJ: Erlbaum.

Doise, W., & Mugny, G. (1984). *The social development of the intellect*. Elmsford, NY: Pergamon.

Goodman, Y., & Wilde, S. (1992). *Literacy events in a community of young writers*. New York: Teachers College Press.

Graves, D. (1989). *Experiment with fiction*. Portsmouth, NH: Heinemann.

Graves, D., & Murray, D. (1981). Revision: In writers workshop and classroom. In R.D. Walshe (Ed.), *Donald Graves in Australia* (pp. 105–118). Rozelle, NSW: Primary English Teachers Association.

Halliday, M. (1978). *Learning how to mean*. Baltimore, MD: University Park Press.

Hooper, F.H. (1968). Piagetian research— education. In I.E. Sigel & F.H. Hooper (Eds.), *Logical thinking in children: Research based on Piaget's theory* (pp. 423–434). New York: Holt, Rinehart, & Winston.

Kasten, W.C. (1984). *The behaviors accompanying the writing process in selected third and fourth grade Native American children*. Unpublished doctoral dissertation, University of Arizona, Tucson.

Kasten, W.C. (1990). Oral language during the writing process of Native American students. *English Quarterly, 22*(3–4), 149–156.

Kasten, W.C. (1995). Literature circles for the teaching of literature based reading. In M. Radencich & L. McKay (Eds.), *Flexible grouping for literacy in the elementary grades* (pp. 66–81). Boston, MA: Allyn & Bacon.

Kasten, W.C., & Clarke, B.K. (1987). A study of third and fifth grade students' oral language during the writing process. *Research Bulletin, 19*(4).

Peterson, R., & Eeds, M. (1994). *Grand conversations*. New York: Scholastic.

Piaget, J. (1928/1977). Logique genetique at sociologigie. In *Etudes sociologiques* (pp. 203–239). Geneva, Switzerland: Librarie Droz.

Trudge, J., & Rogoff, B. (1989). Peer influences on cognitive development: Piagetian-Vygotskian perspectives. In M.H. Bornstein & J.S. Bruner (Eds.), *Interactions in human development* (pp. 17–40). Hillsdale, NJ: Erlbaum.

Vygotsky, L.S. (1978). *Mind in society: The development of higher psychological processes* (M. Cole, V. John-Steiner, S. Scribner, & E. Souberman, Eds. and Trans.). Cambridge, MA: Harvard University Press. (Original work published in 1934)

Webb, R.A. (Ed.). (1977). *Social development in childhood day care programs and research*. Baltimore, MD: Johns Hopkins University Press.

Wood, D. (1988). *How children think and learn*. Cambridge, MA: Basil Blackwell.

## Children's Literature References

Blume, J. (1972). *Tales of a fourth grade nothing*. New York: Dell.

Buss, F.L. (1993). *Journey of the sparrows*. New York: Dell.

Conroy, P. (1972). *The water is wide*. New York: Houghton-Mifflin.

Hunt, I. (1964). *Across five Aprils*. New York: Grosset & Dunlap.

Hunt, I. (1976). *The lottery rose*. New York: Tempo Books.

MacLachlan, P. (1985). *Sarah, plain and tall*. New York: Harper & Row.

Paterson, K. (1977). *Bridge to Terabithia*. New York: Crowell Junior Books.

Voigt, C. (1990). *On fortune's wheel*. New York: Macmillan.

Yep, L. (1975). *Dragonwings*. New York: Harper & Row.

# CHAPTER 6

# Inventing Conversations in Second-Language Classrooms: What Students Say and How They Say It

∞

## KATHRYN F. WHITMORE

Educational research about classroom discourse often deals with what children and teachers talk about, especially regarding issues like content area knowledge, reading comprehension, and behavior expectations. Sociolinguistic research regarding classroom discourse often focuses on the structure of language, including how turntaking occurs and what types of turns are taken by various speakers of different roles. This chapter discusses the relation between the content and structure of classroom discourse. The discussion shows that these connections exist in classrooms that are learning communities. In fact, in classrooms where learners' talk is supported through more symmetric power and trust relationships between teachers and learners, the content and structure of discourse support and extend each other, inviting students to transform their thinking and change as language users and learners.

In this chapter, two examples of classroom discourse involving multilingual and diverse learners illustrate this point. The first excerpts come from conversations in a literature study group in Caryl Crowell's bilingual third-grade classroom in Tucson, Arizona, USA. In order to support children's search to understand the realities of the war in Iraq in 1991, children in Caryl's class were invited to explore children's picture books organized in a text set around the theme of war and peace. Their conversations taught Caryl and me, as a teacher-researcher collaborative team, the essential components of discourse in her room (Whitmore & Crowell, 1994).

The second excerpts are from my teaching at the University of Iowa during a recent graduate course. In a seminar about second language learning and teaching, I joined nine teachers, who had interests ranging from early childhood to college teaching and who were from South America, four different Asian countries, and the United States. As the teacher researcher in this setting, I extended my previous understandings about classroom discourse dynamics in an adult university setting.

An analysis of the speech data in both settings, Arizona and Iowa, reveals how each classroom invented its interactions as a speech community (Hymes, 1972). Findings from content analyses determine what learners and teachers talked about during study sessions, in particular how change was expressed as an indicator of learning. Findings from structural analyses demonstrate how participants talked—how they took turns, initiated topics, evaluated their discourse and participation, and interacted with one another. Together, these analyses demonstrate what specific issues were involved in the invention of these two language communities. I have selected three of the key issues that emerged in data analysis to discuss in this chapter. A *high level of intellectual expectation* describes the significance of the content of talk, understanding the *power and trust relationships* between speakers explains the structure of talk, and viewing *teachers as mediators* provides a theoretical explanation for the relationship between the two.

# Creating Contexts for Inventing Conversations

## The Sunshine Room: A Vicarious Experience with War

The Sunshine Room is a bilingual primary classroom in the southern part of Tucson, Arizona. Here, the school day regularly begins with a good story and some time for personal sharing by the children and teachers. In January 1991, however, the typical early morning routine had changed dramatically. Half a world away, war had broken out in the Persian Gulf. Questions, comments, hopes, and fears took the place of the children's usual stories, and the daily newspaper replaced the typical picture books. For 30 or more minutes each morning the gathering of 24 children discussed the events of the world surrounding them and their country. Questions related to the war, before, during, and after the actual combat, were asked by the children: Where is the Persian Gulf? Why are we at war there? The third graders wondered about how gas masks work and wanted to know if Americans were dying.

Since newspaper articles and photographs provided a limited image of the war with little attention to the human issues that concerned some of the children, Caryl felt a responsibility to provide more accurate information. She later remembered, "To my dismay, most of the [newspaper] articles concerned the technological nature of this war—the weapons, planes, communications systems—and the superiority of American and allied forces. There was little to give my students a picture of the harsh realities that accompany war, the devastation and death at a human level, on both sides of the battle lines."

Caryl developed a text set of picture books that provided children with a humane, historically accurate look at war over time, particularly related to U.S. history. The result was a text set of materials that came to be known as "the war and peace books." Such text sets encouraged discussion, highlighted connections between reading experiences and life experiences, and facilitated understandings of related texts.

Literature study groups made up a large part of the Sunshine Room reading program. They were fashioned after the notion of literature circles (Daniels, 1994; Short, Harste, & Burke, 1996; Short & Pierce, 1990) (see Chapters 3, 5, and 10 for further discussion of literature circles). In literature circles, children read quality pieces of literature based on their own selection and meet in groups to discuss their reading, reactions, and responses. Literature study groups in the Sunshine Room met twice a week with the teacher or teacher assistant who worked with various groups depending on the situation and the needs of the students. However, groups met independently on occasion. In the group described here, the books that became the focus of discussions were selected by group consensus and were passed around systematically before the meeting time to ensure that each child had an adequate opportunity to read the next selection in preparation for discussion.

The war and peace text set was selected by five boys and three girls, and the children gathered around several bins of war and peace books to begin their study. This was the first recorded discussion and the children's first exploration of the text set as a group. As the children browsed through the collection, they shared background knowledge about the issues presented by the books, they questioned one another about what they knew and did not know, they wondered at the brutalities of the events of U.S. history, and they unknowingly established roles among themselves that would endure through their time as a group.

This initial experience generated a pattern that prevailed over the set of meetings to come: Initiations of conversation topics, self-evaluation of discussions and the quality of literature, and rules for interaction as a speech community were established as students posed and resolved questions. The first discussion prompted six weeks of lively discourse, authentic questions, and serious attempts to understand personally relevant social issues through the construction of a social meaning for literature texts.

The startling realities of World War II and Adolf Hitler's involvement in the lives of Jews was the most harsh and captivating topic of the first day's discussion. Aaron, who was the only Jewish child in the group became the expert on this issue, answering queries posed by others to the best of his ability. Seaaira, the most naive of the children about the events of World War II, assumed the role of overt questioner. She was not as knowledgeable about war and U.S. history and was both horrified and fascinated by the illustrations and written texts of the books she explored. The books exposed Seaaira to concentration camps, children's deaths during World War II, and the discrimination against Jews. She was impressed by the seemingly knowledgeable comments of her peers. Aaron and Seaaira's roles were obvious even to them as Aaron asked, "How come you're asking me all these questions?" Seaaira answered, "'Cuz you know more about the war than I do. 'Cuz you're Jewish and I'm not Jewish."

The children read captions, studied illustrations, and skipped through entire volumes rather than reading any one text. Aaron was speaking when the discussion that follows was recorded. (Conversations have been transcribed at the turn level, with elimination of most hesitations and overlaps. A dash, —, indicates an interrupted turn; … indicates part of a turn has been omitted to conserve space; and xxx indicates a brief portion of indecipherable speech. Occasional comments for clarification outside of the original speech are contained by brackets [ ].)

| | |
|---|---|
| Aaron: | I know. They're taking him to the uh, concentration camps. |
| Seaaira: | Cause he's— |
| Travis: | Jewish. |
| Seaaira: | Jewish? |
| Travis: | They want to capture everybody who's different. |
| Aaron: | Yeah. Everybody who's different. |
| Seaaira: | What do they do at the concentration camps? |
| Aaron: | Well unfortunately they kill 'em. |
| Aaron: | 'Cuz they go into like these showers and gas comes out. |
| Travis: | And it's poison. |
| Aaron: | Poison gas comes out and then they die. |
| Travis: | They either get killed, they either get killed in the fence or starvation. |
| Colin: | Huge furnace. |
| Aaron: | Either starvation cause they know the fence is electrocute, will electrocute you. |
| Students: | Or they— |
| Colin: | Seaaira, they stuff 'em in huge furnaces. Aaron, they stuff 'em in huge furnaces. |
| Aaron: | Yeah, I know. |
| Colin: | And turned on the gas. |
| Seaaira: | That's sad. |
| Aaron: | They thought it was showers. |

The children's conversation shows their confrontation with the reality of the historical facts as they sunk in, particularly the understanding that Aaron, as a Jew, may have been involved in such an event. Seaaira asked directly, "Like if you were alive back then you would be getting tooken to a concentration camp?" and Aaron's friends vowed that they would have protected him from the Nazis.

Through their continued discussions, the children sorted out historical fact from child-like innocence as they asked one another questions and searched for solutions together. Connections were frequently made between history and current events. For example, the children were quick to condemn the United States for dropping an atomic bomb in Japan, as is depicted in the picture book called *My Hiroshima* (Morimoto, 1987). They were horrified when they realized that innocent people, including young children, were intentionally bombed by the United States, and they associated the event with the recent bombing of Israel:

Travis:     They could've bombed at least on an air force base, not where people were innocent. That would be just like Iraq coming over here and bombing us, and we're innocent. Or like we going over there and bombing innocent people, which did happen. And Iraq bombing Israel.

Trevor:     They were bombing innocent people that weren't even in the war.

*Rose Blanche* (Innocenti, 1985) was an important text for this group's understanding of war. It recounts a captivating story about a small girl who accidentally discovers a concentration camp and returns repeatedly to feed the prisoners. One illustration in the book prompted several days of discussion about Rose Blanche's motivation for helping the prisoners and the circumstances surrounding her eventual death:

Seaaira:    How come she's waving a Nazi flag?

Aaron:      That's what Travis's question was.

Seaaira:    'Cause right there she is waving a Nazi flag.

Caryl:      What do some of you think about that?

Aaron:      Well, I couldn't, I kind of tried to answer some of his questions about that but I didn't really know it either.

Travis:     I thought that since she was German and she was waving a Nazi flag, I didn't know what was wrong, 'cause she may have pretended to be a Nazi so she wouldn't get captured. That's what I thought.

Aaron:      Well, I think, I don't think she—

Seaaira:    Maybe they were forcing her.

Trevor:     Yeah, but why would she be smiling?

Aaron:      They were forcing her, they would take her—

Seaaira:    To the concentration camp?

Trevor:     But, why would she be smiling then if she was, ya know, if she was being forced?

This conversation continued for over 20 minutes. The depth of the children's unresolved questions urged them to continue the *Rose Blanche* discussion at the next meeting.

Finally, three discussion days later, Colin offered a new hypothesis for the group's consideration. Trevor, whose turn is in italic, reacted strongly to his idea:

Colin:      Ms. Crowell, I think one of the reasons that when she was waving that is because a lot of the people didn't know that the Nazi's were so mean to the, to the Ger, um to all those people.

Travis:     Yeah.

Aaron:      Yeah.

Trevor:     *WOW! I never thought of that.*

Caryl:      You hadn't thought of that before?

Trevor:     No, I think that might be right.

Caryl:      Why do you think so, Trevor? Why does that made sense to you now?

Trevor:     I just didn't know. I just didn't know about that. I thought everybody in the world knew that Nazis were mean.

Trevor's statements magnify his new understandings about the text he read and about the world. They illustrate two important things about the content of the children's talk that occur several times in the discussions. First, Trevor demonstrates the children's willingness to pursue responses to their questions over time without a need for immediate correct answers. Second, he highlights the social nature of the children's learning. Reading the text set and making meaning from the experience is a social transaction that is mediated by oral language. Important questions generated by the group are the focus topics of the discussion and they take time, require extended conversations, and require the suggestion of multiple hypotheses to resolve to the children's satisfaction.

The children in the war and peace literature study group grew in their understandings about why wars happen, about what constitutes a war, and about how its impact is felt on both sides. On the final day they met, the children shared how much they learned about the historical contexts depicted in the books and how their thinking on those subjects had changed. Caryl asked the children to "think about whether or not the books that we've read have had any kind of impact on your thinking, if they've helped you understand a little better about what's going on there [in the Middle East] or changed your thinking in any way." The responses were dramatic:

Trevor:  I've changed my thoughts about war. I used to, like, play war, but now it makes me sick.

Travis:  Now I think about it a lot more...what's going on, what was going on in Iraq and about other stuff.

Colin:  I felt the same way as Trevor did. Now I just don't play that way any more because I think it's so gross, after I read the books.

Aaron:  I did both [play with war toys and act out roles in war games]. But then, when I was reading the books, I didn't play with them that much.

Lolita:  I don't fight as much with my brother any more.

Seaaira:  I thought in wars everybody got killed. But in the Iraqi war, when they were fighting the air war, I didn't believe there was such a thing as a air war. I thought there was only a ground war.

The conversations from the first day of interaction with the books revealed the children's innocence early in the literature study. By the conclusion of the study, however, for a group of 8- and 9-year-old children, their understanding about the realities of war was quite mature. These ideas will be returned to following the description of a group of adult learners who engaged in a study of second-language learning and teaching.

## The Graduate Seminar: International Conversations

During my first semester at the University of Iowa, I was fortunate to meet graduate students from all over the world. As I became acquainted with them, however, I was disturbed by the anecdotes they related about negative experiences they had had, both on campus and in the local community. One student, for example, was recommended by faculty to be tested for an attention deficit disorder when she struggled with a course and requested help. Another student was publicly humiliated in class by a professor who said she was not smart enough for graduate school. The prejudice they experienced was directly related, in my opinion, to the students' developing use and knowledge of English as a second language, and their instructors' parallel lack of knowledge about, and appreciation for, the second-language development process.

In my own classes, I recognized that these students typically were quiet, if not silent, during discussions. I became aware of their frequent wishes to go home and of their accompanying sadness or even physical symptoms, such as acute headaches. Sunjoo's thoughts during another class with me show her emotional state:

> Today I felt such bad. This is not my first time to be sad in the classroom, sitting without understanding. People talked, asked, responded, and laughed. I just sat silently without knowing why they were so happy even without including me…. Even I have spent more than one year, my English has not improved enough for me to listen to people and talk to people and laugh at their jokes and funny stories, why? I feel choked. I want to breath in Korean air, Korean language with Koreans…so after their talking I don't need to be exhausted. (Journal entry, September 15, 1993)

My concern for these students' experiences, coupled with our shared fascination and curiosity about second-language learning and teaching, brought us together as an intellectual and international community of learners. We wanted to converse about litcracy, language, culture, and education. We spent one semester together initiating and sustaining such conversations and spent several additional months continuing our conversations by analyzing the experience.

As the course began, I had two intentions: an academic goal for students to learn about the whole language approach to second-language (L2) learning, and a social goal to provide a safe community where they could talk to one another, compare experiences, and make friends. I hoped students would find their voices, voices that I believed had been silenced by their English as a second language status. It was my intention to demonstrate trust in students as learners, so I immediately engaged them in active roles in the community by sharing responsibility for classroom organization. Two of the students developed the syllabus with the help of the others, and on the first day, during a lively discussion, we considered our questions regarding language learning. In the process of our conversation, we categorized them as learning questions, teaching questions, and practice questions. Examples are presented in Figure 1.

# Figure 1 Questions Raised in the L2 Seminar

**Learning Questions**

Do children and adults learn (in general) the same way?
Do they learn second languages the same way?
If not, what are the differences?
Is it easier for kids to learn a second language? Why?
How are second languages learned?
How is language learned?

**Teaching Questions**

What are our goals for students in language learning and second language?
What is the most appropriate way of teaching second languages?
How can what we know about teaching and learning in general inform L2 teaching?

**Practice Questions**

When should L2 be taught?
What is the role of L1 in L2 learning?
What materials, organization, and learning experiences should we use in our L2 teaching?

Our questions elaborated on one basic issue regarding the relation between theory and practice: How do we create the social context, so essential to a whole language-learning theory, that supports the needs of second-language learners? We negotiated a plan to further our understanding of this issue. In our first meeting, each student agreed to keep a journal to exchange with me and one another, to lead a discussion based on an article of his or her choice, and to complete an action research project that would lead to a paper. Several students chose to work together to conduct studies of their own practice in L2 settings. Javier suggested that we invite guest speakers to address our shared question.

During the weekly discussions that ensued, students talked about three broad topics: the content issues of the course, the linguistic systems of their native languages, and the affective issues related to their experiences as L2 speakers. A good portion of the time, the group responded to readings and discussed issues pertinent to their practice as L2 teachers. As in the Sunshine Room, these topics developed as a result of the students' questions, in this case, about the language context in their own countries. For example, Sunjoo said, "When I read this article I wonder how can I provide whole environment, like social context, because [Korean children] just, practically they don't need English but much later they will need this English very emergently." Janice expressed determination "to figure out, in a practical way, the concept of whole language, in [her] adult [ESL] classroom that has limited resources." Luis also was focused on practice in one discussion, suggesting, "How 'bout if we think of activities that might work in powerless situations and we might come up with a bank of ideas, collective ideas, that belong to the world that have been produced here." And Jie questioned how to support the children who speak various native languages in her country, as well as English, when she is a teacher unfamiliar with their ethnic backgrounds. Like all learners, these students "make sense of new knowledge by projecting it upon what they know already" (Barnes, 1992, p. 22).

The following excerpt is typical. It is lengthy, as turns of talk are longer with adult speakers, so a single representative example is provided for illustration. Notice how Janice, the sole teacher from the United States in the group, initiates a topic through a personal question that engages the others. Later (highlighted in italic), she recognizes herself answering her own question, much like Trevor did in the war and peace discussions. Notice, also, how the students are learning from one another as they build a social meaning around Janice's question.

Janice:    It seems to me in some of my other readings, I'm asking a question. Would we say that active learning is synonymous in many ways with whole language? I was thinking of the beginning Spanish, the beginning language student, I was trying to think of something besides the list of words [referring to an earlier activity idea that I proposed]. I thought, well maybe, what if you taught the students the phrase, "What country were your parents from?" Well, I'm thinking of the context of the United States, since most of us come from immigrant parents. And the students went around and had, I don't know how much time to talk to each other and took a survey so to speak and then as a class we listed the different, we could get into the singular to plural and this many people, but is that a teacher controlled? Because some of the readings, the ideas are to come from the students; they're to be student generated. But the idea came from the teacher. Now that's active learning; the students are actively participating in their second language, but is that whole language? I don't know.

Kathy: That kind of activity could look like a whole language activity in one classroom and look like a non–whole language activity in another classroom. Because I would ask you what relevance does that topic have to do with the bigger picture of the class, for one thing.

(four brief turns omitted)

Janice: So it depends on your goal. And you can mix the two goals—skills and building a community?

Kathy: Absolutely. Yeah, I think so.

Luis: But I think what we should not confuse is active learning with activity. Or have the illusion that when students are busy, busyness means active learning.

Kathy: That's a good point.

Janice: I understand the concept but I don't get it. Because if you're actively using the language—

Luis: Yeah, they could be just listening to a cassette and repeating sentences.

Janice: And you're calling that activity, OK.

Luis: They're occupied. Many people think that's the appropriate way to learn the language. If you listen to a cassette and you repeat it, the manipulation of the structures will lead eventually to the learning of the language. But that is supported by a behaviorist philosophy behind that, so they could be busy, they could be doing things, but they could not be engaged in a real learning situation.

Javier: Or like doing transformation, doing the exercises.

Kathy: Changing the tense, do you mean?

Javier: Changing tenses, or plurals and all that. I mean they are busy doing all that. And this is something they have to learn but then I've seen that in my students. They do that, and later on when they are talking, they never apply those rules.

| Kathy: | How about if we went a step further. You kept all that stuff on the chalkboard and you had the conversation about it and that's all you could get done in your first 50 minutes or whatever. But you kept that on an overhead or something and the next day you come and you write a story as a group with that language, and in the end you duplicate it so everybody takes it home and that's the reading practice for the next time, is the story that they've been part of writing. So that— |
|---|---|
| Janice: | Except that, they don't know any verbs, so then you use that occasion if they've got a verb they want, then you teach them that verb. |
| Kathy: | You're the expert language user in that situation. You're taking what they already know and you're adding to it. And you're doing it, in the process you're demonstrating the process.... |
| Janice: | Would you limit their verb tense? I mean what if, most dialogue has to do with past, present, future, and continuous. |
| Kathy: | What would be a whole language theory answer to that? |
| Janice: | The theory would say, no, you don't, but— |
| Kathy: | Because what's more important? |
| Janice: | Meaning. |
| Kathy: | To make it make sense is more important than to make it inauthentic by, remember all those choices of functions? If you're putting a whole bunch of rules on what it can be about or how it's to be, then it's instructional function. |
| Janice: | But then, say you've got three verb tenses there. I don't know that much about Asian languages to know if this question applies, but that's the killer for me especially when I'm trying to listen to Spanish is the endings are so—[example, then laughter]. So I've got this ending and this ending and this ending and then they have all these so many irregular verbs when they change the core itself, so I'm looking up there and you know, I can't even recognize the verb. |

(two turns omitted)

Sunjoo:     xxx Because, maybe without conscious we listen too much time. I wonder how I could provide this listening environment in the classroom for the Korean student who wants to learn English. So I think if you want to know all these endings, you can just memorize all these ending, but I think it's more effective to just listen and speak much.

Janice:     One time, I think it was second-semester Spanish, we were required to present something to the class. And I chose to memorize a song that had all kinds of—. *Now I'm answering some of my own questions.* It had all sorts of verb tenses and phrases that I didn't get. But I have to say that after, and it took me forever to memorize this silly little song about chickens and a barnyard, I got a Raffi song. But after memorizing that song, those phrases stick with me now and I haven't lost that.

Jie:        I just like to ask about using song as a way to do it. I don't know because there may be some tunes that are sort of universal but then you have in the other language. So what if you presented that but then they say, "Ah." Then, they're using their own knowledge and their own language and you contribute to that. I don't know.

Janice:     Yeah, and genuine interest. I think most people have a genuine interest in music.

Jie:        Because with the young children I try it sometimes and eventually, using those tunes with whatever they know they make up their own songs with the words.

This lengthy conversation focuses on foreign-language teaching methods within a whole language philosophy, a favorite topic for these foreign-language teachers and learners. It illustrates what these teachers talk about in terms of course content. Similar conversations on other days addressed such topics as language development, the difference between being "bilingual" and "speaking a foreign language," holistic assessment, and inclusion of culture in language classrooms.

As we shared our experiences as L2 learners, we also taught one another the linguistics of our native languages, the second broad topic of talk in this class. I often left the students to continue discussions without me, just as Caryl did in the Sunshine Room. This demonstrated our trust in students to teach one another, an essential part of community. On one occasion, Sunjoo, at the invitation of the others, took over the class to present the linguistic system of Korean. Another day, Siu Rong explained the various dialects spoken in Taiwan and the loss of some dialects given the national stature of Mandarin. Verb tense regularities in Spanish also were mulled over. As a result, two students initiated cross-language tutoring with each other on their own time, teaching each other their native Spanish and Mandarin. Students' recognition of one another as experts influenced the sense of community and symmetric power relations in the classroom.

The third topic of frequent conversation was a more personal one. At some point all students shared their experiences as language learners and international students. These sharing times were very personal and often involved sensitive issues regarding race, gender, prejudice, and discrimination. At one point, I invited the students to share their experiences with studying in the United States. One international student described how a professor lowered her grade because he described her English as "so poor." Others described American students' treatment of them as "hostile" and "very competitive" and their own feelings as "tired" and "offended." Although the same students acknowledged they also had positive experiences and relationships, it was important to them to recognize their common experience and to demonstrate the trust necessary to share intimate and emotional stories with one another. As Sunjoo said, "I realized that I am not the only person who has all the terrible and nerve-irritating troubles in adapting to a whole different culture, different people, and a different language-speaking society." The students attributed their success in perservering and not leaving the country to their inner drive and determination.

Final reflections written by each student show how the group's discussions had a transformational effect on their behavior and thinking as students:

Before this seminar, I sometimes thought that I couldn't contribute to the learning of others in the classes I had taken at the University of Iowa. Now, I firmly believe and feel that I shouldn't have any kind of restrictions or limitations to be an active member of the learning community, and express my thoughts, ideas, and beliefs.... I have learned that international students can learn a lot from this culture, but people in this culture can also gain a lot from international students like us. As a learner, I have developed some more confidence in myself, and as a language teacher, I am now more aware of all the factors that need to be taken into account every time a teacher is in front of a class.... Sometimes I thought that I was not in a class but in a weekly meeting where I could express all my ideas and feelings...and for the first time in graduate school I felt I was in control of my own learning: I was a part of the decision-making people, and I had a voice in the decisions taken. (Javier, December, 1993)

...For once in my life (isn't that the first line of a song?) I could just about say what's on my mind in the class in a "foreign" land and not be sneered at. The sense of community the group built over the semester was indeed a great support to my work in other areas of study. It is almost the first time ever in class as a graduate student that I seem to feel an equal to everyone else. (Jie, December, 1993)

A key element in all this process has been the sources of input available to all of us...the peer discussion during the semester has been the perfect fuel to keep our thinking going....You have helped to fill a need I had and that other professors did not seem to see. It was more than a need to learn, to acquire knowledge. It was a need to belong. It was a need to find a surrounding that would also accept and value who I am and what I can offer to my field of studies. A need to be part of that community called university. (Luis, December, 1993)

These written comments emphasize how a sense of community enables students to transform their thinking.

# Looking at the Data: A Content Analysis

A content analysis of the classroom talk in both the Sunshine Room and the graduate L2 seminar reveals how a *high level of intellectual expectation* in a classroom community contributes to change. A structural analysis shows that *symmetric power and trust relationships* are indicated when discourse is not centered in the patterns typical of many classrooms. Finally, *teachers as mediators* explains the theoretical relationship between the content and structure of talk in school. Each of these factors are addressed next.

# High Level of Intellectual Expectation: The Content of Talk

Wells (1989) said that language researchers and educators should be asking how it is that any language event in the classroom enhances the development of literate thinking rather than advocating a compensatory increase in the quantity of talk in classrooms. Literate thinking, in his words, "refers to all those uses of language in which its symbolic potential is deliberately exploited as a tool for thinking" (p. 253). He argued, "From the point of view of intellectual development, therefore, what is important about reading and writing is not so much the communication of information, as the possibility of developing ways of using language as an intentionally controlled tool for thinking and feeling" (p. 254).

Wells' transcriptions of children in grades 3 and 4 while they plan a theme-centered experience of model making illustrate his point. Through the collaborative talk he recorded, listeners see how children's interests extend their knowledge and challenge them to develop their thinking. Situated in a classroom that was a "community of collaborative enquirers" (p. 269), these children "from lower class, ethnic communities in which a language other than English is the main medium of communication" (p. 271) had the opportunity and the support to discover interests and abilities of a high intellectual level. Wells concluded, "Where the aim of the teacher is to facilitate each individual's construction of knowledge through literate thinking and collaborative talk in the context of student-chosen topics of enquiry, all learners will be empowered, whatever the background from which they come" (p. 271).

The literature study and L2 seminar groups were similar collaborative communities, created in response to students' questions about their world. A large portion of each group's discussion time concerned the learners' working to resolve their questions. The children struggled to know why the world event in their lives had occurred; similarly, the focus of the adults' questions was about their past, present, and future lives as second-language users and teachers. Both groups were inquiry centered, which opened the potential for intellectual challenge to the learners' needs and interests. Oral and written language are tools that enabled the learners to meet highly intellectual goals held for them by their teachers and by themselves. Janice described this expectation as "an acceptance of the necessity of hard work to get where you're going and a desire to strive for excellence." She later thought this was, "a value held in common by the class and I think that drew us together, too."

Using their own criteria of asking good questions in response to illustrations and stories that evoked personal and emotional reactions, the children unanimously chose *Rose Blanche* and *My Hiroshima* as their favorite books. Aaron and Trevor articulated the group's mutual agreement:

Aaron:      But these two books are the best.

Trevor:     Yeah, the sadder they are, the gooder they get.

Aaron:      I liked *Rose Blanche* and *My Hiroshima* because they make you kind of really feel it. The author does.

Trevor:     Me, too. Those were my two favorites. I think we like talked about them the most.

Aaron:      The authors made you think. They really made you feel it.

Trevor:     And wonder what it was like.

Similarly, the adults became conscious of the role of authentic questions in stretching their thinking. Janice reflected,

> I need to study what has personal importance to me, in a cooperative setting that is challenging and stimulating where classmates form a community and offer mutual support. I find I also need for some, if not most, of my classmates to come from different backgrounds; it opens my mind to new perceptions I haven't experienced in homogeneous settings. I need a teacher whose experience and insight give depth and meaning to our class discussions and asks challenging, probing questions we hadn't thought to ask ourselves.

The content of the questions these students, both adults and children, asked is of instructional value, but these questions extend far beyond the types asked at the ends of chapters in social studies textbooks, basal readers, or university texts. Rather, these students' questions were driven by a heartfelt quest for knowledge and understanding. Travis pondered, "I wonder what it was like in the war." Aaron explained how the best books are those that make you "really feel it." Luis wondered, "How can we give power to our students?" and wanted to write an article titled *Powerless Situations—Powerful Ideas.* Jie, Sunjoo, and the others asked for a rational explanation of their sometimes traumatic life experiences as language students. These adults and children were tying their real questions about the world to their academic learning experience, meeting Dewey's (1904) goal for curriculum: "to start where the learner is in time, place, culture, and development" (cited in Goodman, 1992, p. 40). In these examples, the children articulated their changed view of war, conflict, and for some, play; the adults saw themselves as competent, intelligent learners and as knowledgeable teachers. The data from these classrooms suggest that learners need to be invited to inquire, be challenged to ask personal questions, and be provided multiple opportunities to seek their own answers through socially mediated experiences, including discussions, in school settings. Students' asking their own questions has a political effect of empowering them as learners, as Wells (1989) suggested. These results are transformative, not merely additive (Barnes, 1992).

## Power and Trust Relationships: The Structure of Talk

Through a detailed analysis of the content of these discussions, I realized these learners have unique power in their talk in school. As I listened, and later when I poured over the transcripts, I realized that this discourse contains structural features that do not match the discourse described as taking place in typical classrooms. The learners determine their own turns of talk on a predictable basis, they gaze at one another as they speak, and they choose what they will talk about. They compete with one another and the teacher for attention and their turn to speak. They freely interrupt one another and they ignore attempted initiations that do not meet the goals of the group, even if they are made by their teacher.

These features contrast strongly with the types of discourse behaviors children display in transmission-oriented, teacher-centered classrooms, where teachers direct discussion. Philips (1983) found that teachers control virtually every component of every speech act in what she called the "official" structure of a classroom. They are the focus of attention while they talk, they allocate turns of talk, they interrupt students without permitting interruptions of their own turns, and they determine how students will be organized and involved. Discourse structures in other classrooms are similarly described (see Board, 1982, for specific references to reading instruction; Moll & Diaz, 1987, for biliteracy development; and Rosebery, Warren, & Conant, 1992, for scientific discourse). Part of a student's job in school is to learn the rules of the official structure of language. Barnes (1992) said, "Anyone who has attended a school knows how the communication system indicates to pupils the boundaries of who they are and what they may do" (p. 17).

In typical transmission classrooms, teachers are known to encourage a teacher–student–teacher turntaking pattern (Cazden, 1988; Mehan, 1979), as mentioned in earlier chapters. Cazden (1988) outlines this common pattern in reference to a typical sharing time. "[They] all have the same basic structure: (1) The teacher initiates the sequence by calling on a child to share; (2) The nominated child responds by telling a narrative; and (3) The teacher comments on the narrative before calling on the next child" (p. 29). This three-part sequence also occurs in college classrooms.

How do the turns taken by both children and adults in the classrooms described earlier in this chapter compare to typical classrooms in terms of amount and type? Since initiations are described clearly by sociolinguists as turns routinely taken by teachers, my data analysis focuses on who initiates talk. My definition of initiation is a turn that begins a new topic, develops into an extended conversation, and draws in other students.

An example of structural analysis is from the conversation initiated by Seaaira about *Rose Blanche* and is presented in Figure 2. In the 17 turns taken during the literature study conversation initiated by Seaaira, Caryl speaks four times and Aaron is interrupted twice by Seaaira. The children ask questions of one another and look at one another while talking. Their turns flow naturally and overlap like normal conversation. Comparitively, the entire L2 seminar conversation (a representative part appeared earlier in this chapter) involved 44 turns. It was initiated by Janice. I spoke 17 times, and 19 turns were interchanges between Janice and me. The style of talk is similar to the children's. Opposed to discussion in typical transmission classrooms, in which teachers are known to talk at least two thirds of the time, and their turns are expected to involve primarily initiating and evaluating, in our classrooms Caryl and I took 22% and 35% of the turns, respectively. In addition, the turntaking pattern is varied, many responses follow a student initiation, and neither Caryl nor I made evaluative responses. Structurally, these discussions more closely resemble conversations outside of school than "school talk."

Analyses of talk in other whole language classrooms confirm the conversational nature of school talk when power is shared with children. Newkirk (1992) reported a meeting of two oral cultures—that of the

## Figure 2   Example of Turntaking Analysis

| Initiation | Student response | Teacher response |
|---|---|---|
| Seaaira (asks question) | | |
| | Aaron | |
| | Seaaira | |
| | | Question |
| | Aaron | |
| | Travis | |
| | Aaron (interrupted) | |
| | Seaaira | |
| | Trevor (asks question) | |
| | Aaron (interrupted) | |
| | Seaaira (asks question) | |
| | Trevor (asks question) | |
| | | Question |
| | Travis | |
| | | Summary |
| | Seaaira | |
| | | Statement |

teacher and that of the children—in primary classrooms. He recognized that when children control the content of talk, being "on topic is socially defined instead of being a self-evident function of the texts under discussion" (p. 83). Paley's (1981) careful descriptions of kindergartners in her classroom show how, when she valued the children's meaning, topics, and ideas, waiting for "teachable moments" to participate or question, they accomplished advanced language and thinking. Simpson (1996) concurred, recommending that if teachers wish to extend their students' critical thinking, "We must listen and respond to their interests and concerns first, then support, encourage, and develop analytical readings as opportunities arise" (p. 126). Such analyses of atypical discourse patterns encourage us to expand our sociolinguistic hypotheses about how face-to-face interaction happens in school.

# Teacher as Mediator:
## Connections Between Content and Structure

From the learner's point of view, language provides a set of strategies for interpreting the world, and a means of reflecting upon this interpretation. Why then is exploratory discussion so infrequent in school lessons? The answer must lie in the social pressures which define what behavior seems appropriate. These pressures are partly traditional—they constrain the teacher as well as the pupils—but *they are under the teacher's control, and therefore open to change.* (Barnes, 1992, p. 115, italics added)

This excerpt from Barnes alludes to a third issue revealed in the analyses of the discussion recorded in the Sunshine Room and in the graduate seminar: The importance of the role a teacher plays in classroom discourse cannot be overstated. Teachers who value their students' knowledge and voices and hold a goal to alter the expected patterns of using language in their instructional settings must be effective mediators in the Vygotskian sense (Moll & Whitmore, 1993). Teachers create the social and instructional contexts that enable students of all ages, but especially those of marginalized backgrounds, to achieve the empowerment we hold as ideal. It is up to the teacher to expect a high level of intellectual engagement from all students and to organize classrooms that share power with students. A closer look at the teachers' turns in the data from these two classrooms provides some specific clues as to how this might be accomplished in learning communities.

Structural analysis at a micro-analytical level reveals that neither Caryl's students nor mine waited for the teacher's invitation to speak or set the agenda for discussions and follow-up activities. Rather, they assumed these roles that usually are reserved for the teacher. During our turns, we asked real questions, often for clarification when a speaker's statement was lacking a cohesive tie to the previous discourse or when a statement was ambiguous. Once, for example, Caryl joined a conversation when children were attempting to sort out the characteristics of Germans, Jews, and Nazis in *Rose Blanche*. Caryl asked, "Oh, you mean why didn't just the regular German people fight back, is that what you mean?" Similar questions asked, "Who are you talking about?" or "What do you mean by that?" I often asked students to provide additional background information or to share personal stories with which I was familiar but other listeners were not.

Caryl and I contribute selectively to the content of the conversations as more experienced learners, by extending arguments and adding information. She, for example, joined the talk when she realized that the children were confused about the history and geography of the atomic bombing during World War II. I added terminology, examples, and academic references to the L2 conversations when appropriate. Also, even from the first conversation, I demonstrated my assumption that the students were professional, knowledgeable educators by suggesting that their work was appropriate for a broader audience, through publications or conference presentations.

Caryl and I were not merely improvising on the standard rules for "lesson language," however. The inventions of discourse were goals from the beginning of the year, not exceptions to the rule. Caryl explicitly stated language rules that encouraged talking in the classroom in a positive, conversational manner. These rules gave the children power. She told them, "Talking is the most important thing you can do in this classroom. You learn best when you talk while you work." Throughout the day, she provided overt guidelines for children's participation in terms of thinking and speaking. Guiding the content of the children's talk she said, "I guess what I want is for kids to know why they think something is a good story." Her stated intentions were followed through in the form that talk took, as all participants were awarded time to speak, and discussion was encouraged. It was not necessary for children to raise hands to obtain a turn during interactive periods, nor was the teacher the only participant who could interrupt utterances, negotiate time or activity, or make evaluative remarks.

Similarly, in the graduate seminar, I used several explicit strategies to mediate L2 speakers' participation in the formal discourse. One strategy is time. I explicitly silenced myself to provide time for students to raise issues and take turns. Siu Rong provided a wonderful example. As a young Taiwanese graduate student who was very uncomfortable speaking in classes, she needed a long time to express her thoughts to the group. Given that time, however, Siu Rong demonstrated repeatedly that her ideas were appropriate, in fact central, to our sustained inquiry, as shown in the following dialogue:

Siu Rong: Um, I heard my friend, one of my friend from Japan, I think teachers, about, like, teacher is still, is still, a problem. 'Cuz like, um, a friend of mine from Japan, she told me that lot of English teacher in Japan, they are Japanese but they, they don't know how to speak whole sentence, they just, yeah, even though, even though they are English teachers that they don't how to con-, con-, speak to Americans, or conversations with the others. So, you know sometimes I'm just wondering, like I think in Taiwan, some of my teachers even though they are English teachers, but they don't know how to—

Kathy: They couldn't come and converse here any better than you guys.

Siu Rong: They're just teaching you grammars, vocabulary and read a text book, that's all. So that's why, I think that's part of the reason why many, many international students from Asia they cannot speak the words in English.

Janice: Because they haven't used English to make meaning.

Siu Rong: Yeah.

This type of teaching requires patience and trust in students' intellectual contributions, showing that their turns are worth waiting for. Notice that even with my overt goal to keep quiet, I was compelled to help Siu Rong—by interrupting!

The structural analyses show that the numbers of learners' turns versus teachers' turns vary considerably across separate discussions due to the changing purpose, or content, of the study sessions over time. For example, both groups met on occasion without any teacher participation, giving students 100% of the turns of talk. At other times, we had more focused goals and were more involved in the talk. In one discussion, Caryl was determined to help the children resolve their questions about *Rose Blanche* so they could move to other topics and books. This required more direct involvement in guiding the children's conversations than she might otherwise have taken. Caryl's purpose for most discussions, however, was to sit back and listen, interested in the children's responses, and intentionally giving them opportunities to speak.

The way Caryl and I moved in and out of our students' talk, making split-second decisions about how to participate, is a form of mediation. It is difficult to see because, as explained in Moll & Whitmore (1993),

> The teacher's guidance is purposely mediated, almost hidden, embedded in the activities. [Thus], learning...is not only an individual achievement but a joint accomplishment between adults and children.... The goal of this mediated assistance is to make [students] consciously aware of how they are manipulating the literacy process, achieving new means, and applying their knowledge to expand their boundaries by creating or reorganizing future experiences or activities. (pp. 38–40)

Both Trevor and Janice (during their turns transcribed in italic on pages 108 and 115, earlier) showed the powerful effect of such mediation on the learners' awareness of the influence of social discourse on their individual thinking.

## Conclusion

Content and structural analyses show that, to be communicatively competent in these two classrooms, learners need to be active participants, take intellectual and emotional risks, voice authentic and personal questions about the real world, take turns as appropriate for the success of the conversation, initiate topics of interest, interrupt if necessary to take a turn, and direct utterances to the real audience during talk. The structure and the content of discourse are dependent on each other; both are crucial in the invention of communicative competence. As Barnes (1992) said, "We cannot make a clear distinction between the content and the form of the curriculum, or treat the subject matter as the end and the communication as no more than a means. The two are inseparable" (p. 14).

The structure enables the learners to develop content that is authentic and is of high academic quality. It alters the form of discussion, demonstrating that all students can be trusted to learn and to participate meaningfully. Without the amount of personal control over turns of talk and initiations, among other structural variables, the content could not emerge as dramatically as it does. However, the richness of the content, the fact that learners have something important to talk about, necessitates and pushes the natural, conversational structure that results. When learners have real questions about their real worlds, they push for helpful responses and interactions. Teachers who are mediators honor the content of their students' talk by altering their own participation. It is the subsequent transformation of classroom discourse that allows for the transformation of students. And, as Wells (1989) stated, as children (and I would add, adults) participate in collaborative talk in response to their own inquiry-driven language event, they become empowered.

## Questions for Reflection

1. How can the conditions that fostered high-quality, authentic talk in the two settings in this chapter be demonstrated in teacher education programs to most effectively teach preservice and inservice teachers about effective classroom language?

2. How might a teacher design a research study to become more metalinguistically aware of his or her role as a mediator in students' talk?

## References

Barnes, D. (1992). *From communication to curriculum* (2nd ed.). Portsmouth, NH: Heinemann.

Board, P.E. (1982). *Toward a theory of instructional influence: Aspects of the instructional environment and their influence on children's acquisition of reading.* Unpublished doctoral dissertation, University of Toronto.

Cazden, C.B. (1988). *Classroom discourse: The language of teaching and learning.* Portsmouth, NH: Heinemann.

Daniels, H. (1994). *Literature circles.* York, ME: Stenhouse.

Dewey, J. (1904). The relationship of theory to practice in education. In C. McMurry (Ed.), *The relation of theory to practice in the education of teachers* (Third Yearbook of the National Society of the Scientific Study of Education, Part I, pp. 9–30). Chicago, IL: University of Chicago Press.

Goodman, K.S. (1992). Why whole language is today's agenda in education. *Language Arts, 69*(1), 354–363.

Hymes, D. (1972). Models of the interaction of language and social life. In J.J. Gumperz & D. Hymes (Eds.), *Directions in sociolinguistics: The ethnography of communication.* New York: Holt, Rinehart, and Winston.

Mehan, H. (1979). *Learning lessons.* Cambridge, MA: Harvard University Press.

Moll, L.C., & Diaz, S. (1987). Change as the goal of educational research. *Anthropology and Education Quarterly, 18*(4), 300–311.

Moll, L.C., & Whitmore, K.F. (1993). Vygotsky in classroom practice: Moving from individual transmission to social transaction. In E. Forman, N. Minick, & A. Stone (Eds.), *Contexts for learning: Sociocultural dynamics in children's development* (pp. 19–42). New York: Oxford University Press.

Newkirk, T., with McLure, P. (1992). *Listening in: Children talk about books (And other things)*. Portsmouth, NH: Heinemann.

Paley, V.G. (1981). *Wally's stories: Conversations in the kindergarten*. Cambridge, MA: Harvard University Press.

Philips, S.U. (1983). The invisible culture: Communication in classroom and community on the Warm Springs Indian Reservation. New York: Longman.

Rosebery, A.S., Warren, B., & Conant, F.R. (1992). *Appropriating scientific discourse: Findings from language minority classrooms* (Working paper No. 1–92). Cambridge, MA: TERC Communications.

Short, K.G., Harste, J., & Burke, C. (1996). *Creating classrooms for authors and inquirers*. Portsmouth, NH: Heinemann.

Short, K.G., & Pierce, K.M. (1990). *Talking about books*. Portsmouth, NH: Heinemann.

Simpson, A. (1996). Critical questions: Whose questions? *The Reading Teacher*, *50*(2), 118–127.

Wells, G. (1989). Language in the classroom: Literacy and collaborative talk. *Language and Education*, *3*(4), 251–272.

Whitmore, K.F., & Crowell, C.G. (1994). *Inventing a classroom: Life in a bilingual whole language learning community*. York, ME: Stenhouse.

## Text Set of Children's Literature About Issues of War and Peace

Adler, D. (1989). *We remember the Holocaust*. New York: Trumpet Club.

Bunting, E. (1990). *The wall*. Illustrated by Ronald Himler. New York: Clarion.

Cohen, B. (1985). *The secret grove*. New York: Union of Hebrew Congregations.

Durell, A., & Sach, M. (Eds.). (1990). *The big book for peace*. New York: Dutton.

Eco, U., & Carmi, E. (1989). *The bomb and the general*. New York: Harcourt Brace Jovanovich.

Eco, U., & Carmi, E. (1989). *The three astronauts*. New York: Harcourt Brace Jovanovich.

Finkelstein, N.H. (1985). *Remember not to forget*. New York: Franklin Watts.

Gauch, P.L. (1975). *Thunder at Gettysburg*. New York: Putnam.

Greene, C. (1987). *Elie Wiesel—messenger from the Holocaust*. Chicago, IL: Children's Press.

*I never saw another butterfly...children's drawing and poems from Terezin Concentration Camp 1942–1944*. New York: McGraw Hill. (Originally published in Czechoslovakia in 1962)

Innocenti, R. (1985). *Rose Blanche*. Mankato, MN: Creative Education.

Kellogg, S. (1973). *The Island of the Skog*. New York: Dial.

Morimoto, J. (1987). *My Hiroshima*. New York: Viking.

Seuss, Dr. (1984). *The butter battle book*. New York: Random House.

Slater, D. (1988). *Why do wars happen?* New York: Gloucester Press.

Tennyson, A. Lord. (1964). *The charge of the Light Brigade*. New York: Golden Press.

Tauchiya, Y. (1988). *Faithful elephants*. New York: Houghton Mifflin.

# PART THREE

## Examining Conflicts and Complexities in Peer Talk

# CHAPTER 7

# Conflict During Classroom Discussions Can Be a Good Thing

∞

## JANICE F. ALMASI AND LINDA B. GAMBRELL

Derek* is a 9-year-old child who lives in a suburban area on the east coast of the United States. Like many other children his age, Derek enjoys sports and is quite active outside of school. On the playground and in the cafeteria, he is social and even a leader. In his fourth-grade classroom, however, Derek is shy and withdrawn. He rarely participates in classroom discussions of literature. His classroom demeanor may be accounted for in large part because he has difficulty reading fluently and difficulty comprehending what he has read. During a discussion of "Orienteering Day" (Razzi, 1986) the seven other members of Derek's peer-led discussion group were engaged in a lively discussion about why the two antagonists in the story would cheat in order to win a race. Several students offered conflicting explanations, and eventually one student synthesized the conflicting ideas to render a reasonable motive. At one point in the discussion the teacher momentarily intervened and tried to draw Derek into the discussion by asking, "Derek, what did you think about the story?" After waiting 35 seconds for a response from Derek, the other students resumed their conversation. Could Derek just be reserved and perhaps overwhelmed by all of the discourse surrounding him?

---

*All names of students appearing in this chapter are pseudonyms and resemble original names only as they relate to gender and ethnicity.

Discussions are speech events in which students and teachers collaboratively construct meaning or consider alternate interpretations of text in order to arrive at new understandings (Almasi, 1996). We know that during literary discussions discourse is lively and can focus on personal reactions and responses to what has been read (Many & Wiseman, 1992; McGee, 1992). We also know that students must engage in a great deal of cognitive strategy use in order to participate meaningfully in the discussions. Participants must use interpretive strategies such as comparing characters, making intertextual connections, or challenging the author's writing style. Additionally, participants must display communicative competence in their interactions with others (Bloome & Bailey, 1992). Such strategies for interaction require that participants initiate topics of conversation, link information that they want to communicate to what already has been discussed, respond to the comments of others, and speak in a manner that enables them to be understood by others. Participating in a literary discussion requires readers to be cognitively and socially literate by being involved in the types of interaction processes that are central to the social transmission of knowledge (Cook-Gumperz, 1986). Could it be then, that Derek was unable to participate because he did not have the cognitive strategies, the social strategies, or some combination of both that would enable him to participate meaningfully and successfully?

Vygotsky (1978) theorized that perhaps the single most effective learning environment is a social one, in which a learner observes and interacts with more knowledgeable others as they engage in cognitive processes that he or she may not be able to engage in independently. Learning in this situation may occur incidentally as the learner observes the cognitive and social processes in which fellow group members engage. Learning also may be direct when teachers or peers function as more knowledgeable others and scaffold the interaction so that the learner becomes capable of achieving more with their assistance than he or she could have independently (Rogoff, 1990; Vygotsky, 1978). Situating literature discussions within this type of learning environment might mean that a child like Derek, who has difficulty participating in discussions, gradually internalizes the ability to participate meaningfully and to monitor his comprehension and, with proper scaffolding, eventually becomes able to do so independently.

# The Role of Conflict in Literature Discussions

Berlyne (1971) has defined *cognitive conflict* as incompatible ideas that occur simultaneously in the mind and that tend to disrupt one another. These disruptions motivate an active search for information that would provide a more adequate cognitive perspective so that the uncertainty might be resolved. These searches for resolution or clarity are known as "epistemic curiosity." While reading, we often engage in such searches for clarity. In a literary sense, the notion of cognitive conflict is consonant with transactional views of literacy (see, for example, Bleich, 1978; Iser, 1980; Rosenblatt, 1938/1976, 1978) that assume readers' interpretations are not static, but are shaped continually by new information acquired from their transactions with the text and other members of their interpretive community (Fish, 1980). For example, while reading we might make a prediction about how a character might act or how a problem might be resolved. As we read on in the text we may encounter information that forces us to reconsider or alter our original ideas, predictions, or interpretations. If we were unable to monitor our understanding while reading, we might not notice the conflicting information presented in the text and retain our original interpretation. This ability to monitor and update one's understanding of text is crucial for developing self-regulated readers who are able to recognize conflicting information and adjust their interpretations accordingly (Baker & Brown, 1984; Paris, Wasik, & Turner, 1991; Pressley, Johnson, Symons, McGoldrick, & Kurita, 1989). Yet, younger and less proficient readers often opt to disengage from the textual world when such conflicts arise (Garrison & Hynds, 1991), and they often do not attempt to make meaning from text as they read (Garner & Reis, 1981). This is often because these readers are not aware of the types of active thinking and processing that should occur while reading independently. Our goal for these readers must be to create learning environments in which they can witness these thought processes and gradually internalize and imitate them as Vygotsky (1978) postulated.

Discussions of literature provide an environment that offers cognitive models of thought processes that occur while reading. Conflicts emerge during literary discussions as participants encounter alternate interpretations, or encounter discourse that forces them to reconsider their own interpretations of text. Such conflicts are more appropriately known as *sociocognitive conflicts* because they involve cognitive processes that are brought about in a social environment (Bloome, 1985; Mugny & Doise, 1978). The value of sociocognitive conflicts during discussions of literature is that they provide students with an opportunity to engage in thought processes (monitoring and updating one's interpretation) similar to those that they use when reading independently. That is, as readers talk about text and attempt to construct meaning, they monitor and update their interpretations in order to communicate their thoughts to others. This process is similar to the type of monitoring and updating that occurs when reading independently. Doise and Mugny (1984) have suggested that sociocognitive conflicts are more likely to be confronted in a social environment, such as a literary discussion, because participants are confronted with a conflict that is not only cognitive in nature, but also social. Learners may not be able to deny or ignore the conflict as easily when in a social context as when reading independently (Garrison & Hynds, 1991). If students observe and engage with others as they collaboratively struggle to make sense of a text, they might eventually use the same strategies while reading independently. The question that arises, then, is what type of social learning environment enables children to observe such sociocognitive processes so that internalization might occur?

As mentioned earlier in this volume, the traditional discussion format that children are most familiar with in elementary schools is actually more of a "recitation" than a discussion (Dillon, 1984; Gall & Gall, 1976). During these recitations, the teacher is the leader and inquisitor, asking questions, and guiding the flow of the discussion (Barr & Dreeben, 1991). The interaction patterns that occur between teachers and students are dominated by recurrent chains of teacher questions and student answers (Cazden, 1986; Mehan, 1979). Teacher-led discussions provide little opportunity for students to interact with one another.

Current research on classroom environments that foster discussion (for example, Almasi, 1995; Alpert, 1987; Eeds & Wells, 1989; O'Flahavan, Stein, Wiencek, & Marks, 1992) has suggested that when teachers assume a restricted role as co-collaborator in constructing meaning as in peer discussions, rather than as a leader or inquisitor as in teacher-led discussions, their students exhibit greater amounts of verbalization in terms of both quantity and quality, leading to higher levels of cognitive processing. When students participate in peer discussions, they are responsible for directing and negotiating the agenda for discussion as well as the flow of the discussion. When students are provided with the opportunity to interact freely with one another, ponder issues, and challenge one another's ideas, they become more cognitively engaged and they are more likely to internalize the cognitive processes to which they are exposed (Almasi, McKeown, & Beck, 1996).

# The Present Study

The study reported in this chapter examined the effects of peer-led and teacher-led discussion environments on students' ability to recognize and resolve sociocognitive conflicts. This study was part of a larger investigation reported elsewhere (Almasi, 1995; Almasi & Gambrell, 1994). In order for us to examine the nature of sociocognitive conflicts in peer-led and teacher-led discussions, 97 fourth graders and their six classroom teachers participated in the investigation for 9 weeks. Students were average and below-average readers who were grouped heterogeneously within each of the six classrooms. Students were matched based on comprehension and their ability to recognize and resolve conflicts as measured by a Cognitive Conflict Scenario Task. Two subgroups within each classroom were formed; thus, there were two groups within each of the six classrooms for a total of 12 groups. A discussion group structure, either peer- or teacher-led, was assigned randomly to each group within each classroom.

Teachers selected nine pieces of literature and provided all the instruction. Each week students were introduced to the literature in a similar manner; that is, each group tapped background knowledge, made predictions, and set purposes. Following silent reading of the text, students responded to it in response journals and then they engaged in a 30-minute discussion of the text. Peer discussions followed a Conversational Discussion Group format (O'Flahavan, 1989) in which the teacher introduced and reviewed the rules that students developed to guide their interaction and their interpretations for the first 5 minutes. Following this introduction, students engaged in a 20-minute discussion of the text in which the teacher was present only as a momentary scaffold, interjecting suggestions for facilitating the interaction or the students' interpretation. At the conclusion of the discussion, the students and teacher engaged in a 5-minute debriefing in which they evaluated their interactions with one another and their attempts to interpret the text. All discussions were videotaped and three (one from weeks two, five, and eight) were selected randomly for transcription and analysis from each group. A total of 36 transcripts were used in the analysis.

## Types of Conflict

The first step in analyzing the data involved identifying where episodes of sociocognitive conflict occurred in each discussion. Three hundred six episodes of sociocognitive conflict were identified in all the discussions. The number of conflicts was almost equal in peer-led ($n = 166$) and teacher-led ($n = 140$) groups. After episodes of sociocognitive conflict were identified, they were read and reread numerous times, and categories and patterns of interaction began to emerge that distinguished peer-led groups from teacher-led groups. Three types of sociocognitive conflicts were present in the discussions: conflicts within self, conflicts with others, and conflicts with text. Each of these types are described in the following sections, and a comparison between peer- and teacher-led groups follows.

**Conflicts within self.** These conflicts represent students' ponderings and questions about the text, or their interpretations, that were confusing or disturbing to them. The critical feature of a conflict within self is that the student overtly verbalizes to the group that something has not made sense to him or her, and he or she is seeking resolution to the confusion. For example, after reading "Something Strange at the Ballpark" (Levy, 1986), several students did not understand why the main character, Gwen, kept wearing disguises in her attempts to determine who had stolen her friend Jill's lucky bat. Examples of students' conflicts within self are shown by these questions: "Why did Gwen go around in that funny-looking nose in the beginning?" and "Why isn't she [Jill] any good without her lucky bat?" These types of puzzlements indicate that the student is aware that something about these characters' actions does not make sense to him or her.

The following example of a conflict within self is taken from a peer-led group's discussion of "Something Strange at the Ballpark":

| Kristen: | Gwen always thought something strange was going on. She always, um, taps her braces. |
| All: | Uh huh. Yeah. |

| Aaron: | Because it says here on page 131, on the first paragraph. It says, "'Because I didn't,' said Erica. 'Maybe,' said Gwen. She walked away tapping her braces." Why does she always tap her braces? |
| All: | Because... |
| Kristen: | Because that's what she does when she's, when something goes strange. |
| Aaron: | [Out of] habit. |
| [Students all talk at once] | |
| Timmy: | Yeah. She's like tapping [as she is] trying to think. |
| Brian: | Probably. |
| | (from Almasi, 1993; Episode 05-41-11) |

In this example, Aaron is experiencing the conflict. He cannot understand why Gwen always taps her braces. His query elicits some brief thoughts that lead to the resolution that it is a habit of Gwen's when she is trying to think.

This study revealed that conflicts within self occurred at different times during peer-led and teacher-led discussions. In both contexts, 43% of the conflicts occurred as students read the text. Students recorded evidence of the conflict in questions in their journals and voiced their concerns during discussion. In peer-led groups, the remaining 57% of conflicts occurred as a result of students' questions and comments. However, in the teacher-led groups, only 17% of the conflicts occurred in response to student comments or questions, and 40% occurred in response to teachers' comments and questions.

**Conflicts with others.** This type of conflict represents a conflicting notion or puzzlement that occurred to an individual while group members were interacting. Prior to the interaction with group members, the individual experiencing the conflict may not have had an internal conflict or may not have been aware that an alternative interpretation was possible. The conflict arises as group members share their interpretations.

In the example that follows, a peer-led group is discussing the story "Grandfather and Rolling Thunder" (Strete, 1986). The conflict that arises between Steve and Bobby is a difference of interpretation based on their personal beliefs and values. Bobby cannot understand why the rodeo operators would put a horse as wild as Rolling Thunder into a

*Almasi and Gambrell*

competition where someone could possibly get injured. Steve takes the stance that danger is the nature of competition and that is the chance one takes if one desires to win.

| Bobby: | What I don't understand is Rolling Thunder; they put him in the rodeo, and he is such a wild horse. Somebody could get killed. |
| Steve: | Um, well, that's why they have him in there. It's a competition. |
| Bobby: | What, so somebody can get killed? |
| Steve: | No. They just want competition. They [the rodeo operators] want to build up competition so like if somebody you know is a real good rider, they want to prove that they're not that good of a rider. See, they're not gonna see how good they really are [unless there is difficult competition]. |
| Bobby: | Yeah, by breakin' their neck. |
| Steve: | Hey, if they want to do it, it's hard luck on them. (from Almasi, 1993; Episode 02-31-05) |

Conflicts with others were not predominant in either peer-led or teacher-led discussions, accounting for 12% and 19% of sociocognitive conflicts in each group, respectively.

**Conflicts with text.** These conflicts arise during discussions when students' responses to questions or statements are in direct conflict with the text. The student's response typically is negated by either the teacher or a peer who directly informs the student that the idea is in contrast to what was stated in the text. The difference between conflicts with text and conflicts within self is in the way that they are resolved. Conflicts with text are resolved when students are told that their ideas are blatantly in conflict. Conflicts within self are resolved when the individuals experiencing the conflict are able to recognize it on their own.

An example of a conflict with text is taken from the following peer-led group's discussion of "Something Strange at the Ballpark." In this excerpt, Tracy experiences the conflict when she makes a statement about how the baseball glove was removed from the character's hand. Brian contradicts Tracy's statement and provides textual support for his view. Another group member, Timmy, validates Brian's point:

| Kristen: | I like when um, the boy was riding his bike, and he went around a corner and then the dog jumped right into his basket and then um... |
| Brian: | ...he [the dog] sinked his teeth into the glove. |
| Tracy: | He [the dog] *jumped* to get the glove off his hand. |
| Brian: | No, he sank his teeth into Jill's mitt, and it yanked the boy off the bike. That's what happened. Just read right here on page 135. It says, "The boy stopped. Gwen and Jill were almost on top of him. The band struck 'Take me out to the ball....' The boy tried to dash across the street in front of the parade. All of a sudden Fletcher [the dog] leapt out of the basket and sank his teeth into Jill's mitt pulling the boy off his bike." First paragraph. |
| Timmy: | You're right. |

(from Almasi, 1993; Episode 05-41-12)

Conflicts with text were more common in teacher-led discussions (60% of all conflicts) than in peer-led discussions (13% of all conflicts).

## Distinctions Between Conflict Types in Peer-Led and Teacher-Led Discussions

Two major distinctions arose between the types of conflicts in which peer-led and teacher-led groups engaged. First, conflicts within self were substantially more frequent in peer-led groups than in teacher-led groups. Second, conflicts with text were infrequent in peer-led groups and significantly more frequent in teacher-led groups (see Table 1). However, conflicts with text accounted for 60% of all teacher-led conflicts. Thus, in peer-led groups, in which students set their own discussion agenda, the majority of conflicts revolved around personal incongruities that the students were able to recognize, verbalize, and attend to during their discussions. In a Vygotskian sense, this means that students in peer-led groups were able to watch and observe as others expressed their puzzlements, and they were afforded the opportunity to express their own puzzlements and actively seek resolution—both key components for internalization. That is, by witnessing the cognitive processes that occur as other students express their puzzlements about text, students like Derek might gradually learn how to engage in similar thought processes. Such

*Almasi and Gambrell*

## Table 1 Frequencies (and Proportions) of Types of Sociocognitive Conflicts Between Peer-Led and Teacher-Led Discussions

|  | Type of discussion | |
| --- | --- | --- |
|  | Peer-led | Teacher-led |
| *Conflicts within self* | | |
| Number of episodes | 125 (0.75) | 30 (0.21) |
| *Conflicts with others* | | |
| Number of episodes | 20 (0.12) | 26 (0.19) |
| *Conflicts with text* | | |
| Number of episodes | 21 (0.13) | 84 (0.60) |
| Total number of episodes | 166 | 140 |

a student might begin by trying such processes in peer-led discussions, and eventually the process might transfer to independent reading in which the student actively monitors his comprehension, expresses puzzlement when text does not make sense, and seeks information to resolve the internal conflict.

The teacher-led groups, on the other hand, had far fewer opportunities for discussing their personal questions. Instead, the majority of conflicts to which they were exposed were brought about during the discussion when others (most often the teacher) took responsibility for noting that a student's response was in conflict with the text, rather than the student's recognizing the incongruity himself. The following example, taken from a teacher-led discussion of "Something Strange at the Ballpark," illustrates how Carla was unable to respond to the teacher's question regarding a boy's punishment for stealing the main character's lucky bat; the result was a conflict with text.

Teacher: What was his [Marshall's] punishment? How was he punished, Carla, do you know?

Carla: He was punished because um, because he took, he took...

Teacher: I know, but what did they do to him to punish him?

| Roger: | I know. It's right here. |
| --- | --- |
| Teacher: | Richard, do you know? |
| Richard: | [reading from text] "The coach was so angry at Marshall, that she didn't even let him play. Marshall had to be the water boy." |
| Teacher: | Right. Okay, Marshall had to be the water boy, so that was Marshall's punishment. He had to be the water boy. (from Almasi, 1993; Episode 05-50-05) |

In this excerpt the teacher has assumed the responsibility for recognizing the conflict and for its resolution. The individual who experienced the conflict (Carla) is not responsible for recognizing or resolving her own conflict. Instead, the teacher seeks resolution from a different individual (Richard), and Carla disengages from the entire conversation after her inability to respond "correctly." This pattern occurred 60% of the time in teacher-led discussions. Thus, passivity, disengagement, or withdrawn behavior may not be an exclusive trait of the low-achieving student, as one may have thought in the case of Derek. As Goodlad (1984) has argued, it may be that classroom culture is the arbiter of opportunity for particular students. Doise and Mugny (1984) have suggested that various authority structures impede communication, making nonparticipation and passivity an alluring alternative to engagement. The evidence presented in this investigation suggests that in teacher-led discussions in which teachers established identities as authority figures and students ratified this role (Bloome & Bailey, 1992), this is a plausible explanation for the discourse and patterns of interaction that were present. Moreover, students in the teacher-led groups were not involved in, nor were they accorded the opportunity to observe, the types of cognitive processing that would enable them to gradually acquire the ability to monitor their understanding by recognizing conflicting information.

## Resolving Conflicts

The three types of conflicts that students confronted during literary discussions suggest that perhaps different types of resolutions might occur not only across types of conflicts, but also across peer-led and teacher-led discussions. Six types of resolutions were evident throughout the 306 episodes of sociocognitive conflict that occurred: (1) telling information,

(2) sharing opinions, (3) using text, (4) relying on the teacher, (5) discussing, and (6) no resolution. Often episodes were characterized by a combination of these six resolutions. However, predominant forms of resolution were clear in nearly every episode. Each type of resolution will be explained briefly in the next section, followed by a discussion of how peer-led and teacher-led groups differed in their use of each type of resolution.

**Telling information.** Often episodes of sociocognitive conflicts were resolved when one student simply provided information to resolve the conflict. As seen in Table 2 on page 142, both peer-led and teacher-led groups used this form of resolution. However, teacher-led groups resolved half of all the conflicts in this manner, particularly those within self and with text. Peer-led groups, on the other hand, told information to resolve only 29% of all their conflicts and used it to resolve all types of conflicts equally.

In the example that follows, the teacher asks who the detectives are in "Something Strange at the Ballpark" and elicits an incorrect response from Mary Ann. The teacher provides some information to clarify Mary Ann's original response and then solicits the correct response from the other students:

Teacher:     Okay, so then she [Jill] tells everybody, hey, this is a great bat. Then she finds out that it's missing. Who decides that they're gonna take over this job of finding the person who stole…

Mary Ann: Um, Mr. McGraw.

Teacher:     Mr. McGraw, Rusty McGraw is the name of the bat. It's a bat. Who's going to be the detective?

Mary Ann: Jill and this other…

All:          I know! Gwen!

Teacher:     Alright. Gwen. Gwen is our detective. (from Almasi, 1993; Episode 05-50-01)

Telling information resolves conflicts quickly and invites little discussion or interaction among group members.

**Sharing opinions.** Students often drew on their personal experiences and shared their opinions about a given issue to create a resolution. As indicated in Table 2, children in peer-led groups used this type of resolution one third of the time to resolve both conflicts with others and con-

**Table 2  Frequencies (and Proportions) of Type of Resolution Used by Peer-Led and Teacher-Led Discussions**

| | Type of conflict in peer-led groups | | | | Type of conflict in teacher-led groups | | | |
| --- | --- | --- | --- | --- | --- | --- | --- | --- |
| | Conflict with self | Conflict with others | Conflict with text | Total | Conflict with self | Conflict with others | Conflict with text | Total |
| *Type of resolution* | | | | | | | | |
| Telling information | 38 (.30) | 4 (.20) | 6 (.29) | 48 (.29) | 18 (.60) | 6 (.23) | 46 (.55) | 70 (.50) |
| Sharing opinions | 47 (.38) | 8 (.40) | 1 (.05) | 56 (.33) | 1 (.03) | 13 (.50) | 4 (.05) | 18 (.13) |
| Using text | 17 (.14) | 4 (.20) | 8 (.38) | 29 (.18) | 2 (.07) | 5 (.19) | 21 (.25) | 28 (.20) |
| Relying on teacher | 0 (.00) | 0 (.00) | 1 (.05) | 1 (.01) | 8 (.27) | 1 (.04) | 12 (.14) | 21 (.15) |
| Discussing | 4 (.03) | 3 (.15) | 1 (.05) | 8 (.05) | 0 (.00) | 0 (.00) | 1 (.01) | 1 (.01) |
| Unresolved | 19 (.15) | 1 (.05) | 4 (.19) | 24 (.14) | 1 (.03) | 1 (.04) | 0 (.00) | 2 (.01) |
| Totals | 125 (.75) | 20 (.12) | 21 (.13) | 166 | 30 (.21) | 26 (.19) | 84 (.60) | 140 |

flicts within self. Teacher-led groups shared their opinions to resolve conflicts considerably less frequently (13%) and used this format almost exclusively to resolve conflicts with others.

The following example is taken from a peer-led discussion of "Something Strange at the Ballpark." The students are pondering the main character's actions. Marie and Brigitte offer their opinions in order to help Frank with his conflict:

Frank: One of my questions were, "Why isn't she good without her bat?"
Marie: Well...
Brigitte: Well 'cause...
Frank: Marie, what were you going to say?
Marie: Because it was like, you know how when you get something, and you think it's really lucky? Like if you find a lucky rock, or like if you find a four leaf clover. That's lucky. You'll think that's lucky—you get luck [from it].
Brigitte: Oooh, well I think that with her bat she kept thinking and thinking and *thinking* that it was lucky 'cause she kept hitting grandslammers...homeruns.
(from Almasi, 1993; Episode 05-11-05)

Conflicts that were resolved by sharing opinions did not involve telling factual or text-based information. Instead, students like Marie drew on personal experiences about things such as lucky rocks and four-leaf clovers and combined these ideas with personal opinions to share a possible explanation to the conflict. Thus, conflicts resolved by sharing opinions required more discourse and interaction among students as they expressed their views and were not resolved as quickly as those in which information simply was told.

**Using text.** Consulting the text in order to resolve conflicts was used nearly equally within both peer-led and teacher-led groups. As might be expected, both groups used this method primarily to resolve conflicts with text.

In the following example, taken from a peer-led group's discussion of the conclusion of "Something Strange at the Ballpark," the students are trying to determine how the thief was caught and why the dog jumped. Several students (Nathan, Justin, and Theo) believe that the dog jumped because someone pulled its tail. Angela believes that the dog jumped because it smelled the scent of the glove on the thief (Marshall). However, after consulting the text they alter their ideas:

| | |
|---|---|
| Nathan: | Why did the dog jump up when someone pulled his tail? |
| Angela: | Because… |
| Justin: | Because someone pulled his tail. |
| Angela: | Nuh uh…he smelt [sic] the scent. He smelt the scent of the glove so he ran after Marshall. |
| Nathan: | [reading from text] "He [the dog] jumped up as if someone had pulled his tail." Nobody pulled his tail. He jumped up *as if* someone pulled his tail, but no one pulled his tail. It said *it* pulled his tail. |
| Justin: | It says right here. It says right here, "Jill tied it [invisible string] to Fletcher's tail." The mitt was a trap! Jill tied it to Fletcher's tail [with invisible string]. |
| Nathan: | [From her] detective kit. |
| Angela: | Oh yeah… I get it! |
| | (from Almasi, 1993; Episode 05-61-12) |

This excerpt shows the triumph with which students emerge from the text after they have found evidence that helps resolve the conflict. At times students engaged in quite a bit of dialogue to arrive at a resolution, although at other times, students merely read the piece of text that resolved the conflict with little debate or interaction.

**Relying on the teacher.** A fourth way that students resolved conflicts was by relying on the teacher. Although the peer-led groups had only one episode (1%) in which the teacher resolved the conflict, teacher-led groups relied on the teacher to resolve 15% of all their conflicts.

In the peer-led instance, a student was retelling a portion of a story, and during the retelling it became obvious that the student had misread the word *crow* as *cow*. After several students had failed to comment on the student's miscue, the teacher, in her role as a momentary scaffold, intervened to ask the student to look more carefully at the word. This was the only instance across all 166 episodes of conflict within all six peer-led groups in which a teacher helped students resolve their conflict.

In teacher-led groups, however, the teacher intervened in nearly 1 of every 7 episodes to assist students with the resolution. An example is taken from a teacher-led group's discussion of "The Mystery of the Roll-top Desk" (Witter, 1989). In the mystery, the main character, Jenny, and her family purchase an antique rolltop desk from an auction. Once the desk is unloaded they soon realize that a mysterious man in a green car is parked outside their home. Jenny begins to suspect that there is something special about the desk that warrants so much interest. One night she and her friend, Al, poke around in the desk and uncover a valuable document signed by George Washington. At the conclusion of the mystery it is revealed that the man in the car is a curator from a museum who hoped to purchase the desk for his museum. The episode that follows occurred as the group was discussing the reward that Jenny and Al received:

> Teacher: Okay, so eventually the museum got them [the desk and the document]. They're [the museum] going to pay for them. What do Jenny and Al get out of this besides their mother getting the money [for the desk]?
>
> Karen: Nothing.
>
> Teacher: Oh yeah, they do get something. It says, "'The museum will pay handsomely for this document Mrs. Marsh,' Mr. Young cut in, 'And of course Jenny and Al will receive a citation for protecting a valuable historic document.'"
> (from Almasi, 1993; Episode 05-10-10)

As shown in this excerpt, Karen experienced a conflict with text that the teacher resolved by reading the portion of text that contradicted her. Thus, the teacher's role in the teacher-led groups often was concerned with not just assisting students as they resolved conflicts, but actually resolving them. The teachers in peer-led groups did not provide this type of support; instead they relinquished, or "handed over" (Edwards & Mercer, 1987) this role to the students, enabling them to assume most of the responsibility not only for recognizing conflicts, but also for resolving them.

**Discussing.** Although all conflicts involved discussion, those episodes that were coded as such were resolved through discussion that involved multiple types of resolution. Few episodes in either peer-led (5%) or teacher-led groups (1%) were coded in this manner. Most often, one type of resolution prevailed. An example of this form of resolution

comes from a peer-led discussion of "The Mystery of the Rolltop Desk."
The students discussed the message that was written on the historic document discovered in the desk and Maggie was confused by its meaning:

> Maggie: [At the] bottom [of the page]. It's in like slanted letters. "Howe's fleet in Chesapeake Bay." The first time I read that I thought it said, "Howe's *feet* in Chesapeake Bay. Plans to attack Philadelphia." That doesn't make any sense.
>
> Jake: Yeah, but maybe they were traveling over the bay.
>
> Sean: To go to Philadelphia?
>
> Jake: See, they're traveling by boat.
>
> Maggie: Oh yeah! It's a fleet…fleet of boats.
>
> Jake: And it's also the Revolutionary War.
>
> (from Almasi, 1993; Episode 05-51-12)

The students obviously were confused about the time and location. When Jake pointed out that General Howe's fleet was traveling by boat, the group was reminded that the document was written during the Revolutionary War. The students referred to the text at both the beginning and the end of the episode. In addition, Jake's comments about "traveling over the bay" and "traveling by boat" were key factors in the eventual resolution. The conflict was resolved through combinations of different resolutions rather than by one in particular.

**No resolution.** At times, episodes of sociocognitive conflict remained unresolved. Table 2 shows that this was most prevalent in the peer-led groups (14%). The teacher-led groups only had one instance in which a conflict was unresolved. Clearly, the teachers in the teacher-led groups assumed an authority role. They made certain that the questions that they asked were answered and that any conflicts that emerged were resolved.

In the peer-led groups, however, students had to negotiate to take a turn to speak. They had to be persistent with any questions, concerns, or comments that they may have had in order to gain entry into the discussion so that their conflicts could be resolved. Often students were earnest in their attempts to initiate a topic for discussion and often interrupted topics that already were being discussed. In such instances the newly initiated conflict often went unresolved if not unheard. The example that follows is from a peer-led discussion of "The Mystery of the

Rolltop Desk." The students had been discussing Al's character traits, perhaps because Al is a less fully developed, secondary character. Shauna interrupts the discussion to ask a completely unrelated question from her journal:

Shauna:    Why did Jenny start to feel nervous after the mom did?
Justin:    Hey! We're trying to answer a question!
           (from Almasi, 1993; Episode 05-51-10)

Clearly Justin felt that Shauna's question was intrusive and informed her that she had violated the group's discussion rule: "Stick to the topic." After the harsh reaction, Shauna retreated and did not pose the question again. Thus, the conflict remained unresolved.

Most often unresolved conflicts in the peer-led groups were a result of interactions similar to the one just described. Their presence highlights the fact that students negotiated their own agenda for discussion and, at times, were awkward in their attempts to gain entry into a discussion. However, over time, the number of unresolved conflicts diminished (12 during week 2, 8 during week 5, and 3 during week 8).

## Ability to Recognize and Resolve Conflicts

The data provide strong support for the premise that peer-led discussions are vastly different from teacher-led discussions in terms of the types of conflicts and resolutions in which students become engaged. Students in peer-led discussions were engaged in and exposed to substantially more conflicts within self than their teacher-led counterparts. These conflicts within self tended to be resolved through the shared opinions of group members. Students in teacher-led groups, however, tended to be engaged in conflicts with text that most often were resolved when the teacher called on another student to tell the information that "correctly" resolved the conflict. Therefore, conflicts were recognized and resolved by a person other than the one experiencing the conflict.

The impact of participation in these environments on students' ability to recognize and resolve conflict was measured by the Cognitive Conflict Scenario Task Posttest. This task was administered to each student individually at the conclusion of the investigation. Students were presented with four different discussion scenarios that each illustrated a conflict of some sort. After each scenario was read to students, five probes were asked that determined whether students could determine who was experiencing the conflict, what the conflict was, and what they might do to resolve the conflict: (1) What is going on in this discussion? (2) What would you do in this discussion? Why? (3) Who is having trouble understanding something in this discussion? (4) (asked only if probe #3 was answered) How can you tell? (5) What would you do in this situation to help? Why? Their responses were coded and scored on a 3-point scale (0 = responses that failed to, or incorrectly identified what the conflict was; 1 = responses that evidenced accurate recognition of what the conflict was during the fourth probe; 2 = responses that evidenced accurate recognition of what the conflict was during the first probe). The results revealed that students in peer-led discussions showed significant improvement over their pretest scores on their ability to recognize and resolve conflicts and that students in peer-led discussions also were much more adept at recognizing and resolving conflicts than students in teacher-led discussions. The data suggest that students in peer-led discussions, having engaged in substantially more conflicts within self, were recognizing and sharing their own internal conflicts and questions about texts and actively seeking resolution with their group members. The results of the Cognitive Conflict Scenario Task corroborate and extend these notions in that they reveal that by performing significantly better than students in teacher-led groups on a transfer task, students in peer-led groups were able to internalize the ability to recognize and resolve conflicts.

# Discussion

This study found that the environments that were provided for students in classroom settings had an enormous influence on their cognitive processing. Students who participated in peer-led discussions of texts were exposed to a social environment that provided them with the opportunity to observe the cognitive and social processes in which their peers engaged as they attempted to construct meaningful interpretations. These students were apt to see others express the cognitive conflicts that arose within themselves as they struggled to make sense of text. They were also likely to see such conflicts resolved by sharing a variety of ideas and opinions and by telling information that would facilitate resolution.

By participating in an environment in which these cognitive and social processes were modeled by their peers, students in peer-led groups eventually were able to internalize these same processes. It is clear that teachers can promote students' social and cognitive growth when they assume a more detached role, intervening only to scaffold or model social or cognitive processes.

## What Happened to Derek?

Although this study documents that peer groups as a whole experienced significant cognitive growth, it also is important to examine individual growth. Derek was an intriguing student because of his passivity during peer discussions. As described earlier, Derek's first entry into a peer discussion was during the second week of the study when the teacher invited him to share his opinion about the text. As the weeks went by, Derek was a concern mainly because the rest of his group was functioning so well that his passivity was quite noticeable. By week five of the investigation, the other students in his group had begun to assume the role that the teacher had taken earlier during week two, and began to invite him to share his ideas during the discussion. In a discussion from week five, Derek participated three times, all at the urging of his peers:

| | |
|---|---|
| Timmy: | Derek, did you want to know anything? |
| Derek: | [Nodding his head negatively] Uh, uh. |
| Aaron: | You knew [all of] the story? |
| Jiaguo: | Did you understanded it? |
| Hillary: | What were your predictions Derek? What'd you predict? |
| Derek: | I was, gonna, wonderin' what that one word is, it was on um, page thirt-, thirty. |
| All: | Disguises. |

(from Almasi, 1993; Episode 05-41-09)

In this interaction, Derek's peers were determined to draw him into the discussion. Despite his reservations, Derek eventually succumbed and inquired about the pronunciation of an unknown word. This was the first time that Derek took a risk and exposed the fact that he did not know a word. Although recognizing inability to decode a word is a cognitive process that is not nearly as complex as recognizing failure to understand a larger portion of text, it is a first step in being able to self-monitor.

Derek's peers continued to encourage him to participate and to model cognitive processes for him through their own interactions with one another. By week eight Derek was a completely different group member. In the discussion during week 8, Derek participated *20 times* without any encouragement from his peers. He asked 5 substantive questions and gave 15 statements in response to the comments and questions of his peers. Some of the questions that Derek asked were patterned after questions and discourse patterns in which his peers had engaged earlier. For example, very early in the group's discussion of "Soup's New Shoes" (Peck, 1986), the students were intrigued by the low cost of Soup's shoes. Within that episode the students found text that identified the time period of the story, and their discussion focused on the economic differences in the value of a dollar in 1930 and today. Derek did not participate in that initial episode, but returned to the topic when he asked, "Why don't they buy a new pair of shoes when they need 'em? They only cost three dollars." Derek obviously was confused by the earlier issue and was seeking resolution—a sure sign that he was monitoring his comprehension and actively listening to the earlier interaction.

In that same discussion, Derek also made a critical comment regarding the main character's actions that was an indirect critique of the author's style:

Derek:     He [the main character] said *honest* a lot in the story.
Hillary:   'Cause Rob kept asking him, "Is that true?" [So] he kept saying, "honest."
Brian:     I think this was a pretty weird story because it was all about shoes and partly about the characters. It's like, hey I got new shoes and that's all they were talking about the whole story.
Derek:     I didn't like it because of that. All's they talk about is the shoes.
           (from Almasi, 1993; 08-41-08)

These comments depict students who are thinking critically about the meaning of a text and attempting to interpret it. Derek was becoming a more proficient participant during discussions. He was able to gain entry into a discussion and sustain topics of conversation with greater ease. The profound changes in Derek came about gradually; it took nearly 8 full weeks for him to "blossom." Evidence from this study suggests that students like Derek can grow cognitively and socially. The challenge is in creating environments that promote such growth.

## Suggestions for Classroom Practice

The results reported here and elsewhere (Almasi, 1995; Almasi & Gambrell, 1994; Almasi, McKeown, & Beck, 1996) provide clear evidence that peer-led discussion groups result in improved reading comprehension, higher level thinking skills, and increased motivation. Although some children may learn the conventions of discussion in their homes, many children in our classrooms need support in mastering this kind of instruction. As we plan and implement classroom instruction, the following points are of particular importance:

1. *Providing opportunities for students to ponder confusing aspects of text or to challenge the text improves their reading comprehension.* Often students think that by exposing their confusion about a text their grade will be affected adversely. That is, students feel that if they overtly express confusion then the teacher will know they do not understand. This type of thinking results in students' viewing discussion as an assessment tool rather than as a tool for constructing meaning (Almasi, 1996). It is important for teachers to create a classroom climate that values good reasoning over correct answers.

2. *Providing opportunities for students to interact with one another and to challenge others' ideas during discussions supports higher-level thinking.* When students add or challenge the comments of others, lively debate is sparked and students reveal that they are listening and responding to their peers. This type of interaction provides students with scaffolding for higher level thinking skills as they observe the cognitive processes of their peers, and it enables them to make similar attempts.

3. *Providing opportunities for students to explore issues that are personally relevant enhances motivation.* Permitting students to decide what aspects of the text they want to talk about during a discussion results in increased motivation and participation. When students have choice in the agenda for a

discussion it becomes personally relevant and enables them to take ownership of the discussion, thereby increasing engagement.

4. *Limiting the amount of teacher talk and teacher questions results in increased opportunities for students to develop discussion skills.* When we support students who engage in peer-led discussions, the discussions provide a means for increased language growth and the development of social interaction skills. We can support children in developing discussion skills by taking a coaching position, intervening momentarily to guide students' interactions or to offer various strategies for interpreting literature (for example, comparing characters or challenging the author's style) that might further the discussion.

# Conclusion

Beginning peer discussions is not an easy task. It requires persistence and patience. As in the case of Derek, it takes children time to learn how to interact with one another meaningfully and to focus on interpretation and understanding of text. However, the benefits of engaging in peer discussions of text are numerous and are well worth the effort. Participation in peer discussions improves students' ability to monitor their understanding of text, to verbalize their thoughts, to consider alternative perspectives, and to assume responsibility for their own learning. Increasing students' opportunities to engage in peer-led discussions also increases their opportunities to learn from and to support one another's learning.

## Questions for Reflection

1. Consider the evidence presented regarding Derek's social and cognitive growth. Are there other explanations, besides the Vygotskian interpretation presented here, that might account for such growth?

2. We might call the notion of providing students such as Derek with a decentralized cultural climate in the classroom that affords him the opportunity to observe the cognition and social processing of his peers "empowering." Whose interests are served in such a process, and is enabling students to find their "voice" as empowering as it may seem?

# References

Almasi, J.F. (1993). *The nature of fourth graders' sociocognitive conflicts in peer-led and teacher-led discussions of literature.* Unpublished doctoral dissertation, University of Maryland, College Park.

Almasi, J.F. (1995). The nature of fourth graders' sociocognitive conflicts in peer-led and teacher-led discussions of literature. *Reading Research Quarterly, 30*(3), 314–351.

Almasi, J.F. (1996). A new view of discussion. In L.B. Gambrell & J.F. Almasi (Eds.), *Lively discussions! Fostering engaged reading* (pp. 2–24). Newark, DE: International Reading Association.

Almasi, J.F., & Gambrell, L.B. (1994). *Sociocognitive conflict in peer-led and teacher-led discussions of literature* (Research Report No. 12). Athens, GA: National Reading Research Center.

Almasi, J.F., McKeown, M.G., & Beck, I.L. (1996). The nature of engaged reading in classroom discussions of literature. *Journal of Literacy Research, 28*(1), 107–146.

Alpert, B.R. (1987). Active, silent, and controlled discussions: Explaining variations in classroom conversation. *Teaching and Teacher Education, 3*(1), 29–40.

Baker, L., & Brown, A.L. (1984). Metacognitive skills and reading. In P.D. Pearson, R. Barr, M.L. Kamil, & P.B. Mosenthal (Eds.), *Handbook of reading research: Volume 1* (pp. 353–394). New York: Longman.

Barr, R., & Dreeben, R. (1991). Grouping students for reading instruction. In R. Barr, M.L. Kamil, P.B. Mosenthal, & P.D. Pearson (Eds.), *Handbook of reading research: Volume 2* (pp. 885–910). White Plains, NY: Longman.

Berlyne, D. (1971). *Aesthetics and psychobiology.* New York: Century-Crofts.

Bleich, D. (1978). *Subjective criticism.* Baltimore, MD: Johns Hopkins University Press.

Bloome, D. (1985). Reading as a social process. *Language Arts, 62*(2), 134–142.

Bloome, D., & Bailey, F.M. (1992). Studying language and literacy through events, particularity, and intertextuality. In R. Beach, J.L. Green, M.L. Kamil, & T. Shanahan (Eds.), *Multidisciplinary perspectives on literacy research* (pp. 181–210). Urbana, IL: National Conference on Research in English and the National Council of Teachers of English.

Cazden, C.B. (1986). Classroom discourse. In M.C. Wittrock (Ed.), *Handbook of research on teaching* (3rd ed.) (pp. 432–463). New York: Macmillan.

Cook-Gumperz, J. (1986). Introduction: The social construction of literacy. In J. Cook-Gumperz (Ed.), *The social construction of literacy* (pp. 1–15). New York: Cambridge University Press.

Dillon, J.T. (1984). Research on questioning and discussion. *Educational Leadership, 42*(3), 50–56.

Doise, W., & Mugny, G. (1984). *The social development of the intellect.* New York: Pergamon.

Edwards, D., & Mercer, N. (1987). *Common knowledge: The development of understanding in the classroom.* New York: Methuen.

Eeds, M., & Wells, D. (1989). Grand conversations: An exploration of meaning construction in literature study groups. *Research in the Teaching of English, 23*(10), 4–29.

Fish, S. (1980). *Is there a text in this class? The authority of interpretive communities*. Cambridge, MA: Harvard University Press.

Gall, M.D., & Gall, J.P. (1976). The discussion method. In N.L. Gage (Ed.), *The psychology of teaching methods* (No. 75, Pt. 1, pp. 166–216). Chicago, IL: The University of Chicago Press.

Garner, R., & Reis, R. (1981). Monitoring and resolving comprehension obstacles: An investigation of spontaneous text lookbacks among upper-grade good and poor comprehenders. *Reading Research Quarterly, 16*(4), 569–582.

Garrison, B.M., & Hynds, S. (1991). Evocation and reflection in the reading transaction: A comparison of proficient and less proficient readers. *Journal of Reading Behavior, 23*(3), 259–280.

Goodlad, J. (1984). *A place called school*. New York: McGraw-Hill.

Iser, W. (1980). The reading process: A phenomenological approach. In J.P. Tompkins (Ed.), *Reader response criticism: From formalism to poststructuralism* (pp. 50–69). Baltimore, MD: Johns Hopkins University Press.

Many, J.E., & Wiseman, D.L. (1992). The effect of teaching approach on third-grade students' response to literature. *Journal of Reading Behavior, 24*(3), 265–287.

McGee, L. (1992). An exploration of meaning construction in first graders' grand conversations. In C.K. Kinzer & D.J. Leu (Eds.), *Literacy research, theory, and practice: Views from many perspectives* (Forty-first Yearbook of the National Reading Conference, pp. 177–186). Chicago, IL: National Reading Conference.

Mehan, H. (1979). *Learning lessons*. Cambridge, MA: Harvard University Press.

Mugny, G., & Doise, W. (1978). Socio-cognitive conflict and structure of individual and collective performances. *European Journal of Social Psychology, 8*, 181–192.

O'Flahavan, J.F. (1989). *An exploration of the effects of participant structure upon literacy development in reading group discussion*. Unpublished doctoral dissertation, University of Illinois, Urbana-Champaign.

O'Flahavan, J.F., Stein, C., Wiencek, J., & Marks, T. (1992, December). *Interpretive development in peer discussion about literature: An exploration of the teacher's role*. Paper presented at the Forty-first Annual Meeting of the National Reading Conference, San Antonio, TX.

Paris, S.G., Wasik, B.A., & Turner, J.C. (1991). The development of strategic readers. In R. Barr, M.L. Kamil, P.B. Mosenthal, & P.D. Pearson (Eds.), *Handbook of reading research: Volume 2* (pp. 609–640). White Plains, NY: Longman.

Pressley, M., Johnson, C.J., Symons, S., McGoldrick, J.A., & Kurita, J.A. (1989). Strategies that improve children's memory and comprehension of text. *The Elementary School Journal, 90*(1), 3–32.

Rogoff, B. (1990). *Apprenticeship in thinking: Cognitive development in social context*. New York: Oxford University Press.

Rosenblatt, L.M. (1938/1976). *Literature as exploration*. New York: Modern Language Association.

Rosenblatt, L.M. (1978). *The reader, the text, the poem: The transactional theory of the literary work*. Carbondale, IL: Southern Illinois University Press.

Vygotsky, L.S. (1978). *Mind in society: The development of higher psychological processes.* (M. Cole, V. John-Steiner, S. Scribner, & E. Souberman, Eds. and Trans.) Cambridge, MA: Harvard University Press. (Original work published 1934)

## Children's Literature References

Levy, E. (1986). Something strange at the ballpark. In V.A. Arnold & C.B. Smith (Eds.), *Winning moments* (pp. 127–140). New York: Macmillan.

Peck, R.N. (1986). Soup's new shoes. In V.A. Arnold & C.B. Smith (Eds.), *Winning moments* (pp. 276–286). New York: Macmillan.

Razzi, J.(1986). Orienteering day. In V.A. Arnold and C.B. Smith (Eds.), *Winning moments* (Level 4, pp. 329–341). New York: Macmillan.

Strete, C.K. (1986). Grandfather and rolling thunder. In V.A. Arnold & C.B. Smith (Eds.), *Winning moments* (pp. 343–362). New York: Macmillan.

Witter, E. (1989). The mystery of the rolltop desk. In B.E. Cullinan, R.C. Farr, W.D. Hammond, N.L. Roser, & D.S. Strickland (Eds.), *Crossroads* (pp. T795–T815). Orlando, FL: Harcourt Brace Jovanovich.

# CHAPTER 8

# Exploring the Complexities of Peer-Led Literature Discussions: The Influence of Gender

∞

## KAREN S. EVANS

W hen I first began exploring the use of peer-led literature discussions, gender was not a focus of my work. I was more excited by the possibilities such instructional contexts might afford students to engage in personal, meaningful conversations about books. As an avid reader who always had enjoyed talking with others about the books I read for pleasure, I wanted to encourage young readers in their efforts to experience this same type of enjoyment. It was not until I started listening closely to the conversations students had in their literature discussion groups that I began to understand that other learning opportunities exist in such contexts as well. These other learning opportunities represent the ways social and cultural issues influence how students respond to the books they read and to one another as members of a discussion group. In particular, I began to notice that gender is an important factor in students' discussions. This chapter explores the ways gender influenced the type of talk and participation patterns found in two fifth-grade literature discussion groups.

# Gender Influence on Students' Responses to Literature

Research suggests that students' response to literature can be influenced by gender in several ways. The three potential types of influence that are discussed in this chapter are (1) boys' and girls' possible predisposition to engage in different types of talk about texts, (2) the text that is being read and the ways in which gender roles are presented within texts, and (3) the group dynamics within literature discussion groups.

## Different Types of Talk

Many feminist theorists argue that gender is an important factor in determining how students interpret and respond to texts. For example, Cherland (1992) found that girls tend to favor a discourse of feeling and boys tend to use a discourse of action. Cherland described a discourse of feeling as one that focuses on the emotion in the text, deals with human relationships, and values caring. In contrast, a discourse of action is concerned with logic, values reason and believability, and seeks meaning in the plot and action. Cherland termed such differences "gendered readings" that result in "gendered talk," and hypothesized that a discourse of action is more likely to be valued in a male-dominated society.

A concern that must be raised, however, relates to the use of labels such as "discourse of feeling" and "discourse of action." Such labels could be interpreted to be synonymous with "girl talk" and "boy talk" and consequently could reinforce gender stereotypes. For example, it is possible that teachers who believe in gendered readings and gendered talk might have different expectations for the ways in which boys and girls talk about the books they have read. Moreover, it is possible that feeling talk and action talk might be valued differently by teachers and students. Such an interpretation would serve to constrain rather than open new possibilities for students' discussions of texts.

## The Text Being Read

The texts students read also may influence their response. Many books reinforce traditional gender roles that may result in limiting students' responses to such books. For example, consider the gender roles found in most fairy tales or adolescent romance novels. In such books, females typically are portrayed as being weak and in need of a man to rescue them, while males are portrayed as strong, intelligent heroes. When reading these types of books, it is likely that students interpret and respond to the content in ways that reinforce gender stereotypes. Rather than discourage the reading of such books, feminist theorists advocate helping students to "read against the grain" (Taylor, 1993; Temple, 1993). Reading against the grain refers to the processes of questioning what is read and arguing with the roles, relationships, and ideas represented in books, especially when reading about people of different sexes, ages, races, and economic or social classes. For instance, in an effort to help students challenge gender roles in society, the teacher in Temple's (1993) study read students the story "Beauty and the Beast" and then asked students questions such as, "Suppose Beauty had been kind and clever but not prettier than her sisters?" and "Suppose Beauty had been a boy in this story and the Beast had been a girl?" Asking such questions generated rich discussion among the students regarding the roles of women and men.

Another method used to challenge gender stereotypes is reading stories to children that reverse traditional gender roles. For example, Davies (1989) read to preschool children feminist fairy tales in which the traditional story line was followed but the stereotypic gender roles were reversed (for example, a strong and intelligent princess rescues the prince). She found, however, that young children had difficulty interpreting the stories. They were unable to see the female as a hero and thought the reason she lost her prince at the end of the story was not because she chose to leave him, but because she was lacking in virtue. Moreover, Trousdale (1995) found that, even though children may like the nontraditional female characters in such stories, they may not necessarily consider such characters "normal" or view their character traits as personally viable alternatives. Davies (1993) also read these types of stories to sixth graders and found that, although these students were better able to entertain alternative gender possibilities, such as an ugly witch who is kind and a female who is heroic, they still were hesitant to accept alternatives to traditional romantic story lines and held on to their notions that beauty was something necessary to attract heroic men.

# Group Dynamics in Literature Discussion Groups

Gender also has the potential to affect students' interpretation of and response to literature through its impact on how students interact with one another in their discussion groups. Group dynamic concerns such as who assumes leadership roles, who is allowed to speak, who is listened to, and who is ignored can be influenced by gender. The concept of positioning (Harré & Van Langenhove, 1991) helps explain the role of group dynamics in literature discussions. Positioning refers to the notion that people take a position in relationship to others in conversational contexts (for example, a skeptic, a leader, or a follower). People also can be positioned by others. How people position themselves or are positioned by others influences how their contributions will be received. For example, if a person who is positioned as an authority on a topic offers an opinion, her or his opinion is more likely to be listened to and valued than the similar opinion of someone who is positioned as unknowledgeable about the topic. In view of the fact that males have been found to consistently dominate discussions inside and outside of classrooms and across grade levels (LaFrance & Mayo, 1978; Lockhead & Hall, 1976; Tannen, 1984, 1990), it is likely that gender has the potential to influence how students position themselves or are positioned by others in literature discussion groups.

Harré and Van Langenhove (1991) argue that positioning is not a static, permanent process, but rather is constantly open to renegotiation by the conversation participants. In other words, members of any conversational context have the choice to accept or challenge the initial positioning of themselves or others. For instance, if during a literature discussion Sally says to Joe, "You need to tell us what you think about that," Sally positions herself as someone who tells others what to do and positions Joe as someone who should listen to her. Joe now has two options: either he can accept the initial positioning and give his opinion or he can refuse Sally's positioning of him by saying, "You can't tell me what to do."

This fluid, changing nature of positioning helps distinguish the concept of positioning from the roles (such as recorder, summarizer, or encourager) that often are used in small-group contexts. Unlike positioning that always is open to change, roles typically are more static. For instance, in most contexts group members are assigned or choose a role and then remain in that role for the duration of the discussion or small-group task. Such separation of roles among students, however, is rare in real contexts. Students may choose to ignore their role, share their role with another student, switch roles with another student, or refuse to allow certain students to assume their roles. It is possible that gender may influence how students negotiate the accepting, rejecting, trading, or sharing of roles within the context of literature discussions.

# Exploring Literature Discussions

The research highlighted in the previous section suggests that gender is an important component in understanding the complex social and cultural contexts of literature discussion groups. The following study describes how gender influenced fifth-grade students' interpretation of and response to literature as well as their positioning of themselves and their group members during their literature discussions.

## Classroom Context

The work discussed here is based on my year as a visiting member in two fifth-grade classrooms in a multicultural elementary school. The teachers had combined their classrooms by opening the dividing wall separating them, and they regularly team-taught for most of each day. Both teachers were well versed in the theory supporting the instructional practice of literature discussion groups and had been using them as a component of their literacy instruction for 2 years. The teachers had designed their literature study to follow a consistent pattern. Each literature study cycle began with the teachers' selecting approximately eight books and giving a brief book talk on each book. Students then had time to browse through the books and select their top three choices. The teachers then formed the groups based on the students' selections. The groups typically ranged in size from three to six students; they usually met three to four times a week and the members decided each time how much they would read before the next meeting. The teachers rotated among the groups; however, since there typically were 10 to 12 groups in all, the teachers were unable to spend a significant amount of time with any one group. The students frequently used literature response logs as a means to respond to their books and to facilitate their discussions.

The teachers read and responded to the students' logs and used them to keep track of the issues and ideas students raised in response to their books.

The teachers spent a great deal of time supporting students in their efforts to respond to and discuss their books. They modeled discussions for the students, brainstormed discussion topics, discussed behaviors that were conducive to productive discussions, and introduced literary concepts. Because they were unable to spend sustained time in the discussion groups, the teachers often provided this type of support during other components of their literacy instruction. For example, during book sharing (a time during the daily class meeting when students or teachers could share a book they read) the teachers raised issues the students could use in their own discussions. Among the issues teachers discussed were author's purpose, author's writing style, different points of view, and how the book related to something else they had read.

## Gathering Data

During the first semester, I regularly visited the classroom during literature study. I took observation notes, visited with students, and joined numerous literature discussions. During the second semester, I was in the classroom every day and began videotaping the students' literature discussions. Two different groups are featured here. Each group met for 6 days for 20 to 25 minutes each day to discuss their book. One group consisted of six girls (Alice, Mary, Valerie, Hannah, Nancy, and Julie), who read the realistic fiction book *Homecoming* (Voigt, 1981). The second group consisted of five students, three boys (Duane, Jimmy, and Bobby) and two girls (Mimi and Vivianne), who read the historical fiction book *The Perilous Road* (Steele, 1958). All six discussions for both groups were videotaped and transcribed.

## Making Sense of the Data

After gathering the data, I read the transcripts to determine students' purposes in their discussions. I identified five different purposes:

1. Constructing meaning (predicting, connecting to personal experience or other texts, or using imagery);

2. evaluating text (such as content, author's writing style, characters' personality);
3. monitoring (asking clarifying questions or discussing unknown words);
4. maintaining conversation (deciding what page to read to in the book for the next discussion); and
5. talking socially (about topics unrelated to the book).

While reading the transcripts, I noticed a qualitative difference in the nature of talk that existed between the two groups. Even though the students might have been using the same purpose in their discussion, the frame of reference they had been using was different. I identified three different types of talk that characterized the different frames of reference: (1) talk that exhibited a personal or lived-through connection with the text, (2) talk that was textbound and relied on the text itself, and (3) talk that used short, repetitious responses that were unelaborated in nature. I also paid close attention to who initiated topics for discussion, who made comments to refocus the group and what the response was to such comments, and what happened when students tried to overtly assume a position of power in the group.

## What the Data Revealed

**Gendered talk.** The analysis of the different types of talk used by each group revealed that the students engaged in talk that was similar to Cherland's (1992) discourses of feeling and action. Student talk that I categorized as personal or lived-through resembled Cherland's discourse of feeling and was found most frequently in the *Homecoming* group. For example, the students felt sorry for the character Dicey for having to assume responsibility for her three siblings; they discussed what characters they thought should get married and what age Dicey should be to have a boyfriend; they agreed that Maybeth was merely shy and not retarded; and they discussed how mean Mr. Rudyard was. Their frame of reference for such discussions often was either personal experience or a personal connection with the characters in the book. For instance, they used their own understanding of dating and marriage to interpret the relationships in the book. They thought Dicey should have lied and said she was 15 when Jerry asked her how old she was because the students that 15 was the appropriate age for being "boyfriend and girlfriend." Julie wanted Dicey to marry Will because "he had a nice personality except he was a little too old." They also empathized with the characters, as evidenced by Mary's reaction when she said, "I'm going on Dicey's side 'cuz you know when they give 'em clothes and she didn't like the clothes they gave 'em, I would say that too."

Student talk that I categorized as textbound more closely resembled Cherland's discourse of action and was most often found in *The Perilous Road* group. Rather than focus on how characters felt or related to one another, this group emphasized what characters did. When discussing the book, they frequently shared specific plot events but they did not address the internal motivation or reasons behind the events. For example, one day the group discussed an event in which the main character of the book, Chris, was caught on a cliff ledge and enemy soldiers were walking past him:

| Duane: | What part of the book did you guys like? |
|---|---|
| Bobby: | I like when he's falling. |
| Mimi: | Oh, off the hill? |
| Bobby: | Yeah, off the cliff. |
| Mimi: | He's all [waving her arms] …he's holding on and they go "he's all mine!" |
| Bobby: | And he's all bleeding and his feet bleeding and stuff. |
| Mimi: | That's the part I like so far because I haven't read anything more interesting in that book. |

The students enjoyed the action of the event but never addressed why Chris was caught on the ledge or how he must have felt while he was stranded there with the enemy so close to finding him. On the surface the two discussion groups appeared to engage in what Cherland termed "gendered readings" that resulted in gendered talk.

The notion of gendered talk, however, raises a concern because of the apparent dichotomy established by feeling versus action, with females typically aligned with feelings and males with action. Hence, the use of labels such as "discourse of feeling" and "discourse of action" becomes problematic as they easily can be seen to fall along gender lines. Viewing feeling and action as interdependent rather than opposites presents one way of interrupting the stereotypic tendency to associate females with feeling talk and males with action talk (Evans, 1996). In other words, it becomes necessary to consider how feeling talk can be active and how action talk can be rooted in emotion. By addressing the interdependence of feeling and action, a broader conception of what is considered active becomes possible. The stereotypic notion of action as opposite to feeling is based on a definition of action as observable, physical behavior. Conversely, feelings often are not physically apparent and consequently are viewed as passive. Feelings, however, are anything but passive. They energize and exhaust us just as physical behaviors do; they simply are not always as overtly apparent. Conceptualizing feeling and action as interdependent rather than opposite opens new possibilities for interpreting the students' literature discussions and raises a new set of questions. For example, how might the *Homecoming* group's conversations that emphasized feelings and relationships be seen as active attempts to understand the book? How might *The Perilous Road* group's decision to emphasize action and plot events relate to their feelings about the other members of their group? These questions are further addressed later in the chapter.

**Reading against the grain.** The discussions in the *Homecoming* group appeared to indicate the girls' tentative efforts to read against the grain (Taylor, 1993; Temple, 1993), particularly in relation to gender stereotypes. This was most evident in their response to the characters of Dicey and her slightly younger brother, James. Dicey obviously was the protagonist and heroine in the book; however, the girls were bothered by the fact that she was "ugly" and "looked like a boy." Dicey's being ugly was brought up five different times during the course of their discussions. At the same time, they disliked James because they viewed him as a "smarty pants" who acted as if he was better than Dicey. The following transcript excerpt from their second day of discussion provides an illustration of the girls' feelings toward James.

| Julie: | I hope James dies; he's like the smarty pants. |
| Alice: | He's a dork. |
| Mary: | He's a brainy kid. |
| Alice: | I know. Why does he have to be so brainy? |
| Nancy: | And plus he thinks he's better than Dicey I think. |
| Alice: | Yeah, he's bossy. |

The girls clearly sided with Dicey, as evidenced by comments that Dicey was their favorite character, by Mary's earlier assertion that she was taking Dicey's side, by their sympathizing with Dicey for having to take care of three children at age 13, and by calling her incredible because she was able to earn money for the family. Their stereotypic gender notions that a female protagonist needed to be attractive, however, often was a cause of disequilibrium for them. They admired Dicey but had difficulty accepting the fact that she was not beautiful. Purcell-Gates (1993) contends that real-life experiences seem to be the key to how readers respond to nontraditional gender roles in literature. Thus, in light of society's emphasis on beauty it is not surprising that these girls had formed a stereotypic image of a strong female character's need to be beautiful. This stereotypic image, however, led to their disequilibrium because although Dicey was not beautiful, they still viewed her as the heroine and respected her for refusing to bow to male authority.

Cherland and Edelsky (1993) suggest that culture promises gendered forms of agency to children: Boys are promised to be agents in the world at large and expect to wield economic and political power, whereas girls are promised to be agents within the family and expect to wield power in personal relationships. As discussed earlier, the texts that students read have the potential to reinforce such stereotypic gender roles and forms of agency. Reading fiction, however, can provide children one possible place in which to experience alternative forms of agency beyond those that are culturally endorsed. For instance, through Dicey, the girls in the *Homecoming* group could experience both forms of gendered agency. Dicey was the breadwinner of her family; she controlled the money, made the decisions, and resisted James's attempts to boss her around. At the same time, she also was the mother figure who exhibited caring and nurturing characteristics toward her younger siblings. By identifying with Dicey, the girls were provided with an opportunity to explore different forms of agency.

Although the girls never completely resolved their conflict, it was encouraging to listen to them as they struggled with their stereotypic notions of leading females in tandem with their dislike of a male who acted as if he were better than a female. Their disequilibrium provided a perfect forum for them to read against the grain and question their gendered beliefs. As advocated by Taylor (1993), they were able to question their beliefs in the course of practical and productive work, which allowed them opportunities to consider new, alternative versions of themselves as females. Without such opportunities, Alvermann and Commeyras (1994) argue, it is likely that gender stereotypes will continue to go unexamined and thereby be reinforced and reproduced.

**Positioning.** How the students in *The Perilous Road* group positioned themselves and one another changed throughout the 6 days of discussion and appeared to be gender related. Initially, Mimi and Vivianne assumed different types of leadership roles. Mimi initiated the most book-related topics for discussion, and Vivianne assumed the role of group monitor. For instance, if students began to play, Vivianne would get them back on task or refocus the discussion on the book. The boys appeared to accept this positioning until the third day of discussion, when they began to challenge the girls' positions of authority. The boys began to tease Mimi about being a dog, and whenever she would try to initiate a topic for discussion, they either would make barking noises in the background or make comments about her being a dog. Mimi resisted their efforts to position her as the brunt of their jokes and used many tactics to discourage them, such as ignore them, hit them with her book, or reply with verbal insults. Unfortunately, her efforts were ineffective and the boys continued to attempt to silence her for the remaining 3 days of discussion.

The boys used a more direct approach to challenge Vivianne's position of authority. On the fourth day, Bobby was telling jokes and Vivianne told him to stop telling jokes or to be quiet. Duane responded by saying, "You can't boss [Bobby] around, Vivianne, like you're the boss of the group." Jimmy also responded that he wanted to talk about jokes, but Vivianne remained firm in her efforts to keep the group on task and said, "Go get to work." When Duane continued to challenge her position of authority with increasing intensity, Vivianne eventually relinquished her position as leader and became a silent member of the group. The boys challenged only the girls' authority positioning; they never challenged one another. Therefore, it would appear that the positioning in this group was influenced by gender.

The girls in the *Homecoming* group also assumed positions of leadership; however, they appeared to be comfortable with multiple leaders and did not challenge members who assumed leadership roles. Mary, Alice, and Julie all assumed leadership positions as evidenced by the number of discussion topics they initiated. Alice positioned herself as the group monitor and consistently worked to keep the group on task. Rather than challenge one another for a position of authority, the girls were able to let the leadership responsibilities ebb and flow among the various members. There was not the jockeying for an authority position found in *The Perilous Road* group. Although this group also joked and laughed, they laughed *with* one another instead of *at* a particular member. They used laughter as a way to bind together the group rather than as a means to silence a member.

The differences in how positioning occurred in the two groups could be due to a different notion of power operating in each group. The notion of power in *The Perilous Road* group appeared to be based on the belief that power is a commodity or property that exists in a limited amount and the only way to get power is to take it from someone else. Because it was the girls who originally assumed positions of power in the group, the boys' notion of power as property limited their options for how they could gain power. In other words, the only way the boys perceived that they could gain power was to take power away from the girls. This notion of power created a competitive context in which the competition for power overshadowed the learning opportunities.

In contrast, the *Homecoming* group displayed a different understanding of power. Rather than view it as a commodity that could be possessed or taken away, this group appeared to understand that power is something to be exercised (Foucault, 1978/1990; Gore, 1993). This notion of power created a cooperative context that allowed different members to exercise their power simultaneously. Instead of using their power in an effort to silence members, they exercised their power in an attempt to help others speak. The vocal members who had assumed positions of authority frequently tried to include Hannah, the quietest member of the group. For example, they would ask Hannah questions such as, "Do you have a vocabulary word today?" "Did you write anything [in your literature log]?" or "What page are you on?" Furthermore, they included Hannah nonverbally by sitting next to her and making eye contact with her. These efforts were not a means to dominate Hannah but rather were a way to include her and let her know she was a valued member of the group.

# Lessons Learned and
# Implications for Instruction

The results of my study raised three main issues for me as an educator who advocates and uses literature discussion groups as a component of literacy instruction. The first issue centers on the occurrence of gendered talk in literature discussions. As revealed by the two groups highlighted in this chapter, students do use gendered talk in their discussions. The all-female group emphasized "feeling talk," whereas the mixed-gender group focused on "action talk." This finding prompted me to begin thinking about how we might highlight this talk as an instructional issue. For example, we could discuss with students the different types of talk they use in their discussion groups, explore what purposes each type of talk serves, and ask students to reflect on which type they are most comfortable using and why. Moreover, teachers could provide modeling of different types of talk in teacher-led discussions and identify the talk when it occurs. As Eeds and Peterson (1991) advise, "[D]on't be afraid to label what the children are talking about when it is appropriate. There is power in naming; this is part of how language is learned" (p. 125).

The potential problem that arises when naming language by using labels such as "feeling talk" and "action talk" and aligning them along gender lines is that teachers will constrain rather than open the possible types of talk available to students. In other words, it is possible that by addressing feeling talk and action talk with our students we might inadvertently reinforce the notion that feeling talk is synonymous with "girl talk" and action talk with "boy talk." As mentioned, viewing both types of talk as interdependent rather than mutually exclusive is one way to interpret them without locking them into specific gender categories. I found this to be a helpful way of reframing the categories of talk when interpreting the students' discussions. Viewing the types of talk as interdependent rather than opposites opened new possibilities for me. For example, I began to see how the girls' use of a discourse of feeling was their way of acting on the world and represented their active efforts to interpret and personally relate to their book. Their discourse of feeling provided a means for them to challenge gender stereotypes and experience alternative forms of female agency. These were active, not passive, processes. Furthermore, I began to realize that the boys' hurtful teasing represented their efforts, however undesirable and inappropriate, to relate to the girls in their group. Therefore, their discourse could be considered to be rooted in feelings. Helping students see the interdependence of the different types of talk represents one way we might begin to break the gender stereotypes often associated with feelings and action and widen the range of discourses available to both male and female students.

The second issue raised for me relates to the influence of the text being read on the type of talk found in students' discussions. Some texts are more likely to elicit lived-through connections than others. For example, *Homecoming* lends itself to a more personal response that emphasizes character feelings and relationships, and *The Perilous Road* lends itself to a discourse that focuses on the action and adventure in the story. Viewing the type of response elicited by a book as an either/or situation, however, raises the same potential problem discussed earlier with gendered discourse. In other words, it is possible that certain books will be considered "feeling/girl" books and others will be viewed as "action/boy" books. Thus, it might be helpful to view the type of response elicited as on a continuum that allows for the possibility of both types of talk to occur in any discussion. For example, even though the *Homecoming* group chose to focus on factors such as character relationships and personal connections, their discussions also included instances in which they retold plot sequences and discussed the actions of the characters. So, it is not a matter of either/or but a matter of which type of talk is more likely to be the predominant discourse in a discussion about a particular text. Furthermore, even though a text may lend itself to a discourse of feeling, it is still possible that discussion members may choose to talk about it using both types of discourse.

The texts students read also represent a means to help students read against the grain and widen the types of discourses available to them. For example, if we want students to challenge gender stereotypes, we might want to make available to them texts that portray characters in non-stereotypic gender roles and discuss their reactions to these characters. We also might read texts that do reinforce stereotypic gender roles and engage students in discussions that question such roles. Yet, merely providing the texts is unlikely to be sufficient in helping students read against the grain. As Davies (1989) found, even young children are unwilling to give credence to stories that present females engaging in stereotypic male roles. The girls in the *Homecoming* group also struggled in their efforts to reconcile their notion of a strong female character's need to be beautiful with their admiration and respect for a female heroine who was unattractive. Therefore, students are likely to need support and guidance as they attempt to read against the grain and challenge stereotypic notions of gender, race, age, disabilities, and economic status.

The third issue raised for me was the importance of the instructional context for facilitating or limiting students' learning opportunities. Although literature discussions often are promoted as a context in which students' voices and multiple perspectives can be heard, I discovered they also can be places where students are silenced. Providing appropriate texts, support, and guidance for students never will be sufficient to help them read against the grain and engage in alternative types of discourse if the texts are being read and discussed in contexts that the students view as unsafe. The *Homecoming* group was characterized by an atmosphere of respect and cohesiveness. In such a context, the girls in this group were able to explore alternative notions of gender roles and engage in conversations that respected and valued others' perspectives and ideas. They appeared to use what Barnes (1992) calls "exploratory talk," which is characterized by false starts, changes in directions, and hypothetical expressions. Barnes argues that this type of talk allows students to formulate and evaluate hypotheses and keeps open possibilities for future interpretations. These features all were evident in the girls' discussions.

Barnes cautions, however, that students are capable of engaging in exploratory talk only if they are placed in social contexts that support it. *The Perilous Road* group provided an example of what happens to the discourse and learning opportunities in a setting that is characterized by disrespect and divisiveness. Rather than explore alternative interpretations of the book, this group focused on simply retelling plot events. They emphasized the "what," not the "how" or "why." This is understandable because offering hypotheses and alternative perspectives involves taking risks. It is difficult to take risks when in an unsafe context in which other members may laugh at or tease the member who makes such contributions. Given the amount of hurtful teasing that was found in *The Perilous Road* group and the boys' consistent challenging of the girls, it is easy to understand why the girls were unwilling to engage in exploratory talk. Unfortunately, if the learning contexts in our classrooms are not characterized by safety and tolerance, it is unlikely that we will ever create spaces where alternative types of talk are encouraged, different perspectives are valued, and reading against the grain is supported.

The need to create classroom communities where risk taking is encouraged and different perspectives are respected was highlighted for me by listening to the discussions of the two groups I studied. As teachers, we may want to make such issues an explicit part of our classroom instruction, specifically as they relate to literature discussions. For example, we might consider engaging students in reflective discussions of the following questions:

Why is it important to encourage all members to participate?

How does hearing ideas from many different people enhance discussions?

How does hearing different perspectives help us learn?

Why might some students not feel comfortable sharing their ideas?

How might we help students feel more welcome in participating?

By reflecting regularly on these issues, it is possible we will facilitate our efforts to create classroom communities where students feel safe enough to risk confronting gender stereotypes and assuming alternative gender roles.

## Conclusion

The conversations I found in the two groups I studied provided me the opportunity to further appreciate the complexity inherent in peer-led literature discussions. The types of talk and positioning found in the groups suggest that gender is an important factor in determining whether literature discussions are places that open or close learning opportunities. It is important to remember, however, that gender is only one factor that influences students' choice of talk and participation patterns. The students in these groups were not only girls and boys, they also were of different economic, ethnic, religious, and social backgrounds. All these factors mutually influence and interact with gender to determine the type of context that will be created, the type of talk that will be used, and the type of positioning that will occur. Although the two groups discussed in this chapter offer a partial understanding of how gender may influence students' response to and discussion of literature, much work remains to be done if we are to fully understand the complex social and cultural contexts we call literature discussion groups.

# Questions for Reflection

1. How might our own assumptions regarding gender and gender roles influence the type of experiences we provide for our students to read against the grain, question gender stereotypes, and explore alternative forms of agency?

2. Do you tend to think of power as a commodity or something to be exercised? How might our own beliefs about power influence how our students position themselves and others in our classrooms?

## References

Alvermann, D., & Commeyras, M. (1994). Gender, text, and discussion: Expanding the possibilities. In R. Garner & P. Alexander (Eds.), *Beliefs about text and about instruction with text* (pp. 183–199). Hillsdale, NJ: Erlbaum.

Barnes, D. (1992). *From communication to curriculum.* Portsmouth, NH: Heinemann.

Cherland, M. (1992). Gendered readings: Cultural restraints upon response to literature. *The New Advocate, 5*(3), 187–198.

Cherland, M., & Edelsky, C. (1993). Girls and reading: The desire for agency and the horror of helplessness in fictional encounters. In L.K. Christian-Smith (Ed.), *Texts of desire: Essays on fiction, femininity and schooling* (pp. 28–44). Washington, DC: Falmer.

Davies, B. (1989). The discursive production of the male/female dualism in school settings. *Oxford Review of Education, 15*(3), 229–241.

Davies, B. (1993). Beyond dualism and towards multiple subjectivities. In L.K. Christian-Smith (Ed.), *Texts of desire: Essays on fiction, femininity and schooling* (pp. 145–173). Washington, DC: Falmer.

Eeds, M., & Peterson, R. (1991). Teacher as curator: Learning to talk about literature. *The Reading Teacher, 45*(2), 118–126.

Evans, K.S. (1996). A closer look at literature discussion groups: The influence of gender on student response and discourse. *The New Advocate, 9*(3), 183–196.

Foucault, M. (1990). *The history of sexuality: Volume 2.* (R. Hurley, Trans.). New York: Vintage Books. (Original work published 1978)

Gore, J.H. (1993). *The struggle for pedagogies: Critical and feminist discourses as regimes of truth.* New York: Routledge.

Harré, R., & Van Langenhove, L. (1991). Varieties of positioning. *Journal for the Theory of Social Behavior, 21*(4), 393–407.

LaFrance, M., & Mayo, C. (1978). *Moving bodies: Nonverbal communication in social relationships.* Monterey, CA: Brooks/Cole.

Lockhead, M., & Hall, K. (1976). Conceptualizing sex as a status characteristic: Applications to leadership training strategies. *Journal of Social Issues, 32*(3), 111–123.

Purcell-Gates, V. (1993). Focus on research: Complexity and gender. *Language Arts, 70*(2), 124–125.

Tannen, D. (1984). *Conversational style: Analyzing talk among friends.* Norwood, NJ: Ablex.

Tannen, D. (1990). *You just don't understand: Women and men in conversation.* New York: Ballantine Books.

Taylor, S. (1993). Transforming the texts: Towards a feminist classroom practice. In L.K. Christian-Smith (Ed.), *Texts of desire: Essays on fiction, femininity and schooling.* Washington, DC: Falmer.

Temple, C. (1993). "What if *Beauty* had been ugly?" Reading against the grain of gender bias in children's books. *Language Arts, 70*(2), 89–93.

Trousdale, A. (1995). I'd rather be normal: A young girl's response to "feminist" fairy tales. *The New Advocate, 8*(3) 167–182.

## Children's Literature References

Steele, W. (1958). *The perilous road.* San Diego, CA: Harcourt.

Voigt, C. (1981). *Homecoming.* New York: Ballantine Books.

# PART FOUR

## Focusing on Ourselves

# CHAPTER 9

# Encouraging Quality Peer Talk with Diverse Students in Mainstream Classrooms: Learning from and with Teachers

∞

TAFFY E. RAPHAEL, CYNTHIA H. BROCK,
AND SUSAN M. WALLACE

Over the past decade, the literacy education field has witnessed many dramatic changes, two of which are particularly important to the research we report in this chapter. The first change is in the importance placed on classroom talk. Initially, many literacy educators had hoped that providing students with high-quality literature and opportunities to share their responses would lead to rich peer talk. However, when research was conducted that closely examined peer talk, educators learned just how complex student discussions could be, and they began raising questions about the influence of settings (such as whole class, small groups, and pairs), participants, and teachers' roles in peer talk.

The second change relates to the population of students who attend schools in the United States. Increasingly, these schools serve youngsters diverse not only in ability, but also in economic, racial, ethnic, and linguistic backgrounds (McGill-Franzen & Allington, 1993; Nieto, 1992). Further, there has been increased attention to the different ways in which boys and girls experience school settings, particularly those involving peer talk (Alvermann, 1996; Evans, 1996). Our definition of diversity has expanded to include a range of factors such as ethnic, racial, economic, and linguistic backgrounds, as well as gender and ability.

These two sources of change in today's schools have influenced the line of research that frames the findings we discuss in this chapter. This line of research, the Book Club Project (see McMahon & Raphael, 1997), began in 1990 as a university and public school collaborative inquiry to develop the Book Club Program. "Book Club" is a literacy instruction curriculum that places, at its core, small, student-led discussion groups known as book clubs* (see Raphael et al., 1992; Raphael & McMahon, 1994) (see also Chapter 1 for further discussion on using book clubs as an instructional tool).

The research team wished to create and examine a literacy curriculum that reflected current theory and practice. First, the curriculum is based in thematically organized units of instruction. Second, the students read a wide range of literature, from trade books to newspaper articles. Third, the instruction integrates the language arts and has the potential for cross-curricular integration. Fourth, the curriculum emphasizes a delicate balance between aesthetic response to literature-as-art and instructional goals of developing competent and independent language and literacy users. Fifth, the curriculum is based in conceptions of learners as active constructors, not passive recipients, of knowledge.

In this chapter, we focus on students who would have traditionally received instruction outside the regular classroom—in English as a second language (ESL) programs, special education, and remedial reading programs. In doing so, we draw on data collected in two studies within the Book Club Project (Goatley, Brock, & Raphael, 1995; Raphael, Wallace, Pardo, & Choo, 1996) and one related study (Brock, 1996). We address three questions that help us explore the intricacies and complexities of diverse children's engagement in peer talk in their mainstream classrooms:

- What characterized the nature of diverse learners' participation in the contexts of peer talk across the three studies?

---

*Throughout this chapter, we use Book Club (uppercase) when referring to the instructional program. We use book club (lowercase) when referring to the small, student-led discussion groups for which the program was named.

- How did peer talk support and extend diverse students' literacy learning?
- What were teachers' roles in supporting diverse students' opportunities to participate in classroom talk?

This chapter consists of four major sections. In the first section, we describe the theoretical framework that undergirds our research. Next, we describe the classroom contexts in the three studies and the diverse learners who engage in various aspects of peer discussion and supporting activities. Using our three questions as a framework for the third section, we present and discuss data that shed light on how peer talk supported and extended students' literacy learning; how the diverse learners participated in these events in contrast to large-group, teacher-led settings; and how teachers supported their diverse students' participation in peer discussions. We end the chapter with recommendations designed to help teachers create supportive instructional contexts to enable their diverse students to engage effectively in classroom talk, becoming full participants in their classroom communities.

# A Theoretical Framework for Researching Peer Talk

We grounded our work in a sociocultural theoretical perspective. Proponents of this view stress the central role of language in facilitating human learning, arguing that human action is mediated by signs (symbol or semiotic systems) and tools (psychological tools such as language) (Wertsch, 1985). Further, as Vygotsky (1978) wrote, mind is constituted through interactions with others in the social sphere. These two emphases—language and the social construction of mind—are critical to understanding the emerging focus on peer talk in today's classrooms; it is through talk that children make sense of their world, and through talk that teachers and students construct meaning.

Vygotsky considered language to be the most important semiotic tool. He maintained that if mind emerges through interactions with others, it is the *semiotic mediation* with others (i.e., not simply social interactions, but language-based social interactions) that shape the mind. Thus, the nature of language and discourse in the context of interactions and the various ways in which we examine that discourse are central to understanding how mind develops.

Vygotsky's notion that mind originates through social interactions suggests that higher psychological processes—such as those involved in reading and writing—initially take place interpsychologically (within social interactions), and that over time they take place intrapsychologically (within the individual) (Wertsch, 1985). Vygotsky (1978) offered his general genetic law of cultural development to describe this process: "Every function in the child's cultural development appears twice: first, on the social level, and later, on the individual level; first, *between* people (*interpsychological*), and then *inside* the child (*intrapsychological*)" (p. 57). To visually represent Vygotsky's general genetic law of cultural development, Harré (1984) introduced a model called the Vygotsky Space, recently adapted by Gavelek and Raphael (1996). The Vygotsky Space shown in the Figure on page 180 is made by crossing two axes—the public/private and the individual/social—to create four quadrants.

The vertical axis labeled Public/Private represents a continuum between completely public and very private activity. This axis characterizes "the degree to which any cognitive activity is visible and thus available for observation" (Gavelek & Raphael, 1996, p. 185). The horizontal axis labeled Individual/Social represents a continuum—from the individual's private world to the social world—of an individual's realization of some learning event. Thus, Public/Private refers to the nature of the *activity* in which individuals engage, and Individual/Social refers to the *individual(s)* involved in the activity.

Learning occurs through interactive processes across quadrants 1 through 4. In quadrant 1 ($Q_I$), people engage with others in their social environment, such as teacher-student interactions within large and small groups. The figure conveys that individuals appropriate information they have experienced within the social environment, transform it in their own unique ways, publicly express their thinking, and receive feedback as they learn about and contribute to the norms and conventions of their community and culture. Learning occurs as a result of this continual and interactive process of internalizing, transforming, re-expressing, and receiving feedback on experiences that first occur in the Public/Social quadrant. Of course, no single learning opportunity reveals all four processes. For example, because appropriation and transformation, rep-

## The Vygotsky Space

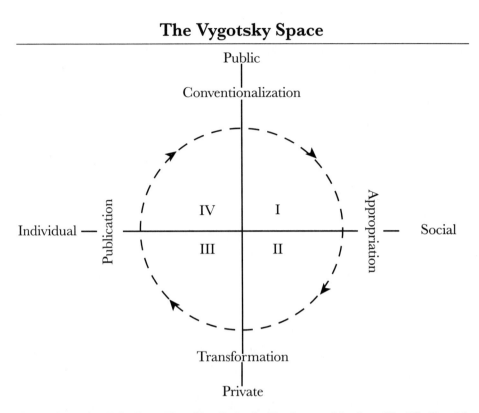

From "Changing Talk About Text: New Roles for Teachers and Students," by J.R. Gavelek and T.E. Raphael, 1996, *Language Arts, 73*(3), pp. 182–192. Reprinted by permission.

resented by quadrants 2 and 3 ($Q_{II}$ and $Q_{III}$, respectively), are not "visible" processes, they must be inferred from a child's public expressions in quadrant 4 ($Q_{IV}$).

Gavelek and Raphael (1996) emphasize that "the Vygotsky Space underscores the complexity of learning and the different entry points a teacher has to observe and make decisions about formal intervention or informal guidance" (p. 190). Teachers first decide that it is important for students to have the opportunity to express their thinking publicly, such as in whole-class or small-group interactions. Next, teachers make decisions about *how* students might publicly express their thinking and the ways(s) that teachers and others could provide feedback to students when they do so (for example, working in pairs, discussing within small groups, or writing individually). The context of peer talk in small, student-led groups such as book clubs or literary circles, as well as in whole-class settings such as community share, provides students the opportunity to see how language is used as a symbol system for understanding and interpreting text and to engage in their own language practices (both social and individual) related to meaningful talk about text.

Students' access to such opportunities is critical for their learning. It is in the public and social spaces that students have the opportunity, through language, to explore ideas, raise questions, and identify points of confusion. The different kinds of classroom contexts implied by the Vygotsky Space make visible the variety of ways in which all students can have access to opportunities to engage in meaningful talk and to do so with the instructional support that promotes their language and literacy development.

# The Context of the Studies

We used case-study designs (see, for example, Bogdan & Biklen, 1992; Erickson & Schultz, 1992) to design and implement the studies that we draw upon in this chapter. Two of the cases present students from Mrs. Pardo's Book Club classrooms: The first case is a book club discussion group consisting of five children diverse in gender, linguistic and ethnic background, and literacy competence (Goatley et al., 1995); the second case is a student named Lenny who had been labeled learning disabled (Raphael et al., 1996). The third case focuses on a fifth-grade child, Deng, from Mrs. Weber's classroom, whose first language was Hmong (Brock, 1996). The Table on page 182 gives an overview of and key information about each case.

## Literacy-Instruction Context

Both Mrs. Weber and Mrs. Pardo are highly experienced teachers, each with a master's degree in reading instruction. Both have made trade books an important part of their instructional programs, although they have structured their instruction quite differently. Mrs. Weber has based her instruction on a combination of texts, including both trade books and the district-adopted basal readers, and Mrs. Pardo has been using Book Club as her reading program since 1990.

# The Three Case Studies

| Mrs. Pardo's Book Club classroom | | Mrs. Weber's Non–Book Club classroom |
| --- | --- | --- |
| Case study of five-member discussion group | Case study of Lenny | Case study of Deng |
| Study reported in 1995 | Study reported in 1996 | Study reported in 1996 |
| Fifth-grade students | Fifth-grade student | Fifth-grade student |
| Text: *Park's Quest* | Text: multiple titles | Text: *Maniac McGee* |

The instructional contexts and thematic units from which the data in this chapter are drawn all occurred during thematically organized, literature-based units. The two case studies of individual children were conducted within units connected to social studies curriculum. Mrs. Weber's students examined social issues such as racism and homelessness as represented in *Maniac McGee* (Spinelli, 1991). Mrs. Pardo's students explored issues of human rights as reflected in biography and historical fiction set within early exploration and within the U.S. Civil War era. The case study of the group examined students' participation during a unit organized around an author study of Katherine Paterson, as they read and responded to *Park's Quest* (Paterson, 1988).

**Mrs. Weber's instruction context.** Mrs. Weber is typical of many experienced teachers. She used a basal reading program for most of her career, but has been moving toward literature-based instruction and cross-curricular integration for the basis of her teaching. She describes herself as working to broaden her instruction from whole-class lessons in which she was, in her words, "pretty much the teacher in charge" to using more flexible grouping and increasing students' opportunities to work in small, peer discussion groups. During the unit centered around *Maniac McGee*, students engaged in 18 whole-group lessons, and on six of the days they also worked on various activities in small groups.

In a typical whole-class session, Mrs. Weber gives students an overview of their focus for the day as they read the story together; both she and her students share responsibilities for reading the story aloud. For example, one day the class focused on contrasts and conflicts related to social issues that society faces. Mrs. Weber began reading the story aloud as the students followed along in their own books. During the lesson, the students in the whole-class setting engaged in 10 topic-centered discussion segments, which Mrs. Weber initiated by asking a question.

In general, Mrs. Weber's whole-class lessons are characterized by a series of topic-centered discussion segments. Although the segments vary in terms of topics discussed, length of exchanges, and nature of activities that accompany the discussion segments, there are four patterns that characterize whole-group discussions. First, Mrs. Weber generally initiates topic-centered segments and brings them to a close. Second, she tends to close a segment by reading on in the story or choosing a child to read. Third, discussions during these segments tend to follow the teacher initiate–student respond–teacher evaluate pattern, described earlier in this volume (Cazden, 1988). Fourth, when Mrs. Weber initiates discussions, she asks general questions or makes general comments that are not directed to any particular child in the class, thus opening the "conversational floor" to anyone in the class.

When students meet in small groups, consisting of four to five children, Mrs. Weber gives them specific focus questions to explore. For example, during one small-group activity, she asked students to focus on characters in *Maniac McGee* and identify a favorite character, discuss him or her within their groups, then create a character map that would convey important and interesting information about the character.

This pattern of teacher-guided, or teacher-controlled, whole-class discussions and indirectly controlled small-group work was typical throughout the units that Mrs. Weber developed. Although more directive than typical Book Club Program classrooms, this kind of instructional context represents an initial departure from the highly controlled activities characteristic of basal reading programs. As such, it is a context that many diverse learners experience in today's school systems.

**Mrs. Pardo's instruction context.** Mrs. Pardo has used the Book Club Program (see Raphael & McMahon, 1994) since 1990, as a member of the original collaborative research team. She usually establishes an overarching theme that helps her create three to six integrated literacy–social studies units over the academic year, with remaining units centered within the language arts. During the 1994–1995 academic year, the overarching theme was "How Did Our Country Develop?" This theme helped her frame issues-oriented units on early exploration, gaining independence, survival in adversity, and human rights versus individual rights.

Integrated units involve two phases: Phase I, the research focus, involves students working in whole-class and small-group settings, as well as in pairs and individually; phase II is the Book Club focus. During the 1994–1995 academic year, Mrs. Pardo's fourth integrated unit focused on human rights within the U.S. Civil War era. During phase I of this unit, the students explored key questions and inquiry about the United States Civil War (see Raphael & Hiebert, 1996). During phase II, students read one of four historical fiction novels set during the Civil War. In addition to the integrated units, Mrs. Pardo usually develops one thematic unit based on genre study (such as fantasy) and one thematic unit based on an author study.

At the center of the Book Club Program are small, student-led discussion groups known as the book club component of the program. Students' book club discussions are supported by a whole-class discussion component called community share, a reading component, and a writing component. A typical Book Club day begins by Mrs. Pardo reading aloud from a novel connected thematically to the literature unit the students are exploring. For example, during the unit focused on the Civil War era, she read from *Across Five Aprils* (Hunt, 1986). Mrs. Pardo reads aloud for many purposes. The book adds to students' repertoire of literary sources related to the unit theme. It provides an opportunity for her to model intertextual connections, fluency, and comprehension and interpretation strategies. Finally, it provides a common text in situations in which each book club group reads and discusses a different text.

Mrs. Pardo follows the read-aloud with an opening community share—a whole-class session that has two different foci: (1) helping students focus on the chapters to be read, summarizing where they had been in earlier discussions that week; and (2) introducing new or reviewing previously taught strategies and skills within the broad categories of teaching language conventions, comprehension strategies, literary elements, and response to literature (see Raphael & Goatley, 1994). During community-share discussions, students work with the whole class to identify important ideas from the text, themes related to the unit, and questions that may have surfaced. Further, community share is a time when Mrs.

Pardo can elicit comments from students that otherwise they may not share. For example, during the unit on the Civil War, Josh had told Mrs. Pardo that one of his ancestors had been a captain in the war. During community share, she asked Josh to volunteer what he had told her about his great-great-grandfather. This led Julianne to comment that she also had an ancestor who had fought in the war, noting that, "he wasn't a captain or anything like that." Then, Lenny mentioned that his ancestors had been slaves during that time, and he later contributed to the discussion of the underground railroad when his peers were not able to describe it. In short, community share helps create an overall sense of a literate and literacy community among the students, and the activity serves as a primary instructional context both for introducing new concepts to the students and for eliciting contributions from a number of students. It exemplifies the public and social quadrant of the Vygotsky Space.

After community share, students read focus chapters for that day. Reading varies, depending on whether a single book or multiple titles are being used within the unit. In the case of the group of students reading *Park's Quest*, all students in the classroom read the same book. Similarly, Lenny's class all read a biography of Christopher Columbus during an early unit on exploration. In contrast, there are times when each book club reads a different book related to the theme. This was the case when each book club read different Civil War historical fiction. Combinations of silent reading, partner reading, and read-alouds are used over the course of the units. After approximately 15 minutes of text reading, students are expected to respond to the literature in their reading logs, again for about 15 minutes. Then, students meet in book clubs for 5 to 20 minutes. Time varies for three reasons. First, early in the academic year the time tends to be shorter because students are in the process of learning how to engage in sustained discussion. Second, length of discussions can vary as a function of the text content. Some texts invite sustained discussion because of challenging ideas or interesting topics, although others invite or require less discussion time. Third, the length of the opening community share can affect the amount of time available for discussion. After students' book club discussions, the session ends as the book clubs come together for a closing community share, led by Mrs. Pardo. She asks students to share what they have discussed in groups, or raises issues she has heard as she observed their discussions.

# Student Context

The two classrooms described in the previous section provide a wealth of data about peer talk within contrasting whole-group, small-group, and paired settings. As we examine the nature of the students' interactions within these settings, we focus on the interactions of a small subset of diverse students, whom we now introduce.

**Focus case-study students: Deng and Lenny.**  Deng and Lenny, students in Mrs. Weber's and Mrs. Pardo's classrooms, respectively, were participants in case studies by Brock (1996) and Raphael et al. (1996). Both Deng and Lenny had been identified by their teachers as being among the least proficient literacy students in their classrooms. Deng had lived in three different refugee camps in Thailand, attending school sporadically and part time prior to coming to the Midwest United States in 1993. At that time, Deng spoke four languages—Hmong, Lao, Thai, and English—although he read and wrote only in English. Deng arrived at Oakland School, the site of the case study, 40 days before the end of the school year and was placed in third grade. He attended a mainstream class part of the day during his fourth-grade year and an ESL pull-out program for the remainder of each day (pull-out programs provide instruction at a site other than a child's regular education classroom). Deng remained in his mainstream classroom all day during fifth grade. Deng was a quiet, diligent student in class; he completed all assignments on time but rarely spoke in class.

Lenny, an African American male, was 11 years old as he entered fifth grade, making him one year older that most of his peers. He had been labeled learning disabled and was educated in a special-education classroom for most of his school career. His reading, writing, and spelling abilities were below most of his regular-education peers, according to both standardized tests and informal assessments of his general classroom performance. Mrs. Pardo, his classroom teacher, noticed that he struggled with the physical act of writing, exhibiting difficulties with letter formation and spelling. Yet, as is often true of students with learning disabilities, his oral interactions reflected greater understanding of ideas and issues and were similar to those of average fifth-grade students. He was an active participant in small-group literature discussions, and, during an informal interview, he stated that discussion provided him with a way to keep up with the story.

**Focus case-study group: Mei, Jason, Jean, Stark, and Andy.** Five students participated in the case study of a group (Goatley et al., 1995) that was one of the book clubs within Mrs. Pardo's 1991–1992 fifth-grade class. They met to read and discuss *Park's Quest*. Mei, Jason, and Jean were in their second year of Book Club, having participated in the program during fourth grade. Mei was from Vietnam and in her third year in the U.S. school system (Raphael & Brock, 1993). The year of the study was her first year of being mainstreamed since her arrival. Jason was an active Book Club participant but had difficulties understanding books when he read them on his own. In an interview early in fifth grade, he described how much he thought Book Club helped him with his reading, and he recalled specific stories and activities from fourth grade that had helped him in his literacy learning. Jean's parents had requested her placement in a Book Club classroom because she had become highly motivated to read after her fourth-grade experiences. Because she had been targeted for remedial reading services, she volunteered to go to school early for the instruction to avoid being pulled away from the Book Club part of the day. Stark had a history of academic and social problems in school and had been labeled learning disabled after district testing. He had received a strong phonics-based remedial program throughout most of elementary school. In fifth grade, he was mainstreamed during Book Club for his reading instruction, but he was given additional instruction in spelling and writing in a resource-room setting. Like Stark, Andy was new to Book Club. He generally was quiet in the classroom. Mrs. Pardo indicated that his reading and writing levels were average for the class. Andy felt that although he did not read much, he thought it was important to read because "it helped him to be smart" (Goatley et al., 1995, p. 359).

# Describing Diverse Learners' Participation in Peer Talk

The three studies described provide data to examine and characterize features of diverse students' participation in peer talk about text, as we address our three guiding questions, outlined earlier. We use the Vygotsky Space as a tool to explore relationships among the talk in the public and social spaces of the classroom (quadrant I, in the Figure), and to explore students' opportunities to appropriate and transform (quadrants II and III) that which they encounter in the social sphere, made visible when they make their thinking public through written or oral discourse (quadrant IV).

## The Nature of Diverse Learners' Participation in the Contexts of Peer Talk

Conventional wisdom argues that students who struggle with literacy are unlikely to be able to participate fully in their regular-education classrooms. Instead, they are said to benefit from learning skills for decoding print, skills they eventually will be able to apply in their own literacy use. Our case study of Lenny and our observations of Stark and Jean within the case study of the small peer-led group suggest otherwise. These students demonstrated not only that they were able to make contributions to the topics at hand, but that they were able to challenge the thinking of their peers identified as more competent literacy users. The examples in this section highlight Lenny and Stark's participation in peer discussions and caution against underestimating the potential of all students to make important contributions in peer-led discussions.

The first example occurred during the early exploration thematic unit in Mrs. Pardo's 1994–1995 fifth-grade class. Lenny and his peers read and discussed a storybook biography, *Christopher Columbus* (Goodnough & Dodson, 1991). In the dialogue that follows, there are two competing topics: Lenny's argument that only the uneducated thought the world was square, and others' attempts to continue taking turns reading from their logs.* Lenny pursues his point, using the text to support his position. Phillip attempts to share the picture he had drawn in his log, while Mandy responds to Lenny:

Lenny:     See, it's right, it says it right. Right here.

---

*The dialogue segments that appear throughout this chapter sometimes are marked with brackets (either one or two [ ]) or side slashes (///) and certain lines of dialogue are indented. Each of these notations shows how the conversations proceeded. One bracket ([) indicates that the students' speech is overlapping, two brackets ([ ]) indicate commentary by the authors about what was happening, and side slashes (//) indicate pauses in speech. Each slash represents about one second of time. The indented lines show where the overlapping speech occurred in the conversation.

| Phillip: | I drew a picture. I don't got it done. Well, I predict that Christopher... |
|---|---|
| Mandy: | They, they did. They said only some people believed that the world was round. |

Lenny continues arguing his position, physically pointing to relevant text sections. Like Phillip, Julianne attempts to share her log entry, but Lenny pursues his focus.

| Lenny: | See. See, right here. The most... |
|---|---|
| Julianne: | I got, I got a character map too. |
| Lenny: | Educated people knew that the earth was round, not all. |
| Julianne: | I said [inaudible], he likes to sail, he has demands, he's persuasive, the Queen gives his demands, wife died... |

Lenny suggests that because neither the King nor Queen were educated, they did not support Christopher Columbus. He uses this argument to answer the original question—why people did not believe Columbus. Lenny apparently gains the group's consensus, as suggested by the end of this segment:

| Lenny: | Yes you did. Only the King and Queen don't know, so how do you... |
|---|---|
| Mandy: | ...and a lot of people didn't know. |
| Lenny: | I know. Only the people who had education knew. |
| Julianne: | Like Christopher Columbus. |
| Lenny: | Yeah. |

Lenny demonstrates that he understands the text and can use it effectively to make a point. Further, he shows his capacity to participate at the level of his regular education peers and to make his own text-based inferences about the reason for the King and Queen's initial lack of support.

A second example of diverse learners' potential to contribute and prompt the thinking of their regular-education peers comes from the *Park's Quest* book club (Goatley et al., 1995). It is Jason, one of the regular-education students, who struggles to make sense of the text and the characters' relationships. His log entry has bold scribbles over the words "Chapter 13, 6-3-92 things that could happen like: If Park figured out if he had a sister" (op cit., p. 368). His discomfort is shown in his opening comment during book club: "This is boring.... This is a boring book. I like *Hatchet*" (op cit., p. 369). When challenged by his peers, he insists that his only problem is boredom with the book. After some conversation, Jason starts formulating a question to express his confusion; Mei jumps in to help him.

Jason:      I got a, I got a question. How could, uh, Thanh and [Park]...

Mei:       Oh, yeah. That's my question.

Some interruptions occur, and Jason finishes his question: "...be brothers and sisters. I don't get it." Jean, Stark, and Mei—all students who traditionally would not have been part of this lesson if attending pull-out programs—try to help Jason make sense of the text.

Jean:      'Cause they got...

Jason:     Because, [because Frank got a divorce and uh, Park, married Park's mother.

Stark:             [Oh, I got it.

Jean:      [Because they got married and then divorced.

Mei:       [From his, from his mother because, because he, [he...

Jean:              [Park married his, her mother.

Mei:       If she, if she said that she had a wife already.

Jason:     [I don't get it. Sorry. I don't get it.

Stark:     [Noo. What I think had happened is when um...

Jean:      When Park got divorced he married that lady.

Stark:     No, not *married*. He was two-timing his friends. If you get what I mean.

Mei:       Don't they get it? Like, like when you come from the war in Vietnam he was mar, married one of the um, [Vietnamese lady and they come over here.

Stark:             [Or no. He was just like...

Mei:       And his wife find out that he had another wife in Vietnam and then...

Andy:      How would she find out?

Jean:      He told her.

Mei:       He find out because like some, something has happened like he was having baby and then she was sending letters to them, something like...

| | |
|---|---|
| Stark: | And then the letters went to the wrong place. |
| Jason: | Na uh, she... |
| Stark: | No, he went home and... |
| Jason: | Now I get it. Now I get it. Alright, so//// |
| Jason: | Park, Park you know, Park's dad is Park Broughton the fourth um, married, a, um, now I get it, married a, um, Vietnam girl, in Vietnam. That, now I get it. Now I get it. |

This transcript segment reveals that Jason was having difficulty understanding some complex character relationships in the story *Park's Quest*. Jason did not understand how Park and Thanh ("a Vietnam girl") could be brother and sister. As the children continue the conversation after Stark's "two-timing" comment, they do not pick up on his suggestion that Park's father had an affair and instead assume that Park's father either had two wives or he divorced his American wife to marry a Vietnamese woman. (Later this same day, the children expressed their confusion to Mrs. Pardo about Park and Thanh being brother and sister, and she explained that Park's father indeed had an affair with Thanh's mother while stationed in Vietnam during the war.)

These examples illustrate that diverse students engage in complex thinking, reflected during peer-led discussions. Further, they make valuable contributions to ongoing conversations—including challenging the thinking of their regular-education peers. Lenny's involvement and persistence in the conversation changed the nature of what was available to talk about and learn. His conversational involvement played a central role in terms of the actual content discussed and ways in which literary arguments were constructed. That is, he transformed what he had experienced in whole-group discussions and applied it to a new small-group context. He knew he needed to bid for a turn to speak, be persistent in keeping his turn to build his argument while still being polite in the group, draw on support available to build an argument, and work to convince his peers with the supporting points available.

Respecting the second example, because the students had the opportunity to engage in talk and to express their thinking publicly, Jason's confusions could be identified. Because Stark understood what was happening in the story and he was in a position to engage with real ideas pertaining to a text-based discussion, he provided input that helped facilitate his peers' thinking and learning (even though they did not fully grasp the implications of his comment). The opportunity to engage in meaningful talk about text benefits both diverse learners and their peers. Diverse learners have valuable contributions to make to the thinking and learning of their peers. These contributions include both the content of conversation and ways to engage in talk effectively.

## Diverse Students' Literacy Learning Supported and Extended Through Peer Talk

Conventional wisdom suggests that students with less competency in the English language may be best served outside the regular-education classroom, working on English skills in an ESL classroom. As we illustrated in the previous section and as both Goatley et al. (1995) and Brock (1996) suggest, diverse learners can engage in meaningful talk about text, can reveal leadership in such situations, and can benefit from the support of their peers. In the following section we draw on two examples to illustrate how diverse children's learning can be supported and extended through peer talk.

Analysis of Mei's engagement in her book club peer discussion group reveals that she assumed an active leadership role during small-group discussions. For example, during the *Park's Quest* book clubs, Mei took 33% to 44% of the turns in the daily peer-led discussions throughout the 3-week unit. The number of turns indicate that she was not reluctant to engage in discussion. Further, when the turns were analyzed in terms of their function (i.e., leadership in focusing the discussion, orchestrating participants turns, or responding to others), she had six times as many leadership turns as her peers. That is, she helped determine the focus of the conversation more than did any of the other four participants. Analysis of Mei's responses to other students' contributions illustrates that she displayed a range of responses, including extending others' comments, agreeing with them or offering an alternative view, clarifying comments, or making a bid for a turn. In short, she was an active group member, assuming leadership in topic focus but participating in responsive ways to her peers' contributions.

Both Mei and Deng relied on their peers to clarify confusions they had about the text. For example, Mei was uncertain about the relationship between two main characters in *Park's Quest*. Rather than raise her questions during community share, she waited until book club.

| Mei: | I have a question. |
| Jason: | Yeah, okay. |
| Mei: | Like, his grandfather... |
| Jason: | Uh huh. |
| Mei: | You know his grandfather? I don't know if, if um, this girl here, the Vietnamese girl, is, is like, related to his grandfather? |

Notice how Mei initiates the topic through her clarification question and how Jason supports her turn through his "yeah, okay" and "uh huh" (from Goatley et al., 1995, p. 364).

Mei rarely spoke during whole-class literacy lessons, and Deng never spoke in any of the 18 whole-class sessions in which he engaged during the unit pertaining to *Maniac Magee*. However, when interacting with two of his peers, Chris and Tran, in small-group discussions, Deng was much more involved. Analysis of Deng's participation during two of the small-group sessions during the unit pertaining to *Maniac Magee* revealed that he spoke approximately one fifth of the time. Deng's overall comments during these small-group discussions fell into the following categories: seeking help, clarification or approval (13%); making suggestions or sharing ideas (43%); agreeing with or confirming someone else's ideas (19%); attempting to gain the conversational floor (17%); and clarifying something he already stated (8%).

Almost half of Deng's comments involved making suggestions or sharing ideas. Often, these suggestions or ideas were in direct response to Tran's questions. Tran played an important role in inviting Deng into the conversation and making it clear that he valued Deng's ideas, opinions, and thoughts. The three exchanges that follow illustrate how Tran brought Deng into the conversation, elicited his opinions and ideas, and gently nudged and guided his thinking about characters' relationships and family. In the first exchange, Tran elicits Deng's view of the main character Maniac's situation and the missing role of family by asking him direct questions, then by asking probing questions to expand on his initial response.

| Tran: | Anything else why you liked the book? Or homelessness or whatever? (Looking directly at Deng) What do you think about Maniac? |
| Deng: | I think, I think Maniac want to be like the best family. |

| Tran: | He wants the best family? |
|---|---|
| Deng: | Yeah. |
| Tran: | Oh, that's good. |
| Deng: | And he want to have mother and dad and sister and brother. |

Through the questions, Deng was able to articulate Maniac's longing to have a life that includes family, and that the "best family" would include a mom, dad, sister, and brother. The second and third exchanges focus on whether Maniac achieved his dream. The second exchange reveals Deng's uncertainty about what might be the best family. Initially, Deng suggests that the family in the story, the Beales, was not the best, shifting his view when Tran seemed surprised at this response.

| Tran: | Do you think he got the best family? |
|---|---|
| Deng: | No. |
| Tran: | The Beales? |
| Deng: | [Responding quickly] Yeah, yeah. |

In the third exchange, Tran, Chris, and Deng continue to think about who or what might constitute a "best" family, while Deng introduces Grayson, an elderly gentleman Maniac lived with until Grayson died, as an alternative "family" to the Beale family. Tran extends Deng's comment, suggesting that having Grayson as a family was a good idea, but would be an even better idea if he had had children so that Maniac would have siblings.

| Tran: | Oh, okay. Do you think they're the best family for Maniac? |
|---|---|
| Chris: | Nobody's the best family. |
| Deng: | Maniac/no, maybe Grayson. |
| Tran: | Yeah, Grayson. Maybe if Grayson, maybe had kids, that'd be another song. |
| Deng: | Yeah. |

Deng's response to Tran's probing question reflects his interpretation of earlier story content that explained character relationships. Earlier in the story, Maniac had been "adopted" by Grayson; like family, they loved each other. Further, Deng agreed with Tran's suggestion that, although Grayson was a good idea as a suggestion for Maniac's family, siblings would be an important addition. Thus, this set of exchanges illustrates Deng's understanding of characteristics of a "traditional" family; Deng's understanding that the Beales would be a good family for Maniac; Deng's understanding that Grayson also would be a good family for Maniac because Grayson and Maniac cared about each other; and the importance of Tran's encouraging Deng to express, clarify, and extend his thoughts and ideas.

The small-group setting provided a place where the voices of both Mei and Deng could be heard. Although Mei was relatively quiet and Deng was totally silent during whole-class settings, both students spoke to test their leadership and ask clarification questions in settings devoted to peer talk. The Vygotsky Space provides a framework for thinking about the significance of diverse learners' participation in large-group and small-group settings. Both are public settings, but the small group provides an important site for students who may not be comfortable going public with ideas they have developed, with confusions they are experiencing, or with contributing to or leading discussions. The whole-group setting provides an important public and social setting for learning new strategies for interacting around text, for reading the text, and for analyzing text events. It also is a site where teachers and peers can model the disposition to engage in literary talk, to understand the range of information sources they can draw on to make sense of text, and to see themselves as competent literacy users. However, it is within the smaller groups that many diverse learners discover opportunities to assume a range of roles, from leaders to consumers of information. They have meaningful contexts in which to try out ways of thinking about text that they have experienced within the whole-class settings. They also take risks in the smaller groups in ways that they do not when facing 25 or more of their peers in a whole-class setting, and they draw on the support from their peers.

## Teachers' Support of Diverse Students' Participation in Classroom Talk

In the previous sections, we discussed several examples of classroom talk in which diverse students engaged with their peers in meaningful ways to discuss and learn from text. The positive nature of these interactions did not happen simply because students were encouraged to talk and were placed in various small-group settings and a large-group setting to engage in talk. Rather, the teachers played a central role in helping children make the most of their opportunities to talk with peers. In the following section, we identify four means by which teachers can support students' classroom talk. We draw on data from Mrs. Pardo's and Mrs. Weber's classrooms to illustrate how teachers can provide this support.

**Creating public and social spaces.** Quadrant I of the Vygotsky Space reflects the public and social space within a classroom—a public forum for modeling ways to interact with text; for explicitly teaching strategies competent readers and writers use as they read, respond to, and create texts; and for all students to participate in their classroom community. Students draw on what they experience in these contexts as they work individually and with smaller groups of peers. For example, Mrs. Weber used the public and social space of the whole-class session to model how novels such as *Maniac McGee* provide windows into the human experience, giving readers a basis from which to think about issues in their own lives and in the lives of others. Throughout the unit, Mrs. Weber built upon events in the book to raise her students' consciousness about societal issues such as racial relations, loneliness, and homelessness. The following exchange occurred in the middle of a discussion about conflicts and contrasts within the novel. Mrs. Weber encourages students to expand on a point Dan first introduces—that Maniac had no parents.

| | |
|---|---|
| Mrs. Weber: | …What else did we see contrasted in the story? What was he [Maniac McGee] without for so long? |
| Sally: | House |
| Mrs. Weber: | Home versus; what's the opposite of having a home? |
| Students: | [several speaking simultaneously] Homeless, homelessness. |
| Dan: | He was without parents for awhile. |
| Mrs. Weber: | Okay |
| Sally: | Still, I mean they're [the Beale family] like parents. |
| Mrs. Weber: | So, we could have "parents"— |
| Chris: | [interrupting] Legal, not legal, but guardians. |
| Mrs. Weber: | —and "none" [referring to a second contrast in the story]. |

This exchange is one of several that brought out contrasts among story characters, some of whom have strong nuclear families, others who have nontraditional families, and Maniac, whose parents were killed when he was young, causing him to be homeless at different points in the story. These discussion foci helped set a stage for later small-group interactions such as the one presented earlier in this chapter among Deng, Tran, and Chris about what would make the best family for Maniac.

In Mrs. Pardo's classroom we observed her use of the public and social quadrant as she read novels aloud to her students, making apparent the processes in which competent readers engage. She used the event to model her thinking, to model strategies for clarifying confusions, and to elicit students' interactions around a common text. The following observation was typical of read-aloud events we observed throughout the year. Mrs. Pardo had just read a segment from *Across Five Aprils* that described one of the characters, Matt, as "ailin'." She read the remainder of the paragraph, then stopped, looked a bit confused, and asked the students, "What happened to Matt?" A student answered that Matt had died, so Mrs. Pardo returned to the text and reread the paragraph to see if they could discover what actually had happened. In the rereading, she emphasized the word "revived," then emphasized words from the next sentence that indicated he was not the same vigorous man. Charles then said, "He's aging!" Mrs. Pardo used this brief read-aloud event to model that competent readers may experience confusions, rereading the text is a useful strategy, and, when evidence is needed to support a point, it is useful to return to the text to gather information. Recall that Lenny used a similar approach during his book club's discussion about why people initially did not believe Columbus. He, too, returned to the text to reread it and then reinforced his argument with text information. Students appropriate experiences they have in public and social settings, using them in similar ways or transforming them to meet their own needs.

A second example from Mrs. Pardo's classroom illustrates how teachers use public and social spaces to provide opportunities for conventionalization—the process involved in moving from $Q_{III}$ to $Q_{IV}$. When a concept is conventionalized, it becomes part of the cultural norms of the classroom. In the following example, Mrs. Pardo drew on one of Lenny's log entries as the basis for students' thinking about alternative entries in their reading logs. Many of Mrs. Pardo's students had, in her opinion, become overreliant on a handout that listed various possibilities for responding to literature. They usually selected a form of responding that was outlined in the handout (for example, "me and the book," which invited them to think about how the book connected to their own lives, or "wonderful words," which invited them to identify interesting or unusual words.) They then wrote their response in their log and labeled it. Mrs. Pardo noticed that in one of Lenny's log entries, he had written something that did not fit any of the response categories on the handout, nor did he attempt to label the response. He wrote simply what he was thinking and feeling. During community share (with Lenny's permission), Mrs. Pardo read Lenny's response to the whole group and emphasized that he had written "from his heart, not from a handout." Students then talked about Lenny's response as combining some of the responses on the handout and also being a bit creative. Toward the end of the brief discussion, Mrs. Pardo suggested that students consider this approach as a new way of thinking about log entries—drawing on their experience with a range of responses, but rather than deciding on a category ahead of time, writing simply "from their hearts." These examples illustrate how the public and social spaces provide important sites for teaching students about new concepts and for valuing their learning, helping conventionalize their transformed ways of using what they have learned.

**Creating private/social and private/individual spaces.** The second and third quadrants of the Vygotsky Space are private, where students can try appropriated skills and strategies and can have a reason to appropriate ways to interact with text, ways to think about text, and ways to respond to text. Students also have opportunities to transform what they have learned in the service of their own goals. Mrs. Pardo used the reading and writing components of book clubs so that students had the opportunity first to individually interact with the text, then to reflect in writing in preparation for later discussion. These were private activities that provided students with opportunities to apply what they had learned in quadrant I as they read and wrote, then gave them a basis for speaking in their book clubs and during community share.

In the earlier example from the *Park's Quest* book club, we discussed Jason's difficulty in trying to make sense of the relationship between Park and his half-sister, Thanh. Jason's written log entry, noted earlier, reveals this confusion. At the beginning of the book club discussion that followed the private writing time, Jason orally expressed the frustration and confusion he had expressed through writing in his log. Thus, the individual time to write in his book club log provided Jason with the opportunity to respond to the text he was reading in a meaningful and authentic way. The writing time allowed him to begin to express his confusion and its source—Park and Thanh's relationship as sister and brother.

**Creating public/individual spaces for students to "go public."** Both Mrs. Pardo and Mrs. Weber provided spaces for children in their classes to "go public" with their thinking as they interacted in small peer groups. Small-group discussions afford students opportunities to make their thinking public in ways that may not be as readily available in large-group discussions and interactions. In the following example, Lenny demonstrates the move from $Q_{II}$ and $Q_{III}$ to $Q_{IV}$ as he makes his log entry reflections public. The example illustrates the dual function of the reading log, first as a place for private reflection, then as a source for later publication of students' thinking. In this example, Mrs. Pardo can see Lenny's strengths (his text understanding, his capacity to use his log entry as support for his oral response, and his use of the log as a "ticket" to enter the discussion with his peers) and the areas where he needs help. When she compares Lenny's oral reading of his log entry to his actual entry, Mrs. Pardo could identify specific problems Lenny was experiencing in conventional spelling, in handwriting, and in punctuation.

Julianne begins the exchange by explicitly asking Lenny, who had not yet participated in the conversation, to contribute. When Jerry responds instead, referring to an earlier part of their discussion, Mrs. Pardo, who was writing fieldnotes while sitting near the group, signals that he should be quiet. Then, Lenny reads from his log. He does not show any one-to-one correspondence between the printed text and his oral contribution; however, he conveys to his peers that, like they had, he is using his printed text, moving his eyes along the lines as he reads, keeping his eyes on the print in front of him and only occasionally looking up at his peers.

| Julianne: | Because she said her dad is in charge of saying whether she can get married to her [inaudible]. Lenny what do you have to say? |
| --- | --- |
| Jerry: | [continuing to talk from an earlier point in the discussion] Man, I'd hate that. People'd be walkin', pullin' up your arm. Uh. And you couldn't stop 'em. This arm. They'd grab this arm with one hand, then pick the other… |
| Lenny: | [reading from the log, eyes tracking his written entry] In this story today, Tall Boy got shot in the back. And by |

the slaves in the tree. But they kept on riding. And then he could not sit on the saddle, so they had to, so they had to tie him up to the saddle. And then he, he could not sit, and then they had to build a sled to pull him up by the strongest horse.

Lenny used the log entry to create a summary of the main points of the text section that they had read for the day. His entry reflects his appropriation of a taught strategy, summarization. By observing Lenny's publication of this entry during book club, Mrs. Pardo had access to what he thought was important in the chapter, how well he could convey events to his peers, and what his log entry actually said—giving her insight into his text understanding that, because of his lack of conventional language, was not visible in the written entry.

Lenny's opportunities to "go public" with his thoughts and ideas facilitated his learning and gave his teacher a window into his thinking. Lack of such opportunities can negatively impact children's learning. We draw on our earlier discussion of the "contrast" transcript segment from Mrs. Weber's classroom to illustrate the importance of providing spaces for diverse students to go public with their thoughts and confusions. From the perspective of an outside observer, the whole-group discussion of contrasts pertaining to having a home and being homeless undoubtedly appeared to be an important opportunity to promote student learning and understanding about the theme of contrast in *Maniac Magee*. However, because most children did not talk during this lesson segment or engage in some type of individual writing activity, it is difficult to know how most students made sense of this and other parts of the lesson.

We now describe Deng's thinking and understanding of the lesson segment by presenting data from a viewing session, in which Deng, the researcher in this study; Brock; and Vue, a high school student who served as translator during the study, met in Deng's living room to watch a videotape of the lesson mentioned earlier. When the class began the discussion segment about constructing large contrast and conflict charts as a group, Deng stopped the videotape of the lesson slightly *before* the conversational segment pertaining to the contrast between having a home and being homeless and *after* the class had already generated several contrasts that the teacher had listed on the chart. He asked, "What are they

*Raphael, Brock, and Wallace*

say?" Brock responded that she was not sure what Deng was referring to and asked Deng if he would like to rewind the tape so that she could help determine what he was asking. They rewound the tape, and Brock heard Mrs. Weber saying, "Are there any other contrasts that we've run across?" The following discussion is in response to the question:

Brock:      Oh, contrasts? Do you know what contrasts are?
Vue:        Contractions or contrasts?
Brock:      [carefully enunciating] Contrast. [looking at Deng] Do you, do you know what a contrast is?
Deng:       [Spoke in Hmong to Vue.]
Vue:        He said, he said, like a race or something?
Brock:      [confused] Like a race?
Vue:        Yeah.
Brock:      You mean like trying to run fast or something? Oh, oh, oh contests!
Deng:       Yeah. [Deng then began talking in Hmong to Vue.]
Vue:        Not contests, contrasts.
Brock:      [to Deng] You thought she said contests?
Deng:       Yeah.
Brock:      Oh, okay.

Deng then asked if a "contrast" is something you "sign your name to." Brock said that she suspected he was referring to a "contract." They talked about the definition of "contract," and Brock mentioned that the word "contract" is different from "contrast." Then they discussed the definition of the word "contrast" and talked about how Mrs. Weber used the word in class. The discussion illustrates that Deng was very confused about the word "contrast," a central concept to the lesson. It was only when Deng had the opportunity to express his confusions that they became evident so that they could be discussed and clarified.

**Being sensitive to diverse students.** The contrast segment in the previous discussion is an important one for mainstream teachers to consider. Several students (the ones who spoke during the whole-group activity) exhibited a sophisticated understanding of the story and related contextual information, such as legal guardians and their roles in American families. Deng's confusion contrasts his speaking peers' sophisticated understandings. Mainstream teachers can support diverse students' learning by realizing that diverse students may be confused about concepts—like the definition of the word "contrast"—that seemingly are common knowledge (but only if they are viewed from a particular cultural perspective). Further, children's physical demeanor in lessons may not reflect their confusion. Videotaped analysis of Deng's physical participation in class revealed that he nonverbally attended to the speakers in his class as did his mainstream peers.

Because diverse students' cultural and linguistic backgrounds may differ significantly from their mainstream peers, educators cannot assume that second-language learners will make sense of lessons in the same ways as their peers. Additionally, nonverbal cues are not sufficient indicators of children's levels of conceptual understanding. Educators must be sensitive to factors that can create challenges for diverse learners. They need to provide meaningful opportunities for them to openly express their thinking and confusions and receive helpful feedback in nonthreatening peer interactions. This type of support and awareness from the teacher can provide the crucial steps needed on the road to successful learning for diverse students.

# Three "Pearls of Wisdom"

The three studies we used to discuss diverse learners' experiences engaging in classroom talk provide a basis for thinking about how teachers can structure their classrooms and the kinds of opportunities they can provide for their students. In the following section, we offer three "pearls of wisdom" that contrast some of the conventional wisdom that undergirds some less desirable teaching practices for working with diverse learners.

## A Language-Rich Classroom Is a Learning Classroom

Our first "pearl" challenges the notion that a quiet classroom is a learning classroom. We are not alone in arguing for the importance of classroom talk, as witnessed in many recently published professional books and articles on this topic. Rather, we wish to highlight that Lenny, Deng, Mei, Jason, and their peers illustrated repeatedly how much they gained from being active observers of, and active participants in, classroom talk. Jason's confusions about the events in *Park's Quest* may never have surfaced in a classroom defined by silent and individual interaction with text. Lenny's novel approach to creating a log entry may have remained his discovery alone rather than becoming part of the class's conventional approach to creating a written response. It was through the classroom talk that teachers and students shared their thinking and learning and mutually influenced each others' interactions with text.

## Students Benefit from Flexible, Heterogeneous Groupings

Over a decade ago, scholars raised questions about rigid grouping practices based largely on "ability" measures (see, for example, Hiebert, 1983). Our data certainly support questioning such practices. Students such as Deng and Mei found their voices in small heterogeneous peer groups. Students such as Jason had resources for clarifying confusions he was willing to share within a small group, though not with the whole class. However, we do not wish to argue that merely putting students together in small-group settings is a guaranteed approach for facilitating their learning. Deng's benefits from small-group participation were attributable, at least in part, to his teacher's spending considerable time and effort teaching her students how to be effective participants in small-group settings. Further, within the small group, Tran actively and overtly served as Deng's advocate, asking for Deng's opinion and offering help and suggestions as they worked. We maintain that it is both the nature of the participants' interactions within the small group and the opportunities to make thinking public and receive continuous, explicit, and immediate feedback from peers that influence learning.

Clearly, small peer-led discussion groups *can* be effective contexts for literacy learning; however, they are effective only when teachers and students work together to create meaningful interactions within those contexts. Further, they are not (or should not be) the only or primary context for promoting diverse students' literacy learning. Finally, as we have illustrated with numerous examples, mainstream children have much to gain from their interactions with diverse peers in small-group settings. That is, the support students gained from their peers in our studies was not always in predicted directions of higher achieving readers and writers supporting those who had more difficulty. Rather, the heterogeneous groups showed shifting leadership and revealed the support students of all reading and writing competencies could provide for their peers.

## Evaluation of Student Learning and Understanding Must Be Ongoing and Multifaceted

Conventional wisdom suggests that teachers can successfully assess student learning through paper-and-pencil exercises and by examining students' overt nonverbal behavior. Our discussion of Lenny's use of his writing log and his subsequent oral discussion highlights the need to give children multiple and varied media for expression. Much of what Lenny thought, knew, and could do was not adequately reflected in writing-related activities. Similarly, not only must we give our students multiple and varied opportunities to express what they think and know, but we also must seek multiple and varied ways to assess their unfolding understandings. We would not have understood Deng's developing understandings (or the lack thereof) without listening to him interact with others in his small-group activities and giving him ample opportunities to express his confusions and concerns through individual questioning.

As educators, we have multiple ways to assess our diverse children's developing understandings during lessons. We can observe how diverse children follow peers' responses or whether they assume a leadership role in interactions; we can engage in occasional informal one-to-one discussions with diverse students to understand how they make sense of classroom activities and lessons; and we can help them seek peer partners who can help them sort through complex and confusing cultural and linguistic conventions. In short, teachers of diverse children must develop multiple and varied ways to evaluate their students' understanding and participation in classroom activities on a continual basis.

## Concluding Comments

Our society is a rapidly changing one, with increasingly diverse youngsters attending school, resulting in teachers commonly working with students who differ from them in cultural, linguistic, social, and academic backgrounds. Our challenge is to create meaningful learning opportunities for *all* of our students, building bridges across culture, language, and levels of literacy competence and drawing on the diversity of our students to enrich our classrooms.

### Author's Note

This chapter was written while the first author was at Michigan State University.

## Questions for Reflection

1. In order to facilitate and nurture diversity in literacy practices, teachers must first understand their own literacy experiences. It is through the valuing and understanding of these practices as ones that are cultural in nature that will allow teachers to value the experiences of their students. How can we help teachers come to understand their own experiences as unique and valuable so that they may value this in their classrooms?
2. How can we help teachers think about ways of changing or rethinking their classroom practices in ways that are more sensitive to diverse learners?

## References

Alvermann, D.E. (1996). Peer-led discussions: Whose interests are served? *Journal of Adolescent & Adult Literacy, 39*(4), 282–289.

Bogdan, R.C., & Biklen, S.K. (1992). *Qualitative research for education: An introduction to theory and methods*. Boston, MA: Allyn & Bacon.

Brock, C.H. (1996, April). *Taking a look at the process: Exploring relationships between assessment, curriculum, and instruction in one teacher's literacy program*. Paper presented at the Annual Meeting of the American Educational Research Association, New York, NY.

Cazden, C.B. (1988). *Classroom discourse: The language of teaching and learning*. Portsmouth, NH: Heinemann.

Erickson, F., & Schultz, J. (1992). Students' experience of the curriculum. In P.W. Jackson (Ed.), *Handbook of research on curriculum* (pp. 465–485). New York: Macmillan.

Evans, K.S. (1996). Creating spaces for equity? The role of positioning in peer-led discussions. *Language Arts, 73*(3), 194–202.

Gavelek, J.R., & Raphael, T.E. (1996). Changing talk about text: New roles for teachers and students. *Language Arts, 73*(3), 182–192.

Goatley, V.J., Brock, C.H., & Raphael, T.E. (1995). Diverse learners participating in regular education "Book Clubs." *Reading Research Quarterly, 30*, 352–380.

Harré, R. (1984). *Personal being: A theory for individual psychology*. Cambridge, MA: Harvard University Press.

Hiebert, E.H. (1983). An examination of ability grouping for reading instruction. *Reading Research Quarterly, 18*, 231–255.

McGill-Franzen, A., & Allington, R.L. (1993). Flunk 'em or get them classified: The contamination of primary grade accountability data. *Educational Researcher, 22*(1), 19–22.

McMahon, S.I., & Raphael, T.E., with V. Goatley & L. Pardo. (1997). *The Book Club connection: Literacy learning and classroom talk*. New York: Teachers College Press; Newark, DE: International Reading Association.

Nieto, S. (1992). *Affirming diversity: The sociopolitical context of multicultural education*. White Plains, NY: Longman.

Raphael, T.E., & Brock, C.H. (1993). Mei: Learning the literacy culture in an urban elementary school. In D.J. Leu & C.K. Kinzer (Eds.), *Examining central issues in literacy research, theory, and practice* (Forty-second Yearbook of the National Reading Conference, pp. 179–188). Chicago, IL: National Reading Conference.

Raphael, T.E., & Goatley, V.J. (1994). The teacher as "more knowledgeable other": Changing roles for teaching in alternative reading instruction programs. In C.K. Kinzer & D.J. Leu (Eds.), *Multidimensional aspects of literacy research, theory and practice* (Forty-third Yearbook of the National Reading Conference, pp. 527–536). Chicago, IL: National Reading Conference.

Raphael, T.E., & Hiebert, E.H. (1996). *Creating an integrated approach to literacy instruction*. Fort Worth, TX: Harcourt Brace.

Raphael, T.E., McMahon, S.I., Goatley, V.J., Bentley, J.L., Boyd, F.B., Pardo, L.S., & Woodman, D.A. (1992). Research directions: Literature and discussion in the reading program. *Language Arts, 69*(1), 55–61.

Raphael, T.E., & McMahon, S.I. (1994). Book Club: An alternative framework for reading instruction. *The Reading Teacher, 48*(2), 102–116.

Raphael, T.E., Wallace, S.M., Pardo, L.S., & Choo, V.M. (1996, April). *Assessing the literacy growth of fifth-grade students: A question of realigning curriculum, instruction and assessment*. Presentation at the Annual Meeting of the American Educational Research Association, New York, NY.

Wertsch, J.V. (1985). *Vygotsky and the social formation of mind*. Cambridge, MA: Harvard University Press.

Vygotsky, L.S. (1978). *Mind in society: The development of higher psychological processes* (M. Cole, V. John-Steiner, S. Scribner, E. Souberman, Eds. and Trans.). Cambridge, MA: Harvard University Press. (Original work published 1934)

## Children's Literature References

Goodnough, D., & Dodson, B. (Ill.). (1991). *Christopher Columbus*. New York: Troll.

Hunt, I. (1986). *Across five Aprils*. New York: Berkeley Books.

Paterson, K. (1988). *Park's quest*. New York: Dutton.

Spinelli, J. (1991). *Maniac McGee*. New York: Harper Trophy.

# CHAPTER 10

# Watching Teachers Watch Children Talk About Books

∽

## JEANNE R. PARATORE, SHEILA GARNICK, AND TRINIDAD LEWIS

With increasing frequency, teachers are using portfolios to assess and document children's literacy learning. Although this change in assessment practice clearly is beneficial and useful for understanding children's writing and their written response to reading (see, for example, Darling-Hammond, Ancess, & Falk, 1995; Stowell & Tierney, 1995), there also is reason for caution. As an assessment practice that often is limited to documentation of children's written work, portfolios fail to capture behaviors and activities that are critically important to students' growth in literacy, but are not written down.

As we thought about ways to respond to our concern about the writing emphasis in literacy portfolios, we considered contexts that might provide teachers with information that would augment the samples of written work that most often make up the literacy portfolio. We discussed teachers' increasing interest in the implementation of peer-led discussion groups and agreed that these instructional settings could provide rich and valuable information about literacies that are not written down. We reviewed the few existing articles that we could find on assessment during literature discussion groups and found excellent suggestions for what teachers *could* do (for example, Matanzo, 1996; Morrow, 1996; Pierce, 1990; Walker, 1996; Watson, 1990), but little evidence documenting how teachers actually use evidence from book discussions to support continued literacy learning. Our search for information led us to pose two questions: (1) When teachers observe children during student-led book discussions, what is their focus? and (2) What influence does the information they gather have on subsequent teaching actions? In this chapter we describe the classroom context in which we examined these questions and what we learned as a result.

## The Context for Observing Children Talk About Books

In the fifth-grade classroom in a small, urban U.S. school where our study took place, the 28 children were ethnically and linguistically diverse. Ten children were Latino, 10 were European American, 4 were Southeast Asian, and 4 were African American. Of the 17 children who spoke English as a second language, most were fluent in English, with the exception of a Russian student who, at the time of the study, had been in the United States for only 2 months and was just learning to speak English. Two children in the classroom were identified as having special learning needs and had Individual Educational Plans; one child currently was in the process of completing the evaluation process required by law to qualify for formal identification. Each of these three children received literacy instruction in the classroom with the other children.

Two teachers, who earlier had expressed interest in the use of peer-led discussion groups, participated in the study. Martha, the classroom teacher, was a first-year teacher who was enthusiastic about learning new instructional strategies. Annie was a Title I (a federally funded remedial reading program) teacher who cotaught with Martha 60 to 90 minutes per day, 4 days per week, every other week throughout the school year. Annie was a veteran teacher with 25 years teaching experience. She held a master's degree in education. In addition, during the previous 7 years Annie had participated in intensive inservice education in literacy instruction by enrolling in both on-site professional development seminars and university-based courses.

### Helping the Teachers Prepare for Literature Circles

The teachers considered themselves to be novices in the use of peer-led discussion groups, or what they commonly called literature circles (see

Chapters 3, 5, and 6 for further discussion of literature circles). Annie had been introduced to strategies for peer-led groups in one of the in-service courses she had taken during the previous year, and she shared this information with Martha. Approximately 4 weeks before the study was initiated, the teachers had introduced literature circles to their students for the first time and engaged children in student-led discussion groups three or four times after that. They considered these first attempts to be "experimental," and they lacked confidence in their ability to support children effectively as they talked about books on their own. When the teachers were approached to participate in this project, they agreed on the condition that they would be mentored in the process of planning and implementing student-led discussion groups. At the onset of the study, they worked with Sheila Garnick, a Title I Director (and a co-researcher on the study), to plan the literature unit. Guided by the work of Martinez and Roser (1995) regarding the selection of texts for use in discussions, the teachers decided that the children would read *Early Thunder* (Fritz, 1967). They chose this particular book for three reasons. First, it was related to the topic that the students were studying in the social studies unit in class (the American Revolution) and, as Martinez and Roser suggested, it would "cause children to tussle with" (p. 36) an important story theme. Second, it was relatively easy to read and, with appropriate interventions, could be accessible to all their students. And third, most of the chapters were reasonably short and could be read and discussed within the allocated instructional period of 60 to 90 minutes.

The teachers and Sheila discussed the literacy behaviors and strategies that they hoped to support and observe as children talked together about the books they were reading. They wanted to gain insight into children's personal response, defined by Rosenblatt (1978, 1985) as the aesthetic stance, and observe what children thought was important about their reading. They also sought to direct children's attention to particular information and events, described by Rosenblatt as an efferent stance. They were guided by the work of Wiseman, Many, and Altieri (1992) in helping children take different perspectives. Because the teachers were interested in helping students understand the cause and effect of events in history in this particular lesson, they decided to focus teacher-led mini-lessons on strategies that would lead children to consider characters' traits, examine characters' motives and viewpoints, and evaluate characters' actions.

Martha and Annie were uncertain about their roles before and during the student-led discussions and they asked Sheila about instances when they might choose to intervene in the students' discussions and how they might do so. Goldenberg's (1992/1993) work on instructional conversations was especially useful in helping them define and explain the role that the teacher would take in supporting the performance of English-language learners in book discussions. They relied particularly on three preparatory steps: They read the book several times, selected a theme to focus initial discussion, and identified and provided the background knowledge students needed in order to make sense of what they would be reading.

To help focus their observations as they circulated among the peer-led groups, the teachers discussed and developed observation forms that they might use to observe and record the literacy and discourse strategies that they had targeted as important. The forms, which teachers referred to as "Clipboard Cruising" forms, differed from day to day depending on what the focal strategies were. One example is provided in the Figure that appears on page 211.

Together Martha and Annie decided to organize students into six discussion groups, each comprising 4 to 6 students of differing literacy and language abilities.

It was agreed that at the start of the literature unit, Sheila would assume the role of demonstration teacher, first modeling the implementation of literature circles and the teacher's role during student-led discussions and then observing the teachers as they assumed instructional responsibility.

## Helping the Children Prepare for Literature Circles

To begin the reading of *Early Thunder*, Sheila chose to build interest in the book and to support shared understanding by reading the first chapter aloud. During the whole-class discussion that followed, Sheila asked the students to think about the characters, their traits, and the motives for their actions. She posed several questions during this discussion: Why did they think the characters were acting in particular ways? What point of view did they have about the events evolving around them? She shared her thoughts about the characters, modeling for the students the ways she considered and examined characters' viewpoints. During this first instructional period, students did not form literature

# Teachers' Observation Forms

| | Gets the floor | Discusses characters' points of view | Shares opinions about characters' actions | Shares ideas from the text (T), pictures (P), personal experience (E), or discussion (D) | Asks for clarification |
|---|---|---|---|---|---|
| Anthony | | | | | |
| Scott | | | | | |
| Israel | | | | | |
| Cathy | | | | | |
| Stephanie | | | | | |

circles, but instead used the remaining instructional time to reread the chapter that had been read aloud and then to record a written response in their journals that described their initial thoughts about the characters and their viewpoints.

## Supporting Children as They Talked About Books

On the second day, Sheila's introductory lesson focused on four areas. First, she reminded students of the key characters and events in the first chapter. She asked them to talk with their peers about what they thought might happen in the next chapter and then to share their predictions. Second, she explained that after reading the next chapter to themselves, they would share their thoughts and ideas with their peers. Students were reminded to pay particular attention to the characters' actions and to examine what events were causing the characters to act in particular ways and why. They were given adhesive notepads on which to write notes as they read; the paper also was used to mark particular phrases or pages that they wished to return to during the book discussion. Third, students were given a few directions about how to manage the tape recorders and microphones that were being used to audiotape their discussions for the purpose of data collection. And finally, they discussed the rules and routines of literature circles. Because the students had been introduced to strategies for peer-led discussion groups earlier, they already were familiar with basic routines. They knew that they needed to give everyone a turn to talk, that they should listen to their peers and try respond to what others said, and that they should support their ideas with evidence from the text and from their own experience.

As the children read silently, all three teachers circulated around the classroom, observing the students' silent reading behaviors, redirecting students who were not immediately on task, and answering occasional questions about words or ideas in the text. After students finished reading and began their discussions, the teachers continued to circulate, taking notes about the literacy and discourse strategies children were using and, at times, intervening in the discussion to scaffold or challenge students' thinking. At the end of the day, Sheila, Martha, and Annie met to discuss the lesson. They talked about what Sheila had done and why, discussed how the students responded and what they had observed as they circulated among the students, and planned the next day's lesson.

On the third day, Sheila again took the lead in preparing students for the day's chapter. She reviewed with the students the events of the previous day and introduced the new chapter. She also reminded them to pay particular attention to characters' traits, actions, and motives. As students engaged in silent reading and peer-response groups, the teachers again circulated among the students. After the students completed their discussions, Sheila again took the lead. She asked them to rewind their audiotapes and asked if a group would volunteer to play their discussion for the class. All the groups were eager to do so. One by one, students listened to the six discussions. At various times throughout the play-backs, Sheila commented on the conversations, pointing out instances when she might have asked a question to seek clarification of an idea or opinion. After listening to all the group discussions, she reminded students that, as they talked about books, they should justify their opinions and ideas with examples from the text, ask questions of their peers to clarify particular ideas or comments, and listen carefully as their friends speak. She closed by saying that these were things she wanted the class to think about each day.

During the next 5 days, Sheila continued to take the lead in preparing children for each day's chapter. She followed the same prereading plan she had followed during the first 3 days, recalling with the students the events of the previous day and sometimes directing their attention to a particular event or episode in the new chapter. She also reminded them of particular reading strategies that they might use to guide their response. As students engaged in silent reading and peer-response groups, the teachers circulated among the students. As the days proceeded, Annie and Martha followed Sheila's lead, intervening when necessary and increasing their documentation of children's behaviors. The Table on page 214 outlines the actions teachers took before, during, and after each day's discussions to support children as they talked about their reading. The team met each day to discuss the process, the notes they were taking, what they were learning about their students, and what they intended to do as a result of their observations.

## Watching Teachers Watch Children

Several sources from our study provided data to answer the research questions we had posed, which follow on page 215.

## Supporting Children as They Talk About Books: Teachers' Actions

| Before discussion | During discussion | After discussion |
|---|---|---|
| 1. Built readers' interest through through read-alouds | 1. Monitored and observed students' silent reading behaviors | 1. Commented on discussions. |
| 2. Directed attention to particular events or episodes in the book. | 2. Wrote notes about the students' literacy and discourse strategies. | 2. Encouraged students to ask their peers clarifying questions about their ideas or opinions. |
| 3. Engaged students in whole-class discussions by posing questions. | 3. Answered students' questions about words or ideas in the text. | 3. Reminded students to justify their opinions and ideas with examples from the text. |
| 4. Shared personal thoughts with the students about the characters. | 4. Encouraged students to ask their peers clarifying questions about their ideas or opiniosn. | 4. Reminded students to listen carefully to their peers during discussions. |
| 5. Modeled ways to consider and examine characters' points of view. | | |
| 6. Encouraged students to share thoughts and ideas with peers and to make predictions about the text. | | |
| 7. Discussed rules and routines of literature circles. | | |

1. In order to learn about teachers' perceptions of and classroom routines for assessment, we interviewed the teachers before and after the study;

2. We took field notes during and immediately after "debriefing" meetings held each day during the 8-day training period, during which teachers discussed what they observed, what they learned, and what they would do next;

3. We collected the observation checklists and anecdotal notes that teachers recorded as they circulated among the peer-led discussion groups and the logs in which they recorded their reflections at various points during the 8-day period;

4. Each of the five peer-led discussion groups audiotaped their discussions throughout the 8-day training period, and the audiotapes from one group (randomly identified as a "focal" group) were later transcribed; and

5. Throughout the 8-day period of the study, an outside observer was present in the classroom. During the 90-minute literacy block, she documented the actions of the Title 1 Director and the teachers. In addition, the observer documented the literacy, discourse, and social behaviors of the peer group identified as the "focal group." Following each observation, all field notes were typed and elaborated with the observer's comments.

Data were analyzed using inductive coding procedures described by Strauss and Corbin (1990). Transcripts and other data were reviewed line by line, labeled, and categorized. We searched across each of the data sources for evidence related to two particular topics: (1) the focus of teachers' observations as students read silently and as they discussed books with their peers, and (2) teachers' response to their observations.

## What Happens When Teachers Watch Children?

During the time that children read and talked about books, the teachers in the classroom were extremely busy. As they circulated around the room, they shifted continually from the role of observer to the role of participant. As we reviewed the data it became apparent that teachers did a good deal of immediate decision making about how to respond to their observations. In some cases, they responded by intervening to refocus or redirect an individual, group, or occasionally the whole class. At other times, they jotted down information for later response or intervention. Their observations and subsequent interventions consistently addressed four areas:

1. students' engagement in the assigned task,
2. students' attention to literacy and discourse strategies,
3. students' comprehension of and response to the text, and
4. the performance of struggling readers.

In the section that follows, the evidence related to each of these areas is presented.

**Observing students' engagement.** Teachers spent a good deal of their observation time monitoring students' engagement in the task. Consistently, a student's off-task behavior triggered some type of teaching action. Most often, the teacher intervened simply by being present and repositioning herself near the student or, sometimes, by placing a finger on a page to redirect the student's attention to the text. Episodes such as the one that follows, recorded by the observer on the second day, were common throughout the 8-day period:

> Sheila walks over to Ira and looks at what he is reading. She asks him why he is not following along and redirects him. A few minutes later Martha walks over to see what Ira is doing. [She was sitting next to Natasha and helping her to follow along.] As Sheila reads aloud, Martha goes over to several of the groups to check on them and then goes back to her seat next to Natasha.

On the day that the observer recorded this episode, Martha wrote a simple statement in her log: "some have difficulty focusing when reading silently." We found the practice of summarizing observations in very brief statements to be common throughout the teachers' anecdotal records. Often, such entries documented the observations of the class as a whole, as in these examples:

> I have seen drastic changes. All participate...
>
> Children are aware the climax of the story is coming—interests are sparked.
>
> Majority are reading with interest.

At other times, entries reflected the teachers' attention to individual students. Watching two students who had completed their reading and were waiting for their peers to finish so that the discussion could begin, Annie wrote, "Children are talking but it is about passages. Which ones were important? What did they mean? Comparing choices."

There also was evidence that teachers used their observations not just to document what children were doing, but also to reflect on and inform their own teaching decisions. For example, after noting that one student was "thumbing through the pages to get basic info instead of reading every word," while another student was "skipping pages," Martha wrote:

> I don't see any true way of telling how much a child has read and understood through the circles. I'm watching some children read key parts to the story and this will be the only area they discuss in conversation. If something comes up that they haven't read, they either don't participate or they fake it. Without posing comprehension questions, do we really understand how much they comprehend? How and in what ways?

Martha's attention to and concern about whether all students were actually reading was on-going and an area for which she continually searched for appropriate instructional interventions. In her final entry in her log she recorded,

> What do I do with the child I know isn't reading? This child is bluffing his way through the lesson pretending to have read and giving input only when necessary.

Teachers' attention to students' engagement remained a central focus throughout the study and was critical in teachers' evaluation of the entire process of student-led discussions.

**Observing students' discourse strategies.** As children talked about books, teachers' observations often focused on their strategies for participating in the discussion. On the first day, Annie's log included the following comments:

> Children don't know where to begin. Jenny tries to revive the group. Quotes section about Daniel letting Mr. Leonard slip away and she asks why?

On the same day, Martha also focused on students' discourse behaviors and tied her observations directly to teaching actions. She recorded these comments:

> Discussions not easily begun. Discussions needed to be teacher motivated. Children need some form of motivation to discuss the story. Without it, the discussion has problems beginning.

Sometimes, teachers noticed gender differences. Martha wrote that "girls do a lot of notetaking, yet it is the boys who answer the questions and begin the discussions."

Attention to students' discourse styles continued throughout teachers' observations over the 8-day period. On the second day, Annie recorded the following notes:

> ...more need to participate; heard a few put downs that could have led to meaningful discussions; need to listen to each other.

On the seventh day, Martha recorded the following:

> Wow—how JoEllen has blossomed—her whole group has come a long way. They have gone from a shy agreeing group to an aggressive passionate disagreeing discussing group.

On the last day, Martha wrote, "Noticed conversations have changed—more participation and more heated discussions." And on the same day, Annie also paid attention to discourse strategies in this observation about one of the groups: "...heads together; leaning in; eye contact; Jake asks personal questions: Would you do that if it were you?"

In another entry on the same day, Annie focused on both the content of the discussion and on the discourse styles:

> Discussion of big decision. Sammy is still reading, but participating. Although Jennella tries to rule, JoEllen and Susie won't allow it.

Teachers' attention to discourse styles also was evident in their final interviews. Their observations helped them to develop an understanding of how group discourse evolves. Martha noted in her final interview that

> it was trial and error and then every group seemed to develop a system. For example, Natasha's group ended up being a two-way conversation and Melanie had to play a role as the mediator for the group...

In reflecting on what they had learned about their students during the literature unit, Martha said:

> Toward the end, the students seemed to be responsible about what they were doing—taking ownership and it also seemed how some kids are getting more involved and seemed to respond more in the discussion and in the journal writing. It went from just telling what happened to really getting into the story.

Annie similarly noted in her final reflections:

> They became more curious and interested about things.... They got a sense of involvement and trust. Increased sense of responsibility to complete the assigned tasks. People in the groups took on different roles and they wouldn't give up until the others responded. For example, students took on roles of the encourager, surrogate teacher, etc.

It was evident that as teachers observed children in their discussion groups, they not only attended to generally held ideas about reading comprehension, but they also assessed strategies not always included as part of the literacy curriculum: students' ability to engage in a constructive discussion, to assume leadership, and to assume responsibility for directing their own learning.

**Observing comprehension and response.** Unlike teachers' observations about children's discourse styles that mostly were written down, teachers' attention to students' comprehension and response to the text was less often written and more often addressed immediately. In numerous instances throughout the project period, teachers abandoned their stance as eavesdroppers or observers and intervened immediately when they observed that students were contributing information without justifying or substantiating their ideas or when students were accepting an idea or point of view without critical evaluation. Teachers' interventions in children's discussions were very brief, usually lasting only 1 or 2 minutes. They occurred quite frequently during the first few days of literature circles and diminished (although they did not stop altogether) as students learned to pay closer attention to text and to critically evaluate their peers' comments.

The following intervention during the first peer-led discussion is characteristic of the teachers' attempts throughout the 8-day period to emphasize the importance of justifying the ideas they were sharing: (In the transcript fragments, a period represents a fall to a low pitch signaling the end of a sentence. Commas indicate the transitional continuity of speaker's thoughts as commonly used in written language. Question marks are used to illustrate grammatical appeals or requests, and short pauses are noted with a sequence of two dots (..). Speakers' utterances are linked together with an equal sign (=) when they are latched together immediately to one another without overlapping. The abbreviation BV denotes Background Voices.)

Ira: I disagree with Dr. West because um (..) he should of told his kids (..) that he was bringing in a new mother. He shouldn't of just like (..) just bring her there one day and say that (..) that's their new mother.

BV: Yeah.

Teacher: Why do you think he should do that? Could you tell them why?

Ira: Um, because um, (..) cause his kid was so unexpected and stuff and um, Hannah, she probably lost her job.

Katie: And that's wrong of them.

Teacher: What makes you think Hannah lost her job?

Ira: No, I didn't say she did (..) She might of because um they don't need her anymore (..) right? Because they have that new person, that new lady.

Sharon: The new wife. Um, I think it wasn't nice of um, ah, the new wife to tell Hannah that she can't cook any more inside the kitchen.

Alex: I don't like the idea of Dr. West having a wife anyways because um, they, him and Daniel lived with each other all of their life and (..) Daniel's mother died when he was small and um, (..) and um, they have Hannah anyways to do all of the housework and um, Daniel doesn't like the idea either because =

Teacher: = Because why? It's important to tell why. Why don't you think Daniel likes the idea?

Alex: Because, because that'll make him upset and um (..) to just unexpectedly have a new mother just like that, and (..) years from having a mother when he was smaller.

Here, as in other instances, the teacher's interventions did not take the discussion in a new direction or introduce a new topic, but rather they directed students' attention to their responsibility to present evidence to support the ideas they had raised.

On the following day, the children's discussion was uninterrupted as the teacher observed them paying attention to the need to justify their ideas and questioning one another in the same ways the teacher had questioned them on the previous day:

| | |
|---|---|
| Katie: | This chapter gave a lot of information. The last one didn't give so much information. |
| Ira: | This one showed a lot about what happened to Peter Ray (..) and who the Liberty Boys are and Peter Ray and Daniel had to save (..) I mean (..) Daniel and Beckett had to save Peter Ray. |
| BV: | (inaudible) |
| Todd: | From what? |
| BV: | Umm… |
| BV: | What did he say? |
| Todd: | From what, I said. |
| BV: | You have to repeat the whole thing. |
| Ira: | Scott said that what did Daniel and Beckett had to save Peter Ray from? |
| BV: | (inaudible) |
| Katie: | I heard that. |
| BV: | (inaudible) |
| Ira: | Daniel wants to beat him up. |
| Susie: | Yeah, because he puts stuff on the doorstep, right? |
| BV: | Yeah. |
| Susie: | Is he really a Whig? |
| BV: | No (..) yeah. |
| Ira: | We don't know that yet. |
| Todd: | He traded. (Overlapping voices) He traded. |

| | |
|---|---|
| Katie: | It's true. It's true. I'll get that. [Cathy pages through the book looking for the information that will substantiate what Scott has said.] |
| BV: | (Inaudible) |
| Ira: | We don't know that yet. |
| Todd: | Peter Ray did (..) Peter Ray is a Whig now 'cause he traded and became a Liberty Boy (..) and all the Liberty Boys are Whigs. |
| BV: | (inaudible) |
| Ira: | They didn't say he was a Whig but Daniel said he's turned traitor. They didn't exactly say he was a Whig. |
| Todd: | Well, aren't all the Liberty Boys Whigs? |
| Ira: | I don't know. |
| BV: | Well = |
| Ira: | = Might just some are Tories. |
| BV: | (Inaudible). |
| Susie: | How come Tories don't put (..) um (..) like put the gross stuff on other people's house just like the Whigs? |
| Todd: | Maybe the Tories are more (..) umm (..) (overlapping voices) |
| BV: | Loyal. |
| Todd: | Maybe the Tories are more (..) um (..) |
| Susie: | Loyal. |
| Ira: | Like Miss Garnick said they are more tamer. |
| Susie: | Loyal. |
| Todd: | Calmer. |
| Susie: | More loyal. |
| Susie: | Yeah, but um (..) how come if [inaudible] didn't tell them to do that to him (..) and they do it to the other people how come the Tories don't do it back to them? |
| Todd: | Because they're calmer, you know, they just don't want to do it. |
| Susie: | Oh, so, they're gonna spend the rest of their life (..) um (..) like = |

| Ira: | = Well, why would they do it when they don't know who's doing it? |
|---|---|
| Susie: | Because they um (..) |
| Katie: | What did you say? What did you say? |
| Ira: | Why would they do it to someone that they didn't know if they were the ones? |

At times, observations made while circulating among the groups prompted an intervention with the whole class. In one instance, as Annie listened to one group, she joined the conversation to remind the students of the events in *The Witch of Blackbird Pond* (Speare, 1958), a book they had read a few weeks earlier, and prompted them to consider how the events in that book and those in *Early Thunder* might be similar. As she moved away from that group, she called for the attention of the whole class and suggested that they all think about *The Witch of Blackbird Pond* in the course of the day's discussion.

In their written anecdotes, the two teachers differed in their focus on comprehension strategies. Annie focused on the behaviors of individuals, and Martha summarized the behaviors of the class. For example, as Annie observed one group, she noted that "Robert agrees and gives reason, uses evidence in text cover; Jenny refers to illustration; Alan poses questions for the group; Sammy didn't stay on the subject." In another day's entry, she noted; "Tany Ban looks back and further explains; Donald looks back in text; Jake asks questions for clarification; Donald refers back to previous chapters."

In contrast, Martha noted that the students were "great at predictions, using the picture at the beginning of Chapter 9." A later entry on the same day suggests that Martha's observations prompted her to examine her teaching practices:

Noticed children confused about ch. 9. Reasons? Could it be because they silent read the full chapter. How many truly read? How many read but had difficulty understanding? Some have difficulty focusing when reading silently. At least when they read out loud they are getting the info whether they are aware or not. Was this a difficult chapter for comprehension? How can I better prepare them for the chapter so when they read it they aren't confused? How much prior knowledge should I give them with each chapter before it is considered to be "spoon feeding?"

Questions such as these persisted for Martha throughout the 8-day period. Informal conversations with Martha several weeks after the study ended indicated that she continued to wrestle with the important and consequential questions she posed during this process of close and intense "kidwatching" long after we left her classroom.

**Observing struggling readers.** Throughout the 8-day period, we observed that teachers were especially attentive to students they believed might struggle during literature circles. From the start, the teachers watched these students carefully during both silent reading and discussion periods and intervened frequently to support their success. Episodes such as the one that follows, recorded by the observer on the first day of the literature unit, occurred repeatedly with different students during the 8-day period:

> Annie comes over and prompts Melanie. She points to the page that Melanie should be on and then Martha joins Melanie. Martha sits next to her and asks Ve Dong to move down one seat. Melanie follows along as Martha helps track the words on the page.

The teachers often supported struggling readers by pairing them with other students during the silent reading period. One student, the young girl who had just arrived from Russia and spoke little English, was joined daily during silent reading with either a teacher or a peer. While the other children in the classroom read silently, Natasha listened to a student or teacher read aloud.

Teachers also intervened during the group discussions when they observed that a particular student was reluctant to participate. We began to refer to this as teachers "bringing lurkers into the discussion."

| | |
|---|---|
| Teacher: | Katie, what about you? Do you have any thoughts about this? Something you would like to share? I noticed you have a sticky note in your hand. |
| Katie: | Oh, oh that's the one that I disagree with Dr. West. |
| Teacher: | Okay, is there anything else you would like to think about. What do you think of his new wife? |
| Katie: | I think, I think she (..) it looks like she is not nice. |
| Teacher: | What makes you think that? |

| | |
|---|---|
| Katie: | Because she's like, she's just walking and she's like [makes a funny facial expression] I don't know. |
| Teacher: | At the microphone. Can't get that face you just made so beautifully. Would you say a little bit more about it so we can all know? |
| Katie: | Like, I don't know. |
| Alex: | You gotta talk louder so that everybody can hear. |
| Katie: | I don't know the word for it. |
| Teacher: | Tell a little bit more about it. Can some (..) |
| Katie: | Like (..) a bad face. Like she thinks she's all that. |
| Teacher: | What does that mean (..) all that? |
| Alex: | She thinks she knows everything. She thinks that she knows everything and that she is the best. |
| Susie: | She thinks she is pretty and beautiful. |

In this discussion excerpt, as in others like it, the teacher's intervention was brief, centered on the student's own ideas, and was critically important in helping less confident students enter the discussion. Consistently, the consequence of the teacher's intervention was that the reluctant student's ideas became the focus of the group discussion, at least for a few minutes.

## Teachers' Perceptions of What They Learned

At the end of the 8-day period, we asked Martha and Annie to talk to us about what they had learned as they watched children talk about books. They shared their insights first in writing and later elaborated during an interview. Their comments addressed four general areas: (1) the differences evident in children's oral and written response to books; (2) the general literacy growth children made when given opportunities to talk about books; (3) their surprise at particular children's strengths; and (4) their lingering questions about the role they should play in supporting children's talk about books.

Both Annie and Martha believed that listening to the discussions extended their understanding of children's comprehension beyond the information they had collected in children's portfolios. This comment from Annie is representative:

> Listening to the discussion helps me better determine comprehension for those students who are not as strong in writing skills. Sometimes the level of understanding demonstrated during conversations is more evident than in journal entries.

They also claimed that they had increased their awareness of their students' general growth in literacy. Annie wrote:

> During the weeks of peer-led discussions I have watched a majority of the children develop measurable literacy behaviors. Children became more responsible for their own work; they got on task easily and developed a routine. I saw students stay with their silent reading, even when the rest of the group was in discussion, but commented when they had something to add. Because they were directly responsible for the working of their group, each took it more seriously—I saw what each child could do in an authentic situation.

Martha's increased awareness of how to connect her students' aesthetic and efferent stances was evident in this comment:

> Literature circles allow the teacher to see how children view literature and how they discuss it. You are able to see what children perceive as important in what they read. You can then discuss why they feel these issues in the story are important to them and in the process find out more about your students and the way they observe and recognize situations. You get insight on the students' analytical thinking processes and how they evaluate situations. This information can help you understand how the student produces and comes up with answers to questions. Helps you to see if comprehension is easily achieved or if there may be some difficulty with the comprehension process.

During the closing interview, Annie emphasized her own struggle at the beginning of the study and her surprise at some of her observations:

> At first, I wasn't quite sure what I was looking for, except acceptable behaviors. I concentrated on taking turns, staying with the group, no put downs, etc. It was very difficult not to get involved in the conversation.... As the days passed, however, I made some interesting observations. I found myself listening more to the conversations the children were having. A routine developed rather quickly. They knew what they had to do and they

got straight to business. What I found interesting was the behavior of the slower readers. I assumed these children would stop reading when the majority of their groups had finished the selection. To my surprise they continued to read through the discussion, but kept an open ear to comment on parts of the conversation. Another surprise was the responsibility displayed by students who were seldom known for their responsibility; the depth of their understanding; and their ability to listen and react to other members in their group; I did not expect these behaviors to develop in such a short period of time.

Finally, as the teachers reflected on what they had learned about their students, they also considered what they had learned about teaching and shared questions that continued to tug at them. These included the amount of time they should dedicate to literature circles, the ways groups should be formed as a matter of routine, the role of the teacher in modeling new strategies, and how they could be certain that *all* students were being held responsible for reading and responding to text. Of particular concern was whether one teacher, unassisted, could manage literature circles on his or her own.

# Discussion

We expected, at the outset, to examine the ways teachers joined the information they gained from observations with the information they gained from students' written work samples. In fact, we saw little evidence that teachers sought to connect their observations to students' portfolio samples. Instead, we learned something more important: We found that teachers used the observed information immediately to initiate corrections or interventions and, by so doing increased children's opportunities to learn. We found that the observation process allowed teachers to achieve what Tharp and Gallimore (1988) described as true teaching: "The teacher assists by providing the structure and the children participate by providing the information" (p. 21).

The observations made by teachers were critically influential in their subsequent teaching actions with both individuals and the class as a whole; consequently, the observations were essential in providing students with effective opportunities to learn. Behaviors they observed on one day clearly influenced their actions on that day and during the days that followed. During this brief period, assessment drove both the type of instruction teachers planned and the actions they took during the course of instruction.

Teachers responded to their observations in several ways: They moved physically closer to students whom they observed to be struggling in the early days of the lesson, using their presence to keep students focused; they increased teacher or peer support for students whom they observed to be disengaged during either silent reading or discussion; and they preceded silent reading and discussion with minilessons deliberately planned to focus students' attention on a particular idea or strategy that they observed to be absent or not fully developed during the previous day's discussion groups.

During the student-led discussions, teachers were not mere observers; their skillful interventions challenged some students to justify their ideas and enabled more reluctant students to take the floor. By so doing, both teachers and students learned that quiet children had some important and interesting ideas to offer. The transcripts provide evidence that time and time again, following the teacher's intervention, a previously unsupported idea was discussed in greater detail and affirmed or rejected. In addition, the transcripts indicate that children drawn into the discussion by the teacher generally remained actively involved after the teacher withdrew.

Perhaps teachers' interventions were successful because they were focused and brief. Using strategies similar to those described by Short and Kauffman (1995), these teachers entered the conversation in ways that did not preempt the students' personal responses. They either started a conversation by asking students what they might like to share or deepened a conversation by asking students to explain a comment made. They then withdrew from the conversation as soon as the unsupported idea was under more thorough discussion or as soon as the reluctant student started speaking and the ideas were "on the table" for discussion. Teachers' actions met Goldenberg's guidelines for an effective instructional conversation: "The conversation is instructional, and the instruction is conversation" (p. 319).

We also found that teachers used their observations not only to assess and document the progress students were making, but also to evaluate the effectiveness of their own teaching. Repeatedly during discussions, in their logs, and in interviews, teachers responded to an individual's or a group's inadequate performance by questioning their own actions and asking what they might have done differently. Teaching changed because of what they observed.

Finally, a comment made by Martha was one we returned to often as we reviewed the data: "Sometimes the level of understanding demonstrated during conversations is more evident than journal entries." It was clear that students' discussions increased the teachers' awareness of the differences between written and oral evidence of reading comprehension, and this awareness extended their understanding of their students' literacy abilities. Although teachers' observations of children's written texts often focused on their ability to conform to standard English, their observations of oral responses consistently focused on the content rather than the form of the ideas they shared. The routine of observing students closely as they talked about books seemed to raise teachers' awareness of the multiple ways students may display their literacies and of the importance of "situated practice" (The New London Group, 1996), in which students are immersed "in meaningful practices within a community of learners who are capable of playing multiple and different roles based on their backgrounds and experiences" (p. 85). Teachers' observations seemed to help them take the first steps toward redefining literacy as "multiliteracies," defined by The New London Group as a focus on "modes of representation much broader than language alone" (pp. 63–64). We believed that these first steps toward redefinition were important as the teachers worked toward a full understanding and appreciation of the literacy knowledge of the linguistically and culturally diverse children in their classroom.

# Conclusion

In their text *Rousing Minds to Life*, Tharp and Gallimore (1988) argue,

Students cannot be left to learn on their own; teachers cannot be content to provide opportunities to learn and then assess outcomes; recitation must be de-emphasized; responsive, assisting interactions must become commonplace in classrooms. Minds must be roused to life. (p. 21)

To meet this challenge, Tharp and Gallimore explain that interactions between teachers and students must be improved and that doing so requires "the most detailed and dedicated examination" (p. 21). We believe that such examination should happen not by outsiders looking in, but rather by teachers looking at their own students, and in turn, at themselves. Annie and Martha taught us quite simply that sharpening the lens through which we see children helps us to sharpen the lens through which we see ourselves.

## Questions for Reflection

1. Think about a student or group of students you might choose to observe during literature circles. What questions would you hope to answer as you watch them read and talk about books?

2. Martha and Annie responded to children's book talk in many different ways. How were their responses similar to or different from those you might expect to occur in your own classroom or in classrooms you visit?

## References

Darling-Hammond, L., Ancess, J., & Falk, B. (1995). *Authentic assessment in action: Studies of schools and students at work*. New York: Teachers College Press.

Goldenberg, C. (1992/1993). Instructional conversations: Promoting comprehension through discussion. *The Reading Teacher, 46*, 316–326.

Martinez, M.G., & Roser, N.L. (1995). The books make a difference in story talk. In N.L. Roser & M.G. Martinez, (Eds.), *Book talk and beyond: Children and teachers respond to literature* (pp. 32–41). Newark, DE: International Reading Association.

Matanzo, J.B. (1996). Discussion: Assessing what was said and what was done. In L.B. Gambrell, & J.F. Almasi (Eds.), *Lively discussions! Fostering engaged reading* (pp. 250–264). Newark, DE: International Reading Association.

Morrow, L.M. (1996). Story retelling: A discussion strategy to develop and assess comprehension. In L.B. Gambrell, & J.F. Almasi (Eds.), *Lively discussions! Fostering engaged reading* (pp. 265–285). Newark, DE: International Reading Association.

Pierce, K.M. (1990). Initiating literature discussion groups: Teaching like learners. In K.G. Short & K.M. Pierce (Eds.), *Talking about books: Creating literate communities* (pp. 177–198). Portsmouth, NH: Heinemann.

Rosenblatt, L.M. (1978). *The reader, the text, the poem: The transactional theory of the literacy work*. Carbondale, IL: Southern Illinois University Press.

Rosenblatt, L.M. (1985). The transactional theory of the literacy work. In C.R. Cooper (Ed.), *Researching response to literature and the teaching of literature* (pp. 33–53). Norwood, NJ: Ablex.

Short, K.G., & Kauffman, G. (1995). "So what do *I* do?": The role of the teacher in literature circles. In N.L. Roser & M.G. Martinez (Eds.), *Book talk and beyond: Children*

*Paratore, Garnick, and Lewis*

*and teachers respond to literature* (pp. 140–149). Newark, DE: International Reading Association.

Stowell, L.P., & Tierney, R.J. (1995). Portfolios in the classroom: What happens when teachers and students negotiate assessment? In R.L. Allington & S.A. Walmsley (Eds.), *No quick fix: Rethinking literacy programs in America's elementary schools.* New York: Teachers College Press; Newark, DE: International Reading Association.

Strauss, A., & Corbin, J. (1990). *Basics of qualitative research: Grounded theory procedures and techniques.* Newbury Park, CA: Sage.

Tharp, R.G., & Gallimore, R. (1988). *Rousing minds to life.* New York: Cambridge University Press.

The New London Group. (1996). A Pedagogy of multiliteracies: Designing social futures. *Harvard Educational Review, 66,* 60–91.

Walker, B.J. (1996). Discussions that focus on strategies and self-assessment. In L.B. Gambrell, & J.F. Almasi (Eds.), *Lively discussions! Fostering engaged reading* (pp. 286–296). Newark, DE: International Reading Association.

Watson, D.J. (1990). Show me: Whole language evaluation of literature groups. In K.G. Short & K.M. Pierce (Eds.), *Talking about books: Creating literate communities* (pp. 157–176). Portsmouth, NH: Heinemann.

Wiseman, D.L., Many, J.E., & Altieri, J. (1992). Enabling complex aesthetic responses: An examination of three literacy discussion approaches. In C.K. Kinzer & D.J. Leu (Eds.), *Literacy research, theory and practice: Views from many perspectives.* Chicago, IL: The National Reading Conference.

## Children's Literature References

Fritz, J. (1967). *Early thunder.* New York: Puffin Books.

Speare, E. (1958). *The witch of blackbird pond.* Boston, MA: Houghton Mifflin.

# Author Index

*Note:* An *f* following a page number indicates that the reference may be found in a figure; a *t* indicates that it may be found in a table.

# Children's Literature Authors

*Note:* An *f* following a page number indicates that the reference may be found in a figure; a *t* indicates that it may be found in a table.

Seuss, Dr., 128
Slater, D., 128
Soto, G., 12*f*
Speare, E., 223, 231
Spinelli, J., 182, 206
Steele, W., 161, 173
Steptoe, J., 37, 44
Strete, C.K., 136, 155
Surat, M., 57, 65

**T**
Tauchiya, Y., 128
Taylor, M.D., 12*f,* 72, 87
Tennyson, A. Lord, 128

**V**
Van Allsburg, C., 12*f*
Voigt, C., 98, 101, 161, 173

**W**
Walker, A., 12*f*
Wiesner, D., 72, 87
Witter, E., 145, 155
Wolstein, D., 44

**Y**
Yep, L., 97, 101

# Subject Index

*Note:* An *f* following a page number indicates that the reference may be found in a figure; a *t* indicates that it may be found in a table.

CLASSROOM(S): acknowledging kid culture in, 61–62; children's connections to culture in, 47–57; implications of Family Studies Inquiry for, 62–64; language-rich, 202–203; learning, 202–203; myth of silence in, 88–101; second-language, 102–128; suggestions for practice in, 151–152; writing, 98–100

CLASSROOM TALK: conflict during, 130–155; content analysis, 117–126; discussion excerpts, 196, 199–201; Sarasota Oral Language and Writing Study, 92, 92$t$; second graders', 26–44; teachers' support of diverse students' participation in, 195–202; Tohono O'Odham Study, 91, 91$t$; during writing, 91, 91$t$, 92, 92$t$

CLIPBOARD CRUISING FORMS, 210, 211$f$

COGNITIVE CONFLICT, 132

COGNITIVE CONFLICT SCENARIO TASK, 134

COGNITIVE CONFLICT SCENARIO TASK POSTTEST, 147–148

COMPLEXITIES, 129–173

COMPREHENSION: enhancement by book clubs, 8; evaluation of, 204; observation of, 219–224; suggestions for improving, 151

CONFLICT(S), 129–173; ability to recognize, 147–148; during classroom discussions, 130–155; cognitive, 132; in peer-led and teacher-led discussions, 138–140, 139$t$; role in literature discussions, 132–134; sociocognitive, 132–152; types of, 135–138; unresolved, 142$t$, 146–147

CONFLICT RESOLUTION, 140–147, 142$t$; ability for, 147–148; discussion excerpt, 141; types of, 140–141

CONFLICTS WITH OTHERS, 136–137; discussion excerpts, 137; in peer-led and teacher-led discussions, 138–140, 139$t$; types of resolution used for, 141–142, 142$t$, 146

CONFLICTS WITH TEXT, 137–138; discussion excerpts, 137–140; in peer-led and teacher-led discussions, 138–140, 139$t$; types of resolution used for, 141–142, 142$t$, 146

CONFLICTS WITHIN SELF, 135–136; discussion excerpts, 135–136; in peer-led and teacher-led discussions, 138–140, 139$t$; types of resolution used for, 141–142, 142$t$, 146

CONSTRUCTING MEANING, 161

CONSTRUCTIVE INSTINCTS, 1

CONTENT. *see also* Text: connections with structure, 123–126

CONVERSATION(S): contexts for, 103–117; instructional, 227; international, 109–117; maintaining, 162; in second-language classrooms, 102–128

CONVERSATIONAL DISCUSSION GROUP FORMAT, 134

CROSS-AGED LITERACY PROGRAM, 66–87; adolescent reflections on, 78–83; debriefing sessions, 79–83; discussion groups, 76–78; facilitating discussions, 78; interactions and learning, 84; lessons learned, 78–84; literacy lessons, 80–82; preparation seminar, 70–76; procedural lessons, 79–80; project description, 70–78; selecting and reading literature for, 71–72; session literacy activities, 77; social lessons, 82–83; theory and rationale for, 69–70; writing, 72–73

CULTURAL DEVELOPMENT: interpsychological, 179; intrapsychological, 179; Vygotsky Space model of, 179–181, 180$f$, 187–188, 195

CULTURAL DIVERSITY, 45–65. *see also* Diverse students; discussion excerpts, 52–55

CULTURE: children's connections to, 47–57; definition of, 56–57; kid culture, 57–62

CURIOSITY: epistemic, 132

# D

DEBRIEFING PREVIOUS DISCUSSIONS, 74–76

DENG (CASE-STUDY STUDENT), 181, 182*t*, 186, 202–203; literacy learning, 192–195; sensitivity toward, 202; teachers' support for, 200–201

DEREK (STUDENT), 149–151; discussion excerpts, 149–150

DISCOURSE: academic, 36; assimilation of, 36–37; authoritative, 36; connecting, 36–39; student, 217–219

DISCOURSE OF ACTION, 157, 163

DISCOURSE OF FEELING, 157, 163

DISCUSSION(S). *see also* Conversation; Peer talk; Talk: about African trickster tales, 34–35; beneficial research-based practices for, 13–17; bringing lurkers into, 224–225; classroom, 130–155; for conflict resolution, 142*t*, 145–146; conflict resolution in, 140–147, 142*t*; conflict types in, 138–140, 139*t*; cross-aged literary, 77–78; debriefing, 74–76; facilitating, 78; literature, 132–134, 156–173; literature circles, 94–98; modeling, 16; peer talk during, 93–98; peer-led, 138–147, 139*t*, 142*t*, 156–173; reflection prompts for, 18, 20*f*; second graders, 34–35; teacher-led, 133, 138–147, 139*t*, 142*t*

DISCUSSION GROUPS: cross-aged literary, 76–78; focus case-study group, 181, 182*t*, 187; literature, 159–160

DISCUSSION SKILLS: suggestions for developing, 152

DISCUSSION STRATEGIES: Save the Last Word for Me, 48; Sketch to Stretch, 48; webbing, 48

DIVERSE STUDENTS, 45–65; being sensitive to, 201–202; discussion excerpts, 188–191; literacy learning, 192–195; participation in contexts of peer talk, 188–192; participation in peer talk, 187–202; pearls of wisdom for working with, 202–204; quality peer talk with, 176–206; teachers' support of, 195–202

# E

ENGLISH AS A SECOND LANGUAGE (ESL) STUDENTS: graduate L2 seminars, 109–126; grouping, 13; Sunshine Room, 103–109, 117–126

EPISTEMIC CURIOSITY, 132

ESL. *see* English as a Second Language

ETHNICITY: Joe's connections to, 54–56

EVALUATION: group assessment, 18; reflective, 18; Self- and Group Evaluation, 18–20, 21*f*; of student learning and understanding, 204; of text, 162

EXPECTATION OF TALK: intellectual, 103, 117–120

EXPERTS: resident, 55–56

EXPLORATORY TALK, 170

EXPRESSIVE INSTINCTS, 1

## F

FAMILY: Brad's connections to, 51–54; Rosanna's connections to, 50–51

FAMILY STUDIES INQUIRY (CURRICULUM), 47–48, 49*f*; acknowledging kid culture in, 61–62; Brad's connections to family and religion with, 51–54; implications for schools and classrooms, 62–64; Joe's connections to ethnicity with, 54–56; Rosanna's connections to family with, 50–51

FEELING: discourse of, 157, 163

FEELING TALK, 168

FICTION, 97–98

FLORIDA: Sarasota Oral Language and Writing Study, 91–93

FOLK TALES: African, 44; African trickster tales, 26–44

FRAMES OF REFERENCE: types of talk that characterize, 162

## G

GENDER, 156–173; influence on students' responses to literature, 157–160

GENDERED READINGS, 157, 163

GENDERED TALK, 157, 162–163; discussion excerpt, 163

GIRL TALK, 157, 168

GOLDENBERG'S GUIDELINES FOR INSTRUCTIONAL CONVERSATION, 228

GRADUATE L2 SEMINARS: classroom talk, 117–126; discussion excerpts, 112–114, 119, 124–125; international conversations, 109–117; reflections, 116–117

GROUP ASSESSMENT, 18; Self- and Group Evaluation, 18–20, 21*f*

GROUP DYNAMICS, 159–160

GROUPINGS: for book clubs, 13, 17; flexible, heterogeneous, 203–204

GROWTH: enhancement by book clubs, 8

GULF WAR: Sunshine Room experience with, 103–117

## I

IMPERIALISM, 61

INDIAN OASIS SCHOOL DISTRICT: Tohono O'Odham Study, 90

INFORMATION: telling, 141, 142*t*

INITIATION-RESPONSE-EVALUATION (IRE) INSTRUCTION, 28, 68

INSTINCTS: constructive, 1; expressive, 1; investigative, 1; social, 1

INSTRUCTION: implications for, 168–171; initiation-response-evaluation (IRE), 28, 68; literacy, 67–69, 181–185; phase-in, phase-out model, 16; questions raised in L2 seminar, 110, 111*f*; teachable moments, 122

INSTRUCTIONAL CONVERSATION: Goldenberg's guidelines for, 228

INTELLECTUAL EXPECTATION OF TALK, 103, 117; high level of, 118–120

INTERNATIONAL CONVERSATIONS, 109–117; discussion excerpts, 112–114; reflections, 116–117

INVESTIGATIVE INSTINCTS, 1

IRE. *see* Initiation-response-evaluation

# J

JASON (FOCUS CASE-STUDY GROUP MEMBER), 187, 202–203; literacy learning, 192–193; participation in contexts of peer talk, 189, 191; teachers' support for, 198

JEAN (FOCUS CASE-STUDY GROUP MEMBER), 187; participation in contexts of peer talk, 188, 190

JOE (STUDENT): connections to ethnicity, 54–56

JOURNALS, 15*f*; reading-response, 18, 19*f*

# K

KID CULTURE: acknowledging, 61–62; definition of, 59; discussion excerpts, 57–58; implications of, 59–61; role of, 57–62; talking about issues of, 57–59

KID TALK, 37

KIDWATCHING, 223

# L

L2 LEARNING. *see* Second-language learning

LANGUAGE. *see also* Oral language; Second language: functions during writing, 92, 93*t*; lesson, 124

LANGUAGE-RICH CLASSROOMS, 202–203

LEARNERS. *see* Students

LEARNING: literacy, 84, 192–195; noisy, 88–101; questions raised in L2 seminar, 110, 111*f*; Sarasota Oral Language and Writing Study, 91–93; second-language, 110; social constructivist theory in, 69; Tohono O'Odham Study, 90–91

LENNY (CASE-STUDY STUDENT), 181, 182*t*, 185–186, 202–203; participation in contexts of peer talk, 188–189, 191; teachers' support for, 198–200

LESSON LANGUAGE, 124

LESSON PLANNING, 74

LITERACY: development of, 66–87; indicators of long-term difficulty with, 67; lessons learned, 67–68, 80–82; multiliteracies, 229

LITERACY INSTRUCTION: Book Club Program case studies, 181–185; context for, 69; Cross-Aged Literacy Program, 66–87; effective, 67–68

LITERACY LEARNING: discussion excerpts, 192–194; diverse students', 192–195

LITERATURE. *see also* Children's literature: fiction, 97–98; selecting and reading for Cross-Aged Literacy Program, 71–72; selection of, 16–17; students' responses to, 157–160

LITERATURE CIRCLES, 94–98; delving into heart of fiction, 97–98; how they work, 95–96; peer talk in, 96–97; student preparation for, 210–212; teacher preparation for, 208–210

LITERATURE DISCUSSION GROUPS: cross-aged, 76–78; group dynamics in, 159–160

LITERATURE DISCUSSIONS, 160–167, 171; classroom context, 160–161; conflict in, 132–134; data analysis, 161–162; gathering data, 161; implications for instruction, 168–171; lessons learned, 168–171; peer talk during, 93–98; peer-led,

156–173; questions to engage students in reflective discussion on, 171; students' purposes in, 161–162

LURKERS, 224–225

# M

MAINSTREAM CLASSROOMS: quality peer talk with diverse students in, 176–206

MEANING CONSTRUCTION, 161

MEDIATION: semiotic, 178

MEDIATORS: teachers as, 103, 117, 123–126

MEI (FOCUS CASE-STUDY GROUP MEMBER), 187, 202–203; literacy learning, 192–193, 195; participation in contexts of peer talk, 189–190

METATALK, 34

MODELING DISCUSSIONS, 16

MONITORING, 162

MOTIVATION: suggestions for enhancing, 151–152

MULTILITERACIES, 228

MYTH OF SILENCE, 88–101

# N

NOVELS: book club selections, 11, 12*f*

# O

OBSERVATION, 207–231; clipboard cruising forms, 210, 211*f*; of comprehension and response, 219–224; context for, 208–212; discussion excerpts, 220–225; kidwatching, 224; of struggling readers, 224–225; of students' discourse strategies, 217–219; of students' engagement, 216–217; of talk about books, 213–215; teacher reflections on, 216–218, 223–224, 226–227; by teachers, 215–225; teachers' perceptions of what they learned, 225–227

OPINIONS: sharing, 141–143, 142*t*

ORAL LANGUAGE: enhancement by book clubs, 8–9; Sarasota Oral Language and Writing Study, 91–93, 92*t*

ORAL READING: cross-aged literary discussion session activity, 77

# P

PAIRING STUDENTS, 17

PARDO, MRS.: Book Club classroom, 181, 182*t*; creating public and social spaces, 197–198; instruction context, 181–185

PEER TALK: about African trickster tales, 26–44; conflicts and complexities in, 129–173; context for, 5–23; cultural diversity in, 45–65; diverse learners' participation in, 187–192; encouraging, 176–206; in literature circles, 96–97; during literature discussions, 93–98; promoting, 29–31; second graders', 26–44; theoretical framework for researching, 178–181; in writing classrooms, 98–100

PEER-LED DISCUSSIONS: conflict resolution in, 140–147, 142*t*; conflict types in, 138–140, 139*t*; influence of gender in, 156–173

PERSIAN GULF WAR, 103–117

PHASE-IN, PHASE-OUT MODEL OF INSTRUCTION, 16

PICTURE BOOKS, 13–16; book club selections, 11, 12*f*

PLANNING LESSONS, 74

POSITIONING, 166–167

POWER AND TRUST RELATIONSHIPS, 103, 117, 120–122

PRACTICE: questions raised in L2 seminar, 110, 111*f*; research-based, for book clubs, 13–17; situated, 228; suggestions for, 151–152

PREPARATION: "Get Ready" ("Take Five"), 30; student, 210–212; teacher, 208–210

PREPARATION SEMINAR, 70–76; debriefing previous discussions, 74–76; discussion, 73–74; instructional foci, 71; planning lessons, 74; purposes, 70–71; selecting and reading literature, 71–72; summary, 76; writing, 72–73

PRIVATE/INDIVIDUAL SPACES, 198–199

PRIVATE/SOCIAL SPACES, 198–199

PUBLIC AND SOCIAL SPACES, 196–198

# Q

QUALITY PEER TALK: encouraging, 176–206

# R

*RACING THE SUN* (PITTS): Brad's connections to, 52, 53*f*

READERS: struggling, 224–225

READING(S): gendered, 157, 163; oral, 77

READING AGAINST THE GRAIN, 158, 164–166; discussion excerpt, 164

READING ALOUD: cross-aged literary discussion session activity, 77

READING COMPREHENSION: enhancement by book clubs, 8; suggestions for improving, 151

READING LOG IDEAS (RESPONSE SHEET), 73, 77

READING-RESPONSE JOURNALS, 18, 19*f*

READING-WRITING CLASSROOM. *see also* Classroom(s): myth of silence in, 88–101

READ-WRITE-TALK PROCEDURE, 79

RECITATION, 1, 133

RECITING BY HEART, 36

REFLECTION: prompts for group discussion and process, 18, 20*f*

RELIGION: Brad's connections to, 51–54

RELYING ON TEACHERS, 142*t*, 144–145; discussion excerpt, 145

RESEARCH: classroom, 26–44; Sarasota Oral Language and Writing Study, 91–93; sociocognitive conflict study, 134–148; theoretical framework for, 178–181; Tohono O'Odham Study, 90–91

RESEARCH-BASED PRACTICES: for book clubs, 13–17

RESEARCHERS: teachers as, 29–39

RESIDENT EXPERTS, 55–56

RESPONSES TO LITERATURE: influence of gender on, 157–160; influence of text on, 157–158; observation of, 219–224; reading–response journals, 18, 19*f*
REWARDS, 16
ROSANNA (STUDENT): connections to family, 50–51

## S

SARASOTA ORAL LANGUAGE AND WRITING STUDY, 91–93; classroom talk during writing, 92, 92*t*
SAVE THE LAST WORD FOR ME (STRATEGY), 48
SCHOOL. *see also* Classroom(s): implications of Family Studies Inquiry for, 62–64
SCHOOL TALK, 121
SEATING ARRANGEMENTS, 11–13
SECOND GRADERS' PEER TALK ABOUT AFRICAN TRICKSTER TALES, 26–44; coding categories, 33, 33*f*; collecting evidence, 31–32; discussion excerpts, 34–35, 38–39; examining evidence, 32–33; lessons learned from, 40–41; rendering evidence, 34–39; unanswered questions, 42
SECOND-LANGUAGE CLASSROOMS: graduate L2 seminars, 109–126; inventing conversations in, 102–128; Sunshine Room, 103–109, 117–126
SECOND-LANGUAGE LEARNING, 110; grouping ESL students, 13; questions raised, 110, 111*f*
SELF-EVALUATION, 18; Self- and Group Evaluation, 18–20, 21*f*; self-assessment, 18
SELF-UNDERSTANDING: conflicts within self, 135–136, 138–140, 139*t*, 141–142, 142*t*, 146; enhancement by book clubs, 8
SEMIOTIC MEDIATION, 178
SENSITIVITY, 201–202
SHARING OPINIONS, 141–143; discussion excerpt, 143; in peer-led and teacher-led discussions, 141–142, 142*t*
SHORT STORIES AND SHORT STORY COLLECTIONS: book club selections, 11, 12*f*
SILENCE, 88–101
SKETCH TO STRETCH (STRATEGY), 48
SOCIAL CONSTRUCTIVISM: key tenets of, 27; principles undergirding, 69
SOCIAL INSTINCTS, 1
SOCIAL LEARNING THEORY: support by book clubs, 9–10
SOCIAL SPACES, 196–198
SOCIAL TALK, 162
SOCIOCOGNITIVE CONFLICTS, 132–133, 148–152; discussion excerpts, 149–150; study, 134–148; types of resolution of, 140–141
SPEAKERS: connecting voices, 34–36; power and trust relationships between, 103, 117, 120–122
STARK (FOCUS CASE-STUDY GROUP MEMBER), 187; participation in contexts of peer talk, 188, 190–191
STRUCTURE: connections between content and, 123–126